Anatomy of a Guerrilla Film: The Making of *RADIUS*

Helmut Kobler

THOMSON
COURSE TECHNOLOGY
Professional ■ Technical ■ Reference

© 2005 by Thomson Course Technology PTR. All rights reserved. No part of this book may be reproduced or transmitted in any form or by any means, electronic or mechanical, including photocopying, recording, or by any information storage or retrieval system without written permission from Thomson Course Technology PTR, except for the inclusion of brief quotations in a review.

The Thomson Course Technology PTR logo and related trade dress are trademarks of Thomson Course Technology and may not be used without written permission.

Microsoft and Windows are either registered trademarks or trademarks of Microsoft Corporation in the United States and/or other countries. Photoshop and After Effects are registered trademarks of Adobe Systems, Inc. Apple, Mac, Macintosh, PowerBook, PowerMac, Mac OS, Final Cut, Final Cut Pro, Final Cut Express, Soundtrack, DVD Studio Pro, LiveType, iDVD, iMovie, Shake, Logic, and Logic Express are trademarks of Apple Computer, Inc. Final Draft is a trademark of Final Draft Inc.

All other trademarks are the property of their respective owners.

Important: Thomson Course Technology PTR cannot provide software support. Please contact the appropriate software manufacturer's technical support line or Web site for assistance.

Thomson Course Technology PTR and the author have attempted throughout this book to distinguish proprietary trademarks from descriptive terms by following the capitalization style used by the manufacturer.

Information contained in this book has been obtained by Thomson Course Technology PTR from sources believed to be reliable. However, because of the possibility of human or mechanical error by our sources, Thomson Course Technology PTR, or others, the Publisher does not guarantee the accuracy, adequacy, or completeness of any information and is not responsible for any errors or omissions or the results obtained from use of such information. Readers should be particularly aware of the fact that the Internet is an ever-changing entity. Some facts may have changed since this book went to press.

Educational facilities, companies, and organizations interested in multiple copies or licensing of this book should contact the publisher for quantity discount information. Training manuals, CD-ROMs, and portions of this book are also available individually or can be tailored for specific needs.

ISBN: 1-59200-910-7
Library of Congress Catalog Card Number: 2005924932
Printed in Canada
05 06 07 08 09 WC 10 9 8 7 6 5 4 3 2 1

THOMSON
COURSE TECHNOLOGY
Professional ■ Technical ■ Reference

Thomson Course Technology PTR,
a division of Thomson Course Technology
25 Thomson Place
Boston, MA 02210
http://www.courseptr.com

Publisher and General Manager, Thomson Course Technology PTR:
Stacy L. Hiquet

Associate Director of Marketing:
Sarah O'Donnell

Manager of Editorial Services:
Heather Talbot

Marketing Manager:
Heather Hurley

Executive Editor:
Kevin Harreld

Senior Editor:
Mark Garvey

Marketing Coordinator:
Jordan Casey

Project/Copy Editor:
Karen A. Gill

Thomson Course Technology PTR Editorial Services Coordinator:
Elizabeth Furbish

Interior Layout Tech:
Sue Honeywell

Cover Designer:
Mike Tanamachi

Indexer:
Kelly Talbot

Proofreader:
Sean Medlock

*This book is dedicated to our team of filmmakers—
the cast, crew, and many generous vendors—who made
RADIUS possible. Guys, you probably didn't know
what you were getting into when you signed up,
but you came through nonetheless. Thank you.*

Acknowledgments

I'd like to thank Andy Trapani, *RADIUS*' producer and my manager, for his long-standing support on *RADIUS* and for his assistance on new projects as we've moved forward.

This book would not have been possible without the support of Kevin Harreld, my executive editor at Thomson, who took a shot on a new kind of filmmaking book. Thanks, too, to editor Karen Gill for helping whip my copy into shape, and to the rest of the Thomson staff for bringing the project to life.

Finally, writing a book can be a lonely endeavor, but I got plenty of moral support from family and friends, for which I'm very grateful. This group includes my mother, grandmother, and especially my girlfriend, Laura, who was always a steady source of comfort and positive thinking. Thanks so much!

ABOUT THE AUTHOR

In a previous life, **Helmut Kobler** founded a video game company. Then he designed, produced, and directed award-winning video games for Windows PCs, the Sony PlayStation, and other gaming platforms.

But Helmut always wanted to try his hand at filmmaking, so he set off to make *RADIUS*. He now runs K2 Films, a small, Los Angeles-based film production company that makes one film at a time, often with a strong Internet component that lets fans play a part in the filmmaking process.

On the side, Helmut writes about cool technology, which he's loved since he was a kid. He's a contributing editor for *MacAddict* magazine, where he writes regularly on subjects from digital video software to action video games. He's also written for *Wired*, *PC World*, *Publisher's Weekly*, *MacWorld*, and other magazines, and he's the author of four *For Dummies* books about Apple Computer's Final Cut video editing software (the latest of which is *Final Cut Pro HD for Dummies*, from Wiley).

Contents

Introduction................xvii

PART 1	PREPRODUCTION	1

Chapter 1 Raising the Cash...................3

My original budget for *RADIUS* was $40,000
for a 20-minute film.......................3

In the end, *RADIUS* went over budget and cost
$60,000 to make............................5

I didn't expect *RADIUS* to make much money....7

I had reasons other than money for
making the film............................8

RADIUS' budget was raised from my savings
account and credit cards..................10

Chapter 2 Writing the Script.................13

I chose to do an action sci-fi film because
it played to my tastes and strengths......13

I didn't want to write the script myself.........15

I met writer Jon Clarke through our producer...15

I paid Jon $1,000 to write the script,
including all revisions....................17

Jon and I signed a written contract............18
We constantly revised the script while it was
    in preproduction.......................19
We even had to revise the script
    after production!......................21
We wrote the script with some strategic
    goals in mind..........................23
A few written scenes were never filmed........25
Jon used Final Draft software to write *RADIUS*....26

Chapter 3   Casting.........................27
We received more than 1,000 headshots
    thanks to a $40 advertisement..............27
We ran casting auditions and saw more than
    100 actors..............................29
We ran our casting sessions out of our
    production office......................30
Actors came prepared to read a scene
    from *RADIUS*..........................30
We tried to keep auditions fun, informal,
    and comfortable........................31
Each actor read his scene twice...............32
We took detailed notes and videotaped all
    auditions..............................32
Finally, we asked actors back for second and
    third readings.........................33
We hired a casting director to find a
    recognizable actor.....................36
Fortunately, we found Matt McCoy
    to play Crim...........................36
We originally cast Rick Schroder to play Crim....38
The original Vesay backed out the day
    before production started..............38
We asked friends to play the four anonymous
    crew members...........................40

Contents

	We paid our cast $25 a day.	41
	We signed an agreement with the Screen Actors Guild.	44
Chapter 4	**Crewing Up**	**47**
	We found most of our crew through referrals.	47
	We found only one person through a want ad, but he was key.	49
	The crew we assembled had considerable experience.	50
	We paid the crew what we could afford.	52
	The crew joined RADIUS, despite low pay, for various reasons.	52
Chapter 5	**Location Scouting**	**57**
	Potential outdoor locations had to meet several criteria.	57
	I wanted to find locations with campgrounds nearby, but our producers nixed that idea.	59
	We served as our own location scouts, with a little help.	59
	We did a two-day road trip looking for locations.	59
	I fell in love with Death Valley, although shooting there was expensive ($1,000 a day).	60
	We also picked a working cinder mine for $250 a day and got a whole new look and feel.	65
	We made three other detailed scouts in our locations.	67
	For our post-CraterMaker blast scene, we found a salt flat off the highway.	68
Chapter 6	**Costume Design**	**71**
	Costume Designer Sal Salamone came from the theater world.	71
	I surveyed a bunch of movies for costume ideas.	72

Contents   ix

    Sal made our soldier's uniforms from painter's
        overalls and fishing vests. 74

    Sal made the Diamone's costume from
        scratch ($300). 77

    Sal sent us a wardrobe supervisor to keep the
        costumes working on set. 79

    We lost the Diamone's costume and had
        to make another one! 80

Chapter 7   Set Design 83

    Production Designer Katherine Ferwerda
        went to work. 83

    We constructed the crashed ship exterior
        from scratch. 85

    We rented a sound stage to do all our
        interior work. 88

    Dim lighting and quick camera work concealed
        the lack of detail in our ship's cabin. 90

    The cockpit was the only set piece we rented. . . 93

Chapter 8   Prop Design 97

    Prop Master Matt McGuire rented and built
        most props. 98

    Matt built the CraterMaker from scratch. 99

    We rented seven functional guns for $400. 101

    When key props were stolen, we had to
        make our own. 104

Chapter 9   Storyboards and Shot Lists 109

    We only did conventional storyboards for
        a couple of scenes. 109

    Video storyboards with placeholder actors
        were much more useful. 113

    Whatever shots we didn't storyboard, we
        identified on a shot list. 115

Contents

Chapter 10	Budgeting and Scheduling	117
	Line Producer Steve Stone created *RADIUS'* budget.	117
	Steve Stone used Microsoft Excel to budget *RADIUS*.	120
	Steve brought along production insurance.	121
	Assistant Director Lou Tocchet scheduled *RADIUS'* production.	123
	Lou used EP Scheduling to plan *RADIUS'* production.	124
	Lou called a final meeting with all key team members.	125

PART 2	PRODUCTION	127

Chapter 11	On the Set	129
	We usually had a crew of 26 people.	129
	Lou made sure everyone was awake and ready to go.	133
	Shooting our scenes involved a lot of preparation time.	137
	We dealt with a number of setbacks on the set.	145
	And we rolled with the punches when we could.	147
	Amazingly, cast and crew morale stayed high.	151

Chapter 12	Cinematography	157
	RADIUS was shot by Philipp Timme.	157
	We found Philipp online.	158
	We shot on 35-mm film, not digital.	160
	We used an Arriflex 35-mm camera, with sound.	162
	We had a lens for every season.	164

Contents　xi

  Working with a 35-mm camera brought
   with it some headaches. 169

  We sometimes went handheld for convenience
   or energy. 175

  The tripod is the most basic camera
   equipment. 178

  The dolly and crane gave us
   smooth movement. 180

  We used other "exotic" camera equipement. . . 186

  We used different approaches to
   light *RADIUS*. 189

  Shooting with a digital video camera has
   several advantages. 196

  MiniDV video cameras usually don't offer
   the quality that other cameras do. 197

  Shooting on DV has some problems. 197

   HD cameras are the latest craze. 198

   It's difficult to distribute your film in
    HD format. 200

Chapter 13　**Pickup Shots** 203

  We finished principal photography missing
   many shots. 203

  Doing pickup shots can be risky. 204

   Reassembling the cast and crew was a pain. . . . 205

   Our cast was changing! 206

   We had to re-create some costumes
    and props. 208

   Our original sets were gone. 211

  The CraterMaker arming scene was a
   particularly complicated pickup shot. 214

Contents

PART 3	POST-PRODUCTION	221

Chapter 14   **Film Editing** 223

Editor Ann Trulove had plenty of experience....223

First, we had to convert our film footage
to videotape. 225

We digitized the taped footage into our
Avid editing system.....................227

Working from the script, Ann built each
scene shot by shot......................228

We had lots of coverage for some scenes,
but others had virtually none. 229

Unfortunately, it took us more than 4
months to edit our 30-minute film. 233

We edited on an Avid, but I would use
Final Cut Pro now. 234

Learn editing basics with Final Cut Pro. 237

    The Browser keeps media clips organized. ..238

    The Viewer plays a media clip. 239

    Use the Timeline to arrange clips in time. ..239

    The Tool palette allows you to edit
    your clips in various ways................240

    The Canvas plays your whole movie........241

When we finished the edit, we "locked" it....243

We still needed to reassemble the edit with
higher-quality footage...................243

We hired a negative cutter to assemble
the keeper shots from *RADIUS'* negative.....244

The cut negative went to a color timer........245

We did our final assembly on a
top-tier Avid. 246

We weighed the difference between film
and video. 248

Chapter 15	**Visual Effects**.....................**251**
	We found Visual Effects Supervisor Adam Howard through a reference.........251
	Adam suggested a brilliant plan to get our effects done cheaply.................252
	...but disaster struck our brilliant plan........254
	It was time to switch to plan B................255
	I recruited a handful of freelance artists......256
	Getting the process started took some organizational skills.....................258
	Our visual effects gear included inexpensive Macs and PCs, Maya, and After Effects.......260
	We set initial deadlines, and then we set them again. And again. 263
	Green screen work allowed us to isolate a character or prop for use in a different background...........................265
	Get yourself a green screen...............266
	Shooting your green screen takes some practice............................266
	Do your compositing work in Final Cut.....268
	We worked on many of the effects remotely...270
Chapter 16	**Music Composition** **273**
	It all started with our music supervisor, Joe Fischer..........................273
	Composer Jeremy Zuckerman was paid $1,000 for his 23-minute score. 274
	Run Lola Run was an initial influence for the *RADIUS* score...........................277
	I edited a lot of placeholder music into *RADIUS*.........................277
	...but I got too attached to our placeholder music. 277

xiv Contents

        Jeremy used Logic Audio software, running
          on a low-end Mac. 281

        When finished, Jeremy output *RADIUS*' score
          to a hard drive. 283

Chapter 17   **Post-Production Sound. 285**

        A team of young engineers at Danetracks
          did all our sound work. 285

        We discovered that some of our production
          sound was too noisy. .288

        We used ADR to record clean dialogue. 289

        We also used ADR to get dialogue that we
          never bothered recording. 292

        We practiced the little-known craft of
          dialogue editing. 293

        We recorded our own Foley sound effects. 293

        Finally, we were ready to start the sound mix. . . .300

        Jeremy secured a professional sound
          mix stage—for free 301

        We started our mix work by "predubbing." . . .303

        We mixed *RADIUS* during a weekend. 306

        We had to decide whether to emphasize
          music or sound effects. 306

        We were glad we recorded our music as
          multiple "stems." 307

        I wish we could have listened to the final
          mix with a fresh perspective. 308

Part 4   **Marketing/Distribution**   **311**

Chapter 18   **Creating a Pro Image 313**

        I commissioned cool concept art by a
          student artist. 313

        I created a promotional card for *RADIUS*. 316

Contents xv

	I launched a Web site that tracked the making of *RADIUS*. 316
	We did early public relations work. 319
Chapter 19	**Film Distribution** **323**
	Film festivals didn't seem like an effective distribution medium......................324
	I decided to publish and distribute a DVD myself. 325
	I wanted to give the DVD special features that would help make it marketable. 327
	I hired a menu designer to create the DVD's menus............................330
	I authored the DVD myself. 331
	How does DVD authoring work?. 333
	The Assets tab showcases what you've imported............................334
	The Menu tab allows you to create button hotspots......................334
	The inspector lets you program menu bottons........................335
	The Track tab lets you play the video and audio stream......................335
	The graphical view is a good way to see the flow of your DVD content...............336
	Video and audio encoding should be done before the authoring process............336
	I replicated the DVDs as DVD-9s, which is a unique process. 337
	I created a Web site to promote and sell the DVD.................................339
	I got set up to accept credit cards. 341
	I've since added Amazon.com distribution.....344

Contents

Chapter 20	**Film Marketing**	**347**
	I had no budget for advertising.	347
	My marketing strategy focused on getting free press.	347
	I came up with multiple marketing "hooks."	348
	I wrote press releases for each of my hooks.	350
	I prioritized the list of print and Internet publications I would approach.	351
	Then I started contacting publications and journalists.	352
	To build credibility, I also sought out promotional quotes for *RADIUS*.	354
Chapter 21	**Lessons Learned**	**359**
	Come up with a unique hook.	359
	Do a small project better, instead of a big project worse.	360
	Find as many experienced crew members as you can.	361
	Find good people—don't settle!	361
	Work with equipment you have easy access to.	363
	Go ahead—get discouraged!	363
	Create a polished image.	364
	Invest in yourself.	365
	Do a "postmortem" review afterward.	366
	Index	**369**

INTRODUCTION

Hi. I'm Helmut Kobler, the author of this book and the director of the film *RADIUS*, which is featured on this book's included DVD. Before getting started, there are a few things I'd like to get out of the way, so here goes...

Why This Book?

Plenty of other books are aimed at independent, guerrilla filmmakers who are looking to expand their filmmaking knowledge, but this book is different in one significant way.

Instead of talking about filmmaking in general terms, *Anatomy of a Guerrilla Film* closely examines a real-world, low-budget indie film (my film, *RADIUS*, which is on the included DVD), showing you all that went right and all that went wrong while making the film.

I truly feel this is the best way to learn about indie filmmaking (other than making movies of your own). By reading this book and watching *RADIUS*, you can see how all the factors that go into making a low-budget film—all the decisions, compromises, setbacks, and victories—actually translate to a final product, on the screen. Personally, I learn a lot better when I can see how theoretical concepts are implemented in the real world—that is, how all the gears really mesh together—and with what degree of success. This book has that going for it in spades.

Plus, as the title suggests, *Anatomy of a Guerrilla Film* is specifically geared toward indie filmmakers working on low, low budgets, who are trying to squeeze efficiency out of each dollar they spend. The challenges I dealt with while making *RADIUS*—figuring out how to recruit a good cast and crew, secure equipment, and maintain reasonably high production values on relatively little money—are the kinds of things you'll probably deal with as you make your films.

Finally, one last unique quality of the book is that its DVD also includes 1.5 hours of Behind the Scenes video (among other things), which follows our cast and crew as we shot *RADIUS*. These videos, apart from the book's text, go a long way toward showing you what it's really like to make an indie film. They have educational value in their own right.

About *RADIUS*

You'll learn quite a bit about *RADIUS* throughout this book, but here are some highlights:

- It's a science fiction action film.
- It's 33 minutes long. (Anything longer would have killed me for sure!)
- We shot it on 35-mm film, instead of video.
- We shot mostly outdoors, against some epic backdrops in Death Valley, California.
- The film features more than 150 visual effects shots.
- We shot *RADIUS* on a budget of about $60,000 (less than the budget of your average TV commercial).
- We had to use just about every trick in the guerrilla filmmaking handbook to get it all done. (For instance, we made our own costumes from thrift-store clothes, built our own sets with materials found at Home Depot, got steep discounts on equipment rentals, found a crew willing to work on our meager budget, and so on.)
- Finally, I created a two-disc DVD about the film (with more than 5 hours of Making Of material). Then I started selling the DVD through a Web site I set up (http://www.radiusmovie.com) and marketed it myself, with some success.

This isn't to say that *RADIUS* is a great film. It's not. In fact, on a good day, I'm able to look at it and say it's a solid film, but it certainly has flaws due to limited resources, overambitious goals, inexperience, or plain old mistakes.

However, if not a great film, *RADIUS* is definitely an *inspired* film. It took on some ambitious goals. (Trying to shoot an action film in one of the harshest regions on earth, with dozens of visual effects, ain't easy!) It also demonstrated tons of resourceful problem-solving in how it stretched each dollar of our budget. And the fact that *RADIUS* became a retail product that people can actually buy (and have bought!) is rare in the indie film world, where most films are never distributed beyond a few film festivals.

This inspired quality is the essence of indie filmmaking, and it makes *RADIUS* a good model for the kinds of films you're likely to make—maybe not perfect, but definitely ambitious and resourceful, the product of blood, sweat, tears, and a great deal of optimism. And that's why I think the lessons I learned while making *RADIUS* can also help you make your films.

> ### THE *RADIUS* STORY
>
> *RADIUS* takes place during a war between humanity and an alien race known as the Gemini.
>
> Humanity isn't faring well, and it launches its fleet into a desperate, last-ditch battle against the Gemini forces. But this battle is actually just a sideshow. It turns out that the humans have discovered the location of a hidden, critical Gemini power center, known as the Vortex. In fact, the humans are sacrificing their fleet in the hopes of sneaking a harmless reconnaissance ship through the chaos and wiping out the Vortex with a massive CraterMaker bomb. This mission is so secretive that most of the ship's crew is unaware of its orders.
>
> *RADIUS*' story starts in the midst of this battle, but things go awry right away, and the recon ship is shot down just shy of the Vortex, before it can drop its payload. So it's up to Dain—the ship's surviving pilot—to arm the CraterMaker with a 30-minute timer and lead her crew on a mad dash to clear the bomb's blast radius. (That's why we called the film *RADIUS*!)
>
> *(continued on next page)*

xx Introduction

> **THE *RADIUS* STORY**
>
> *(continued from previous page)*
>
> Of course, nothing's ever that easy. Thanks to a well-placed spy, the Gemini are alerted to the CraterMaker's threat and are able to send a weapon of their own—a powerful and unpredictable being called the Diamone—to deal with the fleeing air crew and to stop the ticking bomb before it detonates. But the fate of humanity depends on the CraterMaker's successful countdown…
>
> So that's basically the story setup of *RADIUS*. You can, of course, see how the story works out by watching the DVD included with this book.

What's on the DVD

The DVD that's included with this book is the first disc of the two-disc DVD that I originally sold with *RADIUS*. It's packed with stuff, including the following:

- *RADIUS* itself, which lasts 33 minutes.

- Two commentary tracks. The first track features director/producer/writer commentary, and the second track features three of our lead actors.

- More than 1.5 hours of Behind the Scenes footage, showing our cast and crew making every major scene of the film. This material is presented in a unique way; you can watch the film while a small picture-in-picture box pops up at key scenes, showing us making whatever scene you happen to be watching at the moment. If you're interested in seeing this filmmaking material in detail, just press the Enter button on your DVD player's remote control, and you'll jump to a Behind the Scenes movie. When the Behind the Scenes movie is finished, you'll automatically return to *RADIUS*, where you can keep watching for the next picture-in-picture opportunity. (You can also use your Chapter Forward and Chapter Back buttons to quickly jump from one picture-in-picture to the next.)

How to Use This Book

Watch the film first, and then either watch some of our Behind the Scenes material or just jump right into the book. As you read this book, you'll probably want to go back to the film and watch particular scenes again, to reinforce whatever topic you're reading up on.

But don't feel like you have to read the book from start to finish. I'm a big fan of books that let you quickly jump around and find whatever information you happen to be interested in at that moment, so I've written this book with the same goal in mind.

For starters, there's a chapter dedicated to each step of the filmmaking process—casting, location scouting, set design, cinematography, sound, music composition, distribution, marketing, and so on—so you can easily find whatever general topic you're interested in.

Second, I break down each chapter into headings of factual statements—like "We mixed *RADIUS* during a weekend" or "We edited *RADIUS* on an Avid, but I would use Final Cut Pro now" or whatever else. This approach is a bit unusual, but again, it lets you quickly home in on handy information just by scanning my headings.

As for the text itself, I try to be as detailed as possible, often giving you costs for key elements of the film, time requirements, and overviews of whatever went well or poorly as we executed our plan. Some of these details might be overkill for some readers, but they're there if you want the nitty-gritty.

So that's about it. I hope you enjoy this book, the film, and the extras. Better yet, I hope they give you a little added confidence to move forward in making your own films.

And speaking of those films: If you get a chance, let me know about any interesting projects you have going on. You can e-mail me at director@k2films.com, and if you want to be added to a newsletter announcing any new projects on my part, send an e-mail to newsletter@k2films.com. Thanks much, and good luck going forward!

—Helmut Kobler

Part I

Preproduction

Chapter 1

Raising the Cash

When you're setting off to do your own film, the first matter at hand is where you'll find the money to make it and how much money you can ultimately spend (building in margin for error, because there will almost certainly be error!). Here's how that process worked out for me on *RADIUS*. My sense is that most guerrilla filmmakers will find a similar story on their own productions.

My original budget for *RADIUS* was $40,000 for a 20-minute film.

When I decided to do a film and started developing the script, I originally planned to spend $40,000 on what I thought would be a 20-minute film. This seemed like a smart strategy, for a couple of reasons.

First, $40,000 was a budget that I knew I could secure without too much effort. (I'll talk more about fundraising in a moment.) Second, I wanted to make a short film—20 minutes as opposed to a full 90-minute feature—because it seemed like a shorter project offered fewer chances to make mistakes. Anytime you venture into the unknown and do something new, you're going to make mistakes… or at least I do!

Despite a low budget, I think we achieved some pretty respectable production values on *RADIUS*. It would have been *much* harder had we tried to do it within a 90-minute film.

I wanted to play it safe and take on a smaller film that I could do really well, instead of a bigger film that I might do only marginally well. With a smaller film, everything could get more attention and money. We could shoot on film instead of video, and because we wouldn't have to spend as much money on crew and actor pay, we could invest the savings into better visual effects, costumes, sets, and so on.

If you're interested in getting people to notice your film, you need to impress them with the Wow-factor. I think it's a lot less important that you do a full-length feature when you're starting out and instead do something that makes you look good. That way, people will be eager to see what you might do next instead of thinking your attempt was just mediocre.

In the end, *RADIUS* went over budget and cost $60,000 to make.

As you'll learn while reading this book, *RADIUS* went significantly over the initial budget I hoped to shoot it for, thanks to two reasons. First, when I set my target budget, I expected the film to run only 20 minutes long. However, I couldn't be sure of that because we hadn't actually finished writing the script yet (more on that in Chapter 2, "Writing the Script"). In other words, we just guessed that we'd be able to write the initial idea so that it ran for 20 minutes, but by the time we finished all the script revisions (right up until we started shooting!), we had a 33-page script, which turned into a 33-minute running time. And because time is usually money, we had to spend more of that money on just about everything—film, cast and crew pay, and so on.

Our production manager spending my hard-earned cash. I hoped to see some of it come back, but I wasn't really counting on it.

The second reason for going over budget was that many unforeseen hitches came up while making the film, which caused the budget to balloon beyond expectations. Later in this book, you'll learn more about all these unfortunate incidents—from the hidden costs of preparing footage for visual effects to the need for pickup shots we couldn't get during principal photography—but suffice it to say, lots of these extra costs kept cropping up over months of trying to finish the film. It was death by a thousand little cuts. It was quite depressing to sit by and watch more money flow out of the coffers. It was depressing on another level, too, in that I felt like a poor planner and manager. Each budget overrun carried with it a bit of shame, similar to what you might feel when you tell yourself you're not going to eat that whole tub of ice cream in the freezer, and then you go ahead and eat it anyway.

The Gemini Vortex is a good example of the "feature creep" that caused our budget to inflate over time.

Over time, I had a chance to meet plenty of other first- and second-time filmmakers, and they all had the same sad stories of going over budget. I started to feel better, realizing that this phenomenon is pretty common. Overspending stems from a beginning filmmaker's inexperience and the fact that most indie filmmakers always set ambitious goals for themselves, trying to squeeze every drop of blood from the turnip they have to work with. And when you're doing that, you have little margin for error when unforeseen circumstances crop up. (Also, the more ambitious the film, the more likely something will crop up.) Sometimes you have no other choice but to bite the bullet and spend more money.

Lesson Learned

> Expect your first film or two to go over budget until you develop more experience.

I didn't expect *RADIUS* to make much money.

Indie films rarely earn a dime! For an indie film to make money, you need to find some form of distribution, such as theatrical distribution, television, or at least video rental. To get a distributor to choose your film from a sea of others, it needs something to make it stand out in moviegoers' minds.

Very rarely, that unique something can be an unusual story concept that an audience hasn't seen before and especially grabs them. *The Blair Witch Project* is a good example, as is the more recent *What the #$*! Do We Know!?*. But more often, distributors tend to consider only films that have a cast who moviegoers might recognize and that have production values that meet most moviegoers' expectations (in other words, respectable cinematography, sound design, locations and sets, music, and so on). And, of course, hiring a recognizable cast and ensuring professional production values can get relatively expensive, which is then harder, if not impossible, for most indie filmmakers to afford.

Thanks to that expense, most indie films—like *RADIUS*—use unknown or little-known casts and cut corners on production values. (Sets aren't very elaborate, lighting might not be sophisticated, sound might not be 100 percent clean, and so on.) With the odds already stacked against an indie film, it won't get commercial distribution. It's left to play at various film festivals, which might earn awards and perhaps some prize money, but doesn't come close to recouping the film's budget.

At any rate, I went into RADIUS with my eyes open regarding its chances of recouping the money I spent making it. I started with a vague notion that I might be able to sell it directly to people on DVD, but I didn't really know how realistic that course would be and wasn't pinning my hopes on that strategy as I started the film.

I had reasons other than money for making the film.

Of course, I had two reasons to make RADIUS and justify spending tens of thousands of hard-earned cash to make the film.

- **A résumé piece.** I saw RADIUS as a good résumé piece to help get a film directing career started. Here's my logic: If you want to be a film director, your career will hinge on other people deciding to give you directing work. An established studio, financer, producer, actor, or distributor will have to say, at the end of the day, "Yes, I think this person can do it, and I want to work with him." But to get these critical people to work with you, you first need to prove that you can do the work by actually directing a film and demonstrating your talents. That way, you can say, "See? I can do it!" I was hoping that RADIUS would be that film for me—one that showed I could direct an entertaining film and make a small budget go a long way.

    I didn't have major illusions about how far RADIUS would get me—for instance, I didn't think it would land a deal at Paramount directing a $100 million action film. But I did see it being useful in getting me a smaller film to direct, within the conventional Hollywood system—perhaps a $1 million film for cable TV. That would be a realistic next step after doing RADIUS, and if RADIUS got me to that next step, it would easily be worth the money I invested in it. In my mind, RADIUS was a long-term investment in getting a career started that I hoped I would enjoy for the rest of my life.

Making *RADIUS* was a strategic step for me toward someday directing films for bigger studios like this one. But you've got to walk before you can run.

+ **First-class film school education.** I also wanted to make *RADIUS* because I knew it would give me a first-class education in filmmaking. I'm a firm believer that the best way to learn is by doing. I knew that going through the entire process of making a film—from start to finish—would be as educational as any film school I could attend. Because top film schools often cost tens of thousands of dollars in tuition alone—not to mention the cost of making your own student films, which is the whole point—I thought that making *RADIUS* made good economical sense.

Lesson Learned

Don't do your first film expecting to break even or even make a profit. Think of it as an education, a stepping stone to bigger and better things down the road.

RADIUS' budget was raised from my savings account and credit cards.

The truth is, it's usually hard for an indie filmmaker—especially one without much of a track record—to raise money for a film project. The simple reason, again, is that most indie films rarely get an opportunity to earn money.

Knowing this, you can see how it can be hard to find investors for your first couple of films. I recognized this fact of life before starting *RADIUS* and decided that there were too many risks in trying to raise money from other people. First, I didn't want to borrow money from family and friends unless I thought there was at least a fighting chance to make their money back. (I thought there was a slim chance, but not a fighting chance.) Second, I didn't want to try to raise money from other people, because they might back out at the last moment. Many people outside your closest family might say they'll invest in your film but opt out later for any number of reasons—cold feet, a new baby on the way, their latest horoscope, a better investment, and so on. This can really hurt the momentum of your film production, and I wanted to avoid that as much as I could.

My primary source of film financing.

To avoid all these hitches, I simply decided to put up my own money, which meant drawing from two sources: my savings account and credit cards. There's not too much to say about drawing into a savings account, except that if I were you, I wouldn't put all of your savings into a first film. It's better to leave some for your next film project (not to mention vacation, common-sense investments, or whatever else). You need to consider that your first film is merely going to be a step to your next film or two, where you can apply all the painful lessons you learned the first time around, and where you can show off your abilities without them being clouded by the signs of inexperience and unforeseen circumstances that first films typically bear. When it comes to cash you have on hand, make sure to keep a strategic reserve for down the road.

As for credit cards, they're a great source of temporary cash, especially if you use them cleverly and efficiently. Of course, credit cards are notorious for high interest rates, but I found a way around such loan-shark practices, which started with the fact that I had multiple credit cards that I'd opened over the years but rarely used. Each of my credit card companies constantly mailed me offers to either borrow cash or transfer my balances from one card to another at extremely low interest rates (usually from 0 percent to 3.5 percent) lasting for several months. You can probably imagine how I exploited these offers: I took one credit card company up on its offer for cheap cash, but when the offer's term was about to expire months down the road (and big interest rates were about to kick in), I transferred that balance to the next credit card that also happened to be making a low-interest offer. And there you have it: For more than two years, I simply moved thousands of dollars' worth of loans from one card to another and never paid more than 3 percent interest during the whole process.

Carefully moving balances from one credit card to another let me finish the film.

As long as you have a couple of credit cards in good standing, you should be able to do the same thing, but keep two key points in mind. First, this isn't free money; you'll eventually have to pay off your loans. This sounds obvious, of course, but remember that the road to hell is paved with good intentions, and plenty of people have found themselves struggling under heavy credit card loans when they didn't expect to. Don't borrow money that you're not *absolutely, positively sure* you can pay back eventually. No film is worth a personal bankruptcy or marring of your credit rating.

Second, be careful about how you manage the credit cards that you're taking low-interest loans on. There are specific rules for how you pay the monthly interest due on the cards, and if you go afoul of these rules—for instance, if you make an interest payment that's late by even a day—the whole deal could be off, and your loan could suddenly be subject to conventional interest rates (highway robbery). After you take these loans, remember that you're playing with fire, and be sure to read all the fine print that accompanies the low offers. If you're diligent, you can tame the fire, but if not, you're going to get burned.

Lesson Learned

> Expect to fund the bulk of your film yourself or with the help of close family and friends whose expectations are set realistically low. Finding "investors" isn't likely.

CHAPTER 2

WRITING THE SCRIPT

Most films start with the script, except for guerrilla films. A guerrilla film really starts with the budget; then the script has to be tailored to whatever money you think you can raise.

What kind of story should you choose? (It's probably not a good idea to write a $100 million action flick if you expect to actually make it!) And should you write the script yourself? If not, where do you find a writer? Also, how do you work with that person so that he's motivated and working at his best, while delivering exactly what you're looking for?

I chose to do an action sci-fi film because it played to my tastes and strengths.

I knew I wanted to do a film, but what kind? Of course, when you have a low budget, doing a sci-fi action film isn't the natural choice. Many times during production, I wished I had done something easier that didn't involve tons of visual effects, exotic locations, endless camera setups, and so on.

I chose sci-fi action for two reasons. First, sci-fi action is a passion of mine, and I knew I'd be enthusiastic about doing that kind of film. Sure, it would've been much easier and cheaper to do a film about a bunch of 20-somethings sitting around their apartment discussing the meaning of life, but my heart would not have been in it.

Choosing the science fiction genre didn't exactly make our work easier, but it was something I could get passionate about.

Second, I thought I had skills that would make me a decent sci-fi action director. I had directed and produced action video games for five years. Games had taught me some valuable lessons about pacing and creating a sense of excitement, which I thought I could apply to film. Sci-fi action would play to the strengths I already had, as opposed to comedy or drama, which I love as an audience member but don't feel like I have a natural sense for.

Lesson Learned
Do a film that you can not only afford, but that also will fire you up.

I didn't want to write the script myself.

Before deciding to work with a screenwriter, I briefly considered the idea of writing a script myself. I backed away from the idea, though, because I had never written a script before and had no idea where my strengths and weaknesses as a writer would lay. Plus, I thought that simply directing a film for the first time would be enough of a learning curve, and I didn't want to complicate things unnecessarily.

Of course, there's a certain satisfaction to writing your own material, not to mention an ego boost when you see "Written and Directed by..." next to your name. And if you already have an original idea that you're passionate about, maybe writing your own screenplay is the thing to do.

But I'm really glad that I didn't do the screenwriting alone. I just love the creative process of working with a writer—sitting in a coffee shop, brainstorming a bunch of ideas, cracking jokes about the more outlandish ones, and so on. It's fun, and it's nice to know that someone else will then go home and do the heavy lifting of actually making worthwhile ideas work on the page. In the end, I think I'll always enjoy working with a writer as opposed to writing solo.

Lesson Learned
Don't feel that you have to be an auteur and write your own movie besides directing it. If that suits you, great, but working with a screenwriter can give you important creative input while freeing you from the in-the-trenches struggle to get good ideas on the page. Plus, it's fun to work with someone!

I met writer Jon Clarke through our producer.

Jon was a 26-year-old writer at the time, living in Los Angeles. He had studied anthropology in school but constantly found himself writing stories on the side, so he decided to try screenwriting full-time. When I met Jon, he was in the classic position of many ambitious, talented screenwriters who are just getting their start: He had written a number of spec scripts (*spec* being short for *speculative*, meaning he did them on his own, hoping to sell them after they were done), which had gotten him an agent in Los Angeles, a bunch of meetings with development executives, and some small opportunities, including sale of a story to the *Outer Limits* TV show.

Jon Clarke with the final *RADIUS* script. Well... final for that moment, at least.

Jon and our producer, Andy Trapani, knew each other from their college fraternity days, and Andy recommended I talk to Jon to try to come up with a sci-fi short story. I read some of Jon's stuff, we hit it off, and we decided to work together. Finding a screenwriter for *RADIUS* was pretty painless and straightforward. However, had Andy not made an introduction, my plan was to find writers by posting ads on the Internet and with various film groups I knew of (see related sidebar later in this chapter). Still, I'm glad Jon and I found each other via a reference. The fact that Andy was a mutual friend instantly made it easier to work together and helped build some quick trust and camaraderie.

I paid Jon $1,000 to write the script, including all revisions.

Jon was going to write *RADIUS*' script from scratch, so I knew he'd spend dozens of hours coming up with a first draft and then subsequent revisions. Given the work involved, it was appropriate to pay him *something*, but I obviously couldn't afford a lot. We agreed on $1,000, which would include two sets of revisions based on changes I might ask for. In the end, Jon probably did four revisions for that money and spent a lot of other time on the film, from attending casting sessions to lending moral support on the set in Death Valley to doing a cameo as a flight crew member. (He's the crew member who dies in the crash.)

Coming up with a dollar figure to pay a writer is not difficult. The goal is *not* to pay the writer a market value for his time and skills. That's certainly a worthy aspiration when you're making bigger films with real budgets, but for a guerrilla film, it's just not feasible. Instead, you need to find a writer who doesn't care about the money as much as he cares about seeing his work produced as a real film. (For writers without significant credits, this should be a top priority, because pointing to a real movie made from their script gives them credibility.)

Given this, it shouldn't be hard to find a smart writer who is willing to write a script or give you a prewritten script for free. In *RADIUS*' case, though, I wanted Jon to feel like I was serious about making a movie so that he would throw himself into the work and give it all he had. Paying him $1,000 was intended to be a small compensation for his time. It was also a sign that I wasn't treating his work lightly. Lots of people say "Oh, I'm going to make a film. Would you do this for me?" and then nothing happens. If I wasn't willing to sacrifice something, how could Jon really know that his time and effort would be worthwhile?

Lesson Learned

> A screenwriter is a key part of your team. Paying the writer something tells him that you're serious about your commitment to make the film.

Jon and I signed a written contract.

Jon and I created a written document to spell out what we had verbally agreed to. It was drafted by Jon's agent and clearly stated that I would own the rights to the story and characters created in the *RADIUS* script but that Jon would have a share in any profits that might come from licensing *RADIUS* for comic books, video games, novels, television, or other electronic media. We agreed to determine that share on a case-by-case basis and submit any disagreements to an independent arbiter if we couldn't agree ourselves.

Naturally, we weren't really expecting *RADIUS* to become anything more than a short film, but *just in case*, we wanted to agree ahead of time about how any future success would be handled. This helped Jon feel he wasn't going to be cut out of any rewards that his work created down the road and gave him a sense of ownership. (That's always a great way to motivate people!) It also let me feel secure that if another company ever came along and wanted to do something with the *RADIUS* property—for instance, a feature-length sequel, a comic book, a video game, or a line of fine bed linens—I would have sole control over the rights and could quickly make decisions about what to do, rather than having to convince an equal partner before moving forward.

Of course, the actual agreement that said all these things was written in plain English and only ran about two pages in length. Suffice it to say that a real lawyer would have added pages and pages of legalese that tried to account for every conceivable scenario that might come up. But who had the money to pay for that service? In the end, we were doing a guerrilla film, and within our limited means, we just tried to make each other feel comfortable by putting some basic notions on paper.

> When I've wanted to find a good script or a good writer since finishing *RADIUS*, I've taken a couple of different approaches. First, I've cast a wide net by posting ads on Internet sites that focus on screenwriting or where writers tend to hang out. (I've used Google to sniff out plenty of sites with writers' forums and advertised on the New York and Los Angeles sites of Craigslist.com.) But I've never had great results with ads, because they motivate so many writers to send in sample scripts. The vast majority of the scripts aren't very good, and it takes a lot of time and energy to go

through the hundreds of responses that a couple of ads might raise. Tip: If you do solicit scripts, insist that people send you a synopsis of their idea first. Then ask for a full script if the synopsis sounds interesting. Some writers just send a script, without realizing that there's no way you'll have the time to read all the scripts you're likely to get.

Likewise, I've spent a lot of time on Web sites that offer libraries of spec scripts that writers make available for possible purchase. But again, these sites tend to attract writers who have no other way of getting their scripts into circulation, which means you'll run into a lot of amateur scripts. Finding a good script this way is like the needle-in-the-haystack scenario. Many scripts sound incredibly derivative or just plain strange, and you tend to go numb looking at summary after summary.

Nowadays, I try a more refined, focused approach—that is, looking for writers who have already risen a bit above the rabble, which generally means that their work is more professional. Screenwriting competitions are a good tool. Let the judges go through all the submissions, and then you can approach the winning writers after the dust has settled. Also, seeking out winning films at festivals can be a good way to meet competent writers who have other scripts available, or who would be willing to work with you on new ones. Two venues I watch are the online festivals at http://www.instantfilms.com and http://www.48hourfilm.com.

We constantly revised the script while it was in preproduction.

Jon started *RADIUS* by writing a one-page treatment for the idea that sketched the major beats of the story. (The premise of the film is that there's a war between humans and Gemini, and the humans are in a desperate position.) Then he went on to produce a 20-page first draft a couple of weeks later. After we had that draft, Andy Trapani (producer) and I felt secure enough to start preproduction—that is, casting, designing costumes, scouting locations, and so on. While this was happening, Jon kept revising the script per feedback from Andy and me—once, twice, three times, and finally four times before shooting.

Why all the revisions? On some occasions, our preproduction work gave us a clearer picture of what the script had to be. For instance, we originally had our aircrew soldiers carrying pretty high-tech guns that shot lasers and energy grenades, but as we looked for props, we realized we couldn't afford anything beyond conventional guns that were more readily available.

Jon's being fitted for a costume here, because we planned on giving him a cameo that never made it into the film. Still, Jon was on set for most of *RADIUS'* production and lent a lot of appreciated moral support.

Another reason for our script revisions was what we called *feature creep*, which is basically where you just keep coming up with ideas and can't resist adding them. We added several scenes or elements of scenes over time.

- We originally had Vesay running to get to higher ground but never actually making radio contact with a rescue ship. However, we realized that having him make contact and expecting a rescue would add suspense and some satisfaction as he's caught in the CraterMaker blast a moment before being saved.

- Early on, we intended the Gemini elders to appear in a much simpler vortex—in other words, a dark room with some moody, colored lights (instead of shooting the actors against a green screen and adding tons of visual effects). But our visual effects supervisor, Adam Howard, thought we could do something more compelling with even frugal effects, so we upgraded the vortex.

- The first two drafts of our script never revealed Dain as a Gemini. Instead, she just distracted the Diamone until the CraterMaker counted down to zero and survived the blast by diving into the Diamone's protective shield. But when we came up with the idea of Dain being a Gemini herself, we loved the idea of the Diamone appearing to kill her, only to find that she also had a twin who could stop him in the end.

Adding all this stuff over time was fine, and I'm ultimately glad we did it. But, of course, by the time production started, our script had grown from about 20 pages to more than 30! And that meant our budget crept up, too! For more, see Chapter 1, "Raising the Cash," and Chapter 10, "Budgeting and Scheduling."

Lesson Learned

It's easy to keep adding to a script until you've burst your budget. Sometimes it's worth it, but proceed with caution.

We even had to revise the script after production!

Even after we shot the film, Jon did some additional work on the script. For instance, when we assembled a rough cut (that is, a kind of rough draft of all the edited video, without visual effects or much sound design) of *RADIUS*, we showed it to friends and found that people didn't really understand the opening premise of the film.

Our first impulse was to open the film with a couple of sentences explaining this background scenario. But then we came up with the less conventional idea of Dain sending a video letter to someone she loved, like a last farewell before her big battle. (I actually got the idea from a letter written by a Civil War soldier to his wife before the Battle of Bull Run, which is featured in Ken Burns' Civil War documentary). So Jon wrote up Dain's opening letter, and we shot it on video and added it to the beginning of the film. (Note: Even with Dain's opening letter, some audience members have *still* been confused about *RADIUS*' backstory. That makes me wonder if a simple text explanation would have been more efficient!)

We wrote Dain's opening letter after we got test audience feedback, and then we shot it on video.

Likewise, we found that some test audiences didn't quite understand what the Gemini elders were talking about when they discussed the need to destroy the CraterMaker bomb and give the Diamone his marching orders. So Jon took another stab at rewriting their dialogue to be more to-the-point. We could substitute any subtitled dialogue we wanted, because the Gemini speak a language that Jon made up from scratch!

The same test audience feedback sent us back to rewrite the meaning of some lines for our Gemini elders.

What I'm still curious about is why this audience confusion didn't come up during our writing phase, before we shot *RADIUS*. We had friends read our near-final script revisions, and no one said they didn't understand the story elements that became problems later on. In the end, I think a script reads differently from a story captured on film. Also, we should have been more rigorous in getting detailed feedback from our test readers. If I had to do it over again, I would have given the script to a wider array of people—not just close friends—and would have followed up by asking readers specific questions about their understanding of the story, looking hard for gaps.

Lesson Learned

> Have lots of people read your script before shooting, and get detailed, specific feedback. If possible, don't just rely on friends.

We wrote the script with some strategic goals in mind.

Besides just trying to come up with an interesting story, Jon wrote with a couple of strategic goals that I had given him, to make the most of what the production would have to work with. For instance,

I told Jon to make sure that the story largely took place outdoors. That way, we wouldn't have to deal with many set pieces, which are expensive to rent or build, and we could shoot in natural daylight, avoiding the cost and complexity of set lighting.

Setting *RADIUS* in the desert was an early goal before we wrote the script. We thought it would save money, but it carried its own costs, including crew lodging, extreme temperatures, and a slower work pace, to name a few.

Another strategic goal was that Jon tried to create at least one character in the story who had an interesting role but wouldn't have to carry the whole movie and who would only be featured in a limited number of scenes (for instance, the characters of Kyle or Crim). The reason: We hoped to lure one established, recognizable actor to *RADIUS* and thought that a small role would make it easier for such an actor to say yes. Plenty of other indie films use these kinds of roles. One that comes to mind is Guy Ritchie casting Sting in *Lock, Stock, and Two Smoking Barrels*. Sting has a tiny part, but it gives the film some added cachet.

For Crim, we eventually cast Matt McCoy, who's done plenty of work in mainstream films and television.

If you're planning to make a film, I'm sure you can identify some strategic goals for your script to meet. Writing in a cool, limited role for a marquee actor is great start. Also, perhaps you have access to some unique props or set pieces that are a bit out of the ordinary—you know, a friend who works at an ice rink or funeral home, or someone with a boat, jet ski, and so on. If so, build a story around those elements.

A few written scenes were never filmed.

As we got close to shooting the script, we tried to make it as tight as possible, so there were no scenes or smaller moments that weren't absolutely necessary. Still, after we were in production, we twice found ourselves so behind schedule that we had to cut out a page or two of material. (See Chapters 11–13 for more.) And I was surprised at how, when times were desperate, we could cut material but still not adversely affect the story. When you know what went missing, you tend to regret the loss because it removes a little depth from your story. On the other hand, your audience doesn't know what it's missing.

Jon used Final Draft software to write *RADIUS*.

A couple of commercial word processors are designed specifically for screenwriting. The most popular is Final Draft (http://www.finaldraft.com; $229, or $149 if you're a student). Jon used this package to write *RADIUS* and all his other scripts. Final Draft packs lots of handy features, but the biggest help to screenwriters is its ability to quickly and automatically fill in character names, scene headings, transitions, and locations as you type. This way, you can concentrate on your writing instead of worrying about manually formatting everything according to script standards. Another nice trait of Final Draft is how easily it can track revisions from one draft of your script to another, so you can see quickly how the story has changed over time and go back to old material if necessary.

But do you really need to spend a couple hundred dollars on screenwriting software when you probably already have a copy of Microsoft Word on your computer? My opinion: Not really. Software like Final Draft is a luxury item—that is, appreciated but not necessary—and I've since met other writers who work from Word and use its features to mimic what Final Draft does. For instance, you can use Word's style sheets to set up conventional script formatting, and Word can track revisions over time. (The feature can be confusing until you get the hang of it, though.) Plus, if you want to e-mail your script to other people and allow them to make edits (for instance, inserting their comments directly into your copy), they can make those edits using their copy of Word instead of needing a copy of Final Draft.

Lesson Learned

> Screenwriting software is helpful, but you can write a script reasonably easily without it—and save more than $200!

CHAPTER 3

Casting

Casting *RADIUS* was an exhausting process, but I had a blast because casting is where you get the first clear glimpse of what your movie will turn out to be. It's one thing to read about a character in a script, but it's another to see that character in the flesh. Anyway, we expected to cast the movie with a largely unknown cast, but we hoped we might find at least one seasoned actor whose face some audience members might recognize. And although we didn't have much in our budget to pay our actors, we had other things to offer...

We received more than 1,000 headshots thanks to a $40 advertisement.

We kicked off *RADIUS*' casting drive by running an ad in *Backstage West*, which is a biweekly Hollywood newspaper for the acting community. (Nowadays, *Backstage* runs a big casting Web site for the entire U.S., so visit http://www.backstage.com.) Only a few lines long, our ad merely said that *RADIUS* was an independent sci-fi film, that there was pay (some films advertised in *Backstage West* don't pay anything), and that we were looking to cast a number of roles:

- Dain, female, mid to late 20s, military bearing
- Crim, male, mid to late 30s, rugged, steady war veteran
- Vesay, male, mid to late 20s, self-interested, opportunistic

Actors regularly check *Backstage West* for new casting calls (as do their agents and managers) and respond by mailing their headshot to the address you list in your ad. After about 2 weeks, we had received more than 1,000 headshots in the mail—all for a little indie movie that nobody had ever heard of!

A small ad, like this one, was all we ran in *Backstage West*.

Our one little casting call brought in a deluge of headshots.

Of course, when you're operating in Los Angeles, New York, or a few other major cities that have large entertainment communities, this is the kind of response you can expect. (For actors, it's just part of the job to print up a thousand head shots and mail them out for every role that might even remotely suit them.) But if you don't have a large acting community in your area, you should still be able to find actors through local film groups (for instance, the IFP has offices in many cities—check out http://www.ifp.org), local colleges, and theater groups. It will take a little detective work, but you should definitely be able to find some sources for talent.

We ran casting auditions and saw more than 100 actors.

We went through our 1,000 headshots and set aside any actors that had a "look" we thought would match each of *RADIUS*' characters. Next, producer Andy Trapani brought in Beau Windham, a friend of his, to run our casting sessions. We paid Beau a few dollars. Mostly, it was good experience for him, because he was thinking about becoming a professional casting director at some point. Beau set aside some days for casting each character, called back the actors we wanted to see, and scheduled them to come in for an audition.

Beau spent a lot of time on the phone, scheduling one audition after another. He also had a small cameo in the film, as the air crew member who didn't survive the crash.

We ran our casting sessions out of our production office.

We had rented three adjacent offices to serve as production headquarters during *RADIUS*' preproduction, and we used one of these offices as our casting room. If you don't have a production office for your film (which is helpful but not essential), you'll definitely need to secure some space for your auditions. If I were you, I'd rent or otherwise borrow a small office for a couple of days or evenings so that you have a semiofficial place for actors to go. (Having actors visit your home will give them the creeps.) You'll want a medium-sized room for the auditions and some spare space where actors can sit or stand while they wait their turn. A hallway will do. One tip: Post a clipboard somewhere so that arriving actors can sign in and audition on a first-come, first-served basis.

We did all our casting out of this near-empty office.

Actors came prepared to read a scene from *RADIUS*.

Actors audition by reading what are called *sides*, which is a show business term for a scene that the producers want to see them perform. In our case, we picked scenes that really defined each of our characters. For instance, potential Dains read the scene in which Dain arms the CraterMaker warhead, and potential Vesays read the scene in which Vesay argues with Dain about returning to the ticking CraterMaker bomb.

We didn't want actors to arrive at the audition and read our sides cold, because too much of the actor's effort would be spent just trying to read the lines properly, instead of actually performing them. So we sent our sides to a service called ShowFax (http://www.showfax.com), which has an automated computer system that actors can use to have sides either emailed or faxed to them before their audition. (Actors pay $1 a page, usually.) When actors came to see us, many of them already had their lines memorized or were at least familiar with the scene they would be reading.

We tried to keep auditions fun, informal, and comfortable.

I developed a real appreciation for what actors go through during the audition process. Each actor starts an audition with the knowledge that, statistically speaking, the odds are against them, because many actors are reading for the same part. And yet, they try to stay positive. They drive themselves to an audition (often taking time off from paying work), wait among their competitors for a half an hour or more, and then have to "perform" a role they don't know well, in a setting that bears *no* resemblance to the material they're reading, and in front of complete strangers. And when the auditions are finished, they rarely know if the "powers that be" liked their performance. Chances are, they'll never hear back from the producers.

In other words, auditioning is a tough process. It can easily undermine the actor's ability to do a good job.

With that in mind, we tried to make things as comfortable and friendly as possible. It helped that Beau Windham was running the audition, because he was also an actor and liked to joke around with the actors to break the ice. Also, Beau would introduce anyone else in the room. For instance, I was usually there, as was producer Andy Trapani, and sometimes writer Jon Clarke—and I think we came across as friendly and enthusiastic.

Lesson Learned

Anything you can do to make actors feel at home and show that you appreciate them coming in can help get a good performance (not to mention that it's kind).

Beau explains a scene to an actress.

Each actor read his scene twice.

Beau would start each audition by describing to the actor what his character's scene entailed. For instance, he'd explain the character's general temperament, how the scene being read fit into *RADIUS*' overall story, and what the character would be feeling and going through at the moment. Then Beau would step back and let the actor read the scene. Beau would read any other parts that the scene called for so that the actor had someone to interact with.

After that first reading, Beau would give me a chance to give some additional direction—for instance, to emphasize that Dain has a really urgent bearing after arming the CraterMaker, or to call attention to Vesay's disbelief and disgust when Dain insists that he go back to defend the CraterMaker. Then we would have the actor read the scene again and see how they would do. Even if we realized from the first reading that the actor was wrong for the part, we would give them a second reading, just in case.

We took detailed notes and videotaped all auditions.

As I said, we saw more than 100 actors over several days, and that volume of fresh faces can get overwhelming, with one face blurring into the next. To help with that, after each actor left the room, we would take a moment to discuss the audition and Beau would take some notes. Also, we videotaped each performance so that we could go back and see the audition again with a fresh perspective. (You would be surprised how an audition will strike you differently when watched on a different day.) For this reason, I highly recommend you videotape all your auditions. You can be discreet about it—the camera can be off to the side—and there's no need to ask the actor to play to the camera.

Lesson Learned

> Having a video record of your auditions helps give you a fresh perspective on an actor's performance.

We kept a video camera running for each reading an actor did. If you do the same, remember to have the actor state their name and affiliated agency (if any) directly into the camera before they start.

Finally, we asked actors back for second and third readings.

If we liked the actor's original audition (and it still held up on videotape later on), we asked him back for a second audition, usually scheduled a week or two later. This time, we had the actor read the scene he originally read, but we tried to refine the performance further. Plus, we added a new scene to the mix, getting a better idea of how the actor handled his or her character's range through *RADIUS*' story. We also saw a handful of actors for a third audition.

What I found, though, was that it usually took only two auditions before we knew we had the right person for a role. When Catalina Larranaga first auditioned for Dain, she had a strong, confident quality that emerged immediately, and we only had to tune it slightly to see that it could work. Likewise, we pretty much knew that Paul Logan would be our Diamone after his first visit with us. We went through a second audition with him just to confirm that initial instinct. (By the way, you can see footage from Catalina's and Paul's auditions in the Special Features section of this book's DVD.)

Catalina Larranaga's first casting read (top), and a shot of her in the movie (bottom). We thought she'd make a good soldier.

Finally, we asked the actors back for second and third readings.

Paul Logan as the Diamone.

We hired a casting director to find a recognizable actor.

As I mentioned in Chapter 2, "Writing the Script," we had created a couple of roles in the film that we thought would be ideal for a known actor—that is, an actor whose face and credits might be recognized by general audiences and give us a bit more credibility. We thought the role of Crim might be attractive to such an actor. Crim is a cool character who heroically dies in a big action sequence, and his part only required about three days of shooting time, which wasn't a big commitment. We also thought that the role of Kyle, Dain's commanding officer and a Gemini spy, might be attractive to an established actor, because that character has an interesting role in *RADIUS*' story and would require only one day of shooting time.

Late in our casting process, we hired an established casting director named Rosemary Weldon to find a known actor who might want to get involved. It cost us $500, which was a painful amount of money to part with, but we thought it was strategically worth the cash. Rosemary went on to approach a number of actors, such as Matthew Modine and Charlie Sheen, emphasizing that *RADIUS* was a cool, ambitious film in a hot new genre (Internet film). But in the end, none of these leads worked out…

Fortunately, we found Matt McCoy to play Crim.

We were thrilled when Matt McCoy agreed to play Crim. Matt had plenty of mainstream credentials—he had played a memorable character in the original *Police Academy* movies and then had a starring role in the hit thriller, *The Hand That Rocks the Cradle*. Matt also had a supporting role opposite Kevin Spacey in *LA Confidential*, played the recurring character of Lloyd Braun on *Seinfeld*, and has appeared in a bunch of other films and TV shows.

So Matt is a "real" actor who general audiences might recognize and who would help lend our short film some added credibility. When we were explaining *RADIUS* to anyone whom we wanted to become involved in the film—be it potential crew members, vendors, press, or anyone else—we would say "…and it stars Matt McCoy,

Fortunately, we found Matt McCoy to play Crim. 37

who you'd recognize from *The Hand That Rocks the Cradle*, *LA Confidential*, and *Seinfeld*." Even if people didn't recognize Matt's name, they recognized his credentials. It added to the overall impression that *RADIUS* was going to be a short film that stood out, which in turn encouraged people to get involved.

Matt McCoy, before and after.

The way we landed Matt was a lucky break. Despite hiring a casting director to find a recognizable cast member, we found Matt through a casual reference. It turned out that our visual effects supervisor and visual effects producer—Adam Howard and Kelly Granite—knew Matt because their kids attended the same school. So Adam and Kelly asked Matt if he would be interested in getting involved with *RADIUS* for a few days, and he came on board.

We originally cast Rick Schroder to play Crim.

RADIUS' writer, Jon Clarke, had actually served as Rick Schroder's dialogue coach during his first season on *NYPD Blue*. They had become friendly, so Jon asked Rick if he was interested in taking a part in an ambitious little Internet film. (This was when everyone thought that Internet film was "the next big thing," and Steven Spielberg and Dreamworks' Jeffrey Katzenberg had launched Web sites dedicated to Internet films.) Jon and I went to meet with Rick on the set of *NYPD Blue*, and he agreed to come on board, playing Crim.

Of course, I was thrilled, but the whole thing fell apart because Rick's manager and agent couldn't see the upside. Rick had just gotten his career back on track by joining *NYPD Blue*, and his advisers thought that doing a short film with a team that no one had heard of didn't make strategic sense.

A few weeks later, Rick backed out. Fortunately, I had held off telling other cast members, crew members, and friends and family that we had cast Rick in the first place (not wanting to jinx it), so his departure wasn't the demoralizer it could have been.

Lesson Learned

Don't count your chickens until they actually show up on set.

The original Vesay backed out the day before production started.

We had cast another actor to play Vesay, but he called the day before production started to tell us that he had to back out. The reason:

The original Vesay backed out the day before production started.

He had just been called to do an audition for the hit TV show *Ally McBeal*—a big opportunity for actors just getting their careers off the ground—and the audition was scheduled right smack in the middle of our Death Valley shooting.

Suffice it to say that this felt like a huge blow at the moment. Andy Trapani, our producer, broke the news to me just as I was getting ready to drive out of Los Angeles with the rest of *RADIUS*' cast and crew. (I got to sit helpless in a car for 2 hours, wondering how we were going to find a new Vesay in less than 18 hours. Other than this particular actor, our auditions hadn't uncovered any others that I was enthusiastic about.)

But the departing actor said he had a friend who'd do a great job playing Vesay, so Andy called this new prospect—actor Michael Yavnieli—and the two met immediately so that Andy could see Mike's demo reel. A couple of hours later, Mike was heading to our set, ready for a week in the desert.

Mike Yavnieli as Vesay.

What started off looking like a disaster turned into one of the true miracles of our production. I had never even met Mike until he arrived on set and couldn't imagine how we would recover from the setback of losing a major actor. In the end, though, Mike did a fantastic job playing Vesay, and I couldn't imagine anyone else playing that part.

Lesson Learned

With a little luck, you can recover from even a major catastrophe.

We asked friends to play the four anonymous crew members.

The members of Dain's flight crew—the guys who are killed one by one—were all friends of ours who lent a hand. We cast these friends because we knew it would be hard to find strangers who would want to join us in the desert for low pay, with no speaking parts. (Speaking roles are preferable to actors, because these roles highlight their abilities.) These guys did us a huge favor by joining up but also got something in return: Because they were all part-time actors in Los Angeles, *RADIUS* was a chance to get on a set again and enjoy the process of making a movie.

Doug Purdy had gone to college with producer Andy Trapani and writer Jon Clarke.

Paul Belosic (right) was Doug Purdy's roommate, and Carlton Bruce (left) worked with Paul at the same restaurant in Los Angeles.

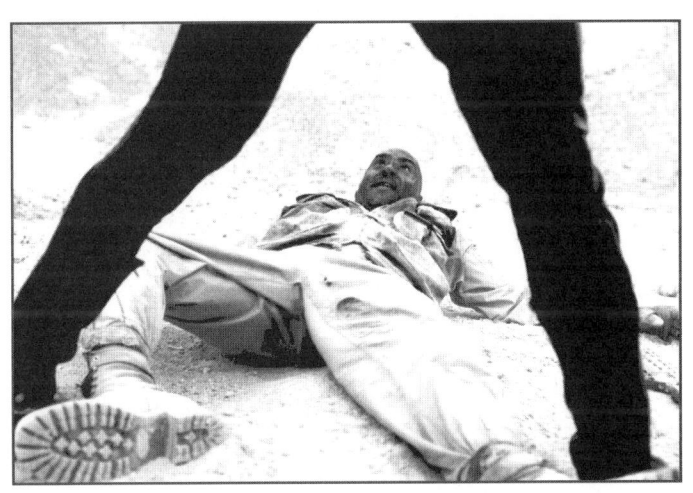

David Bolton was a friend of our Making Of camera crew.

We paid our cast $25 a day.

The exception was Matt McCoy (Crim), whom we paid $75 a day, given the fact that he was a more senior, established actor. We also offered Matt what are called *points* in the film business, which is a percentage share of whatever profits a film makes. Major studios regularly offer points to actors, writers, directors, and producers, but these studios are notorious for using accounting tricks to make even a profitable movie look like it lost money (usually by spreading studio overhead costs to individual film budgets, making them seem more expensive than they really are). Realistically, only top-tier Hollywood talent sees much money from points deals, and few people really pin their hopes on them. Similarly, I don't think Matt had expectations that his points in *RADIUS* would generate a return, but we offered him points for two reasons. First, it was a way of showing appreciation for Matt's participation—even if it would only be a symbolic gesture. Second, on the off-chance that *RADIUS* actually *did* make some money, Matt would be sharing some of that.

RADIUS' other actors—from our leads to the actors who played our anonymous flight crew members—made $25 for a day's work. Of course, I wish we could have paid our cast more, because they certainly deserved it. But in the end, $25 was pretty much all we could afford. (We *did* cover people's lodging and meals during production—we weren't *that* cheap!)

You might wonder why actors would work for so little. Basically, actors getting started in their career need exposure—that is, they need to be cast in various roles that will expose them to audiences and to industry casting directors, directors, and producers who might call on them for other projects down the road.

The way actors get exposure is, of course, by appearing on camera and showing off their skills. But because they don't have recognizable names or faces and few credentials, it's rare when they're cast for mainstream productions such as commercial films and TV shows. So a great place to start is in the indie film realm, where film productions aren't looking for recognizable casts.

Of course, not just any indie production will do—it's useless for an actor to appear in a film with a really bad script or horrendous production values, because the actor would be embarrassed to put that work on their demo reel. (A *demo reel* is a videotape or DVD that features small samples of the actor's work in various productions. Besides going to auditions, it's the main tool that an actor has for getting work). Actors look for productions that will make them look good.

We paid our cast $25 a day. 43

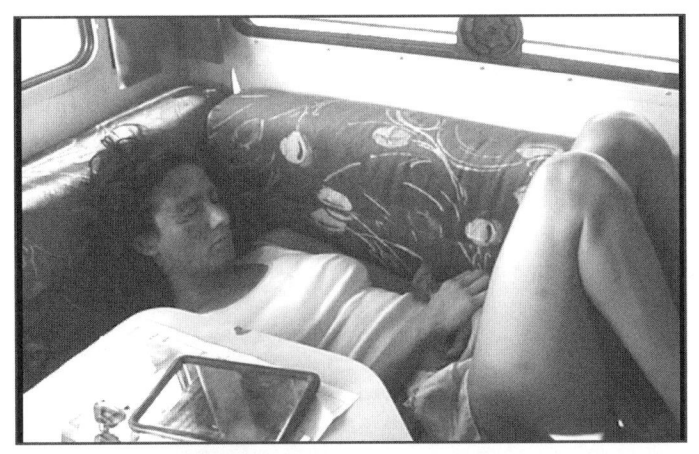

What we couldn't pay in cast salary, we made up with luxurious accommodations. Seriously, we were lucky the cast were such good sports about all this.

And that explains why our actors got involved with *RADIUS*. I think we convinced our cast that the film would look and feel semiprofessional, which would in turn make the actors look good in their featured roles. That's why working on *RADIUS*, regardless of pay, was worthwhile; it was one of many small strategic investments the actors would make as they worked their way up the ladder.

Finally, a couple of other factors played a part. For instance, the fact that *RADIUS* required only a few days of work helped make the commitment bearable for our cast. And then there's the simple fact that actors just love to act. (You have to love that profession to deal with all the rejection and uncertainties that go with it!) Provided an actor has the time, most would much rather act than just sit around the house or do whatever else they do to pay the bills.

Lesson Learned

Appearing in a good film can be much more important to an actor than his paycheck. Don't let your low budget discourage you from casting the best actors you can find.

We signed an agreement with the Screen Actors Guild.

The Screen Actors Guild (SAG) is the major union that represents working film and TV actors. Pretty much all actors aspire to join SAG, because it has established agreements with all major production companies in the entertainment business, and those agreements guarantee a number of benefits that all SAG actors enjoy: good pay scales (including allowances for overtime), reasonable working conditions, the promise of screen credit, and so on. Of course, not everyone can join SAG. Before you can become a member and start paying dues, you have to work a specific number of days on SAG-approved productions, and not just any old indie film will do.

Anyway, if you cast your movie with all non-SAG actors, you don't have to worry about getting involved with SAG—you can just negotiate a deal with each member of your cast and not worry about SAG's requirements, which can be daunting for guerrilla film productions that are making every penny count.

But trouble arises if you want to cast a SAG actor, too (even just one), because every SAG member agrees not to perform in productions that haven't been endorsed by SAG and that don't give actors the deal that SAG thinks they should have. This is serious business: If a SAG actor is caught acting in a nonsanctioned production, the actor can get in a lot of trouble with his union (penalty fees, expulsion, and so on). Likewise, if a film producer is found working with SAG talent but without an agreement, SAG might forbid other actors from working on the producer's other projects in the future.

Of course, *RADIUS*' cast featured a mix of SAG and non-SAG actors (for instance, Matt McCoy, playing Crim, was certainly a SAG actor, but most of our flight crew actors were not), so we felt compelled to make an agreement with SAG. Fortunately, the union has some unique, special-case contracts that are geared toward ultra-low budget indie films like *RADIUS*, and we ended up signing a version of a contract that SAG had developed for Internet and online films, because that's what we expected to be (which allowed for low and deferred pay, and so on). I don't think SAG still offers that particular contract, but it does offer one called an Experimental Film Agreement, which works in a similar way. If you want to see the details of that agreement, in addition to others that SAG offers to indie films (based on budgets and distribution expectations), go to http://www.sagindie.org.

Was signing a SAG agreement absolutely necessary for *RADIUS*? Probably not, because we were a tiny film that hardly was done for monetary gain. Even if we had not signed an agreement, we would probably have been a faint little blip on SAG's radar, hardly worth following up with. But you never actually know, and for our SAG actors' benefit and our desire to have a good relationship with SAG for future productions, it was worth making a deal.

Lesson Learned

SAG makes it reasonably easy to go legit when working with SAG actors. In the long run, it's probably worth doing the extra paperwork.

CHAPTER 4

CREWING UP

RADIUS' crew comprised a few dozen people who worked on the show in preproduction, production, and post-production. We started the process of raising our crew with a few key questions—namely, how to find good people, how much value to put on experience, and how to motivate people to work for pretty meager pay.

We found most of our crew through referrals.

When I was toying with the idea of doing a film, I had no idea how I would find the crew to shoot it. In general, I imagined running a lot of ads at film schools, film organizations like the IFP (http://www.ifp.org), and film-related Web sites. The prospect of building a crew one at a time was daunting, and I expected to find people who were probably short on experience and therefore willing to work for the little money I could pay.

Instead, I found the vast majority of a seasoned crew from referrals—that is, one crew member recommended someone else, who came on board and then recommended someone else, and so on. Here's how it all worked:

Besides me, the first person to get involved in *RADIUS* was producer Andy Trapani. Andy and I had been friends from working in the video game industry, and that's a good foundation to build on!

Chapter 4 ◆ Crewing Up

Almost immediately, Andy brought on board Steve Stone, a friend of his, to be our line producer. Steve worked regularly as a line producer for music videos and knew a lot of people. So he introduced us to a wide array of people he had worked with in the past, such as Production Designer Katherine Ferwerda and Costume Designer Sal Salamone. Steve also asked his industry contacts for other good referrals and was able to find our first assistant director, our sound engineer, our script supervisor, and our production manager.

Producer Andy Trapani hired…

Line Producer Steve Stone, who quickly brought on other major positions on our crew

Production Designer Katherine Ferwerda

Costumer Designer Sal Salamone

Assistant Director Lou Tocchet

Script Supervisor Veronique Fletcher

Sound Recordist John Taylor

Production Manager Michael Silberman

What's more, after we recruited someone as a department head (that is, a key crew member who has other people working for him, such as the director of photography, the production designer, and the assistant director), those heads then brought in people they liked to work with. For instance, Philipp Timme, our director of photography, brought on board his own gaffer and key grip. (See Chapter 12, "Cinematography," for descriptions of these jobs.) Likewise, these guys brought on electricians and grips they liked to work with.

The benefit of this viral process was that there were already a lot of personal relationships established on our crew ahead of time, which was a huge advantage when things got rough and we still needed people to get the job done, despite the low pay. In fact, I would never want to do a film with a group of random people who are all strangers to each other. Not only would it be less fun day-to-day on set, with none of the familiarity and joking that goes on when people have worked together before, but you would have no idea if this kind of crew would be able to pull together when it counted.

Lesson Learned
> You can build a crew quickly by referrals. An added benefit is that your crew will have an instant cohesion.

We found only one person through a want ad, but he was key.

In fact, the only crew member we found without a reference was Philipp Timme, who became our director of photography. We had placed a free ad on Cinematographer.com, saying that an ambitious short film was looking for a director of photography, and Philipp was one of a handful of people to respond. He had a great résumé, having shot a number of European made-for-TV movies, and he'd served as the visual effects DP for Hollywood movies like *Armageddon*, *Dante's Peak*, and *Independence Day*. (Philipp shot the famous scene of the White House blowing up.)

Finding Philipp was a lucky break—not only because of the skill he brought to the production, but also because he ended up introducing us to a whole new set of people. These included Visual Effects

Supervisor Adam Howard, who then introduced us to Matt McCoy (Crim). Had we not bothered to cast our net out with an ad, we would never have found Philipp.

Lesson Learned

> There's little to lose by casting a wide net when you're looking for key members.

Director of Photography Philipp Timme brought along his entire camera crew.

The crew we assembled had considerable experience.

Given what we could spend, I originally thought we would build a crew that was pretty short on experience but long on passion for making an ambitious film. I've always believed that many liabilities that come from a person's inexperience can be overcome by natural talent and lots of raw enthusiasm, and I thought that if we found such people, we would be able to get the film done. I still believe that. There were certainly cases in which we *did* hire people who didn't have experience doing a particular job (more on this in a moment). But when an experienced line producer like Steve Stone came on board, he turned to people whom he knew from previous jobs.

The crew we assembled had considerable experience. 51

We ended up with a pretty seasoned crew who had been through lots of other productions before (mostly indie films or TV shows), and looking back, I'm really glad it worked out that way. Because when we were on set and every second counted, pretty much everyone—from the makeup artist to the director of photography to the assistant director to the second assistant camera person—had been through the filmmaking gauntlet before. Each person knew how the whole process was supposed to work and what their role in that process was to be. (In fact, I was the one exception, because all this was new to me!) I'm certain that this level of experience saved lots of time by avoiding mistakes and miscommunications on set.

Everybody knowing their job well saved a lot of time on set.

If you're making your own film, keep this benefit in mind. If you have infinite time to shoot your movie (for instance, bringing together a small cast and crew on a succession of weekends, where the clock isn't ticking quite so urgently), having an experienced crew isn't so important. But if time is of the essence—for instance, you only have your cast or sets or equipment for a finite time—an experienced crew can be well worth it. And if you can't stock your crew with experienced people in all positions, at least fill some key positions (such as the director of photography or the assistant director) with experienced people.

> **Lesson Learned**
>
> If time is of the essence, an experienced crew is well worth it in terms of avoiding mistakes and miscommunications on set.

We paid the crew what we could afford.

Almost everyone who worked on *RADIUS* was paid something (in cash, usually), although certainly not a lot. For instance, here's a sample of what people were paid:

- **Andy Trapani**, producer. Andy worked either part-time or full-time on *RADIUS* for about 4.5 months and also stayed involved during post-production. Pay: $2,500.
- **Philipp Timme**, director of photography. Philipp met repeatedly with me on shot lists during preproduction, and we drove out to Death Valley on three occasions for location scouts, which were all-day affairs. Then he logged about 10 long days of production work. Pay: $500.
- **Katherine Ferwerda**, production designer. Katherine designed and oversaw the construction of all the set pieces for *RADIUS*—that is, the ship's interior, and its exterior after it crashed. Besides all the time spent designing the sets and searching for materials, she spent days building set pieces. Pay: $750.
- **Mike Bogen, grip.** We had a few grips and production assistants on set, because there was always a lot of gear to move up and down hills by hand. Grips put in 12–14 hour days, in extreme heat, at $100 a day.

You can find other information about how much we paid different departments in other chapters of the book.

The crew joined *RADIUS*, despite low pay, for various reasons.

Given what we could pay, how is it that crew members were willing to get involved with *RADIUS*? People had different reasons, but I think these were the major factors at work:

The crew joined *RADIUS*, despite low pay, for various reasons.

◆ **People liked that we were an ambitious film, trying to do something new.** When we were making *RADIUS*, the concept of Internet films was new and hot, and we were positioning ourselves as one of the most ambitious Internet films ever made. We printed up promotional cards for *RADIUS* even before starting preproduction, had commissioned some nice concept art, had developed a professional-looking press kit, and had launched a Web site that tracked the making of the film day-to-day. (See Chapter 18, "Creating a Pro Image," for more.) Naturally, potential crew members saw all this stuff—which is rare for a short little film—and thought that *RADIUS* had something going for itself. People like the idea of being involved in something that's going to break ground in some way or get attention, and that definitely helped us get talented, experienced people to work with despite our limited budget.

Concept art like this helped persuade potential crew that we were going the extra mile.

- **It was a short commitment, so the potential for pain was limited.** The beauty of doing a short film is that most people only have to work for a handful of days, and then their work is done. (For instance, principal photography lasted only six days, including a weekend.) For many crew members, this kind of a short commitment can be done almost as a lark, without losing other paying work or being too inconvenienced. So I think a lot of people were willing to work with us because the pain factor was so limited. Had *RADIUS* been a full-fledged feature film, it would have been much harder for crew members to justify the sacrifice that would've been required.

- **It was fun to work with a friend.** As I said, we brought a lot of *RADIUS*' crew together through referrals of friends and colleagues. I think a lot of people came on board simply because a friend was asking if they wanted to get involved on this crazy little short film.

Adam Howard liked the chance to work with Philipp Timme again.

- **Experience and credit.** In many cases, people joined our crew and did a significant amount of work to earn experience and get a credit that they didn't have on their résumé yet. For instance, composer Jeremy Zuckerman had recently graduated from Cal Arts, but he had no professional music credits beyond some student work he'd done. For Jeremy, the chance to compose the entire score for an action film was a way to start building his professional reel and point to some significant work he'd done in the "real world." Likewise, a group of young interns at a company called Danetracks did all of *RADIUS*' sound work, putting in unpaid time on their evenings and weekends. They did it largely for the hands-on experience so that they could be better prepared for real work, whenever it came around.

RADIUS was Jeremy Zuckerman's first shot at scoring a film.

- **Better to work than not to work!** Pretty much everybody who works in film production is a freelancer, and most people find themselves with chunks of free time between jobs. At some point, sitting around the house gets old, and many people are willing to take on a cheap job if it means making a film.

Lesson Learned

There are plenty of incentives beyond money that can attract crew members to your film.

CHAPTER 5

LOCATION SCOUTING

RADIUS' budget was small, but we thought that we could make the film seem much bigger than it really was by shooting it against some epic outdoor locations. We also liked the idea of shooting outdoors, because we thought it would save money on lighting equipment and either renting or building sets.

Potential outdoor locations had to meet several criteria.

Following are the five criteria we needed a location to meet before we could shoot there:

- **A dead planet.** As much as possible, I wanted the locations to support the idea that our flight crew had crashed on a dead, barren planet. I wanted it to feel totally threatening and inhospitable to the characters and have no hint that it could support life (that is, not a tree or bush in sight).

- **An epic feel.** In other words, I imagined capturing some wide-angle shots of our crew against a backdrop of desolate terrain that rolled on for miles—the stuff that you wouldn't expect to see in a low-budget film and that would give *RADIUS* higher-than-usual production values.

Chapter 5 ♦ Location Scouting

This early concept art shows the kind of epic backdrops we hoped to find for *RADIUS*. Our logic: If our budget couldn't be big, at least our locations could be.

- **A variety of terrain types.** We also needed to find a variety of locations that supported all the different terrain types our script called for—for instance, the rocky canyons that the flight crew runs through, the high peak that Vesay reaches for rescue, and the wasteland created by the CraterMaker bomb blast.

- **Affordable to rent.** Generally, you have to pay the owner of the location to shoot there (either a private party or the government). Obviously, we needed to find a location that we could afford to spend multiple days in.

- **Accessibility.** It's one thing to find great locations, but we also needed them to be fairly close to each other so that we could shoot at least two locations in a single day. We knew that if the locations were too far apart, we'd lose a day or two of time just getting our crew from one place to another. What's more, we needed nearby, affordable motel accommodations for our cast and crew. Ultimately, we hoped to find motels that were 20 minutes or less from our sets—anything more could start to waste precious time driving instead of shooting.

I wanted to find locations with campgrounds nearby, but our producers nixed that idea.

Ever in the money-saving spirit, I briefly floated the idea that we could save money by having our cast and crew stay in tents and sleeping bags instead of motel rooms. Producer Andy Trapani and Line Producer Steve Stone seemed stunned for a moment. Then they explained that I shouldn't mention that idea to potential crew members, because no one would join up. Of course, they were right; I can't imagine working a 14-hour day in extreme heat and then retiring to a tent and sleeping bag.

We served as our own location scouts, with a little help.

When bigger movie productions need to find unique locations, they often turn to professional location scouts—that is, people who keep big picture databases of spots that are filmmaker friendly and who handle all the logistical work of reserving the locations. Of course, we couldn't afford this kind of service, but our line producer, Steve Stone, happened to know a few scouts who gave him some quick recommendations and loaned Steve a few pictures from their files. These free leads gave us the start we needed.

We did a two-day road trip looking for locations.

With map in hand, Steve Stone, Andy Trapani, and I rented a car and set off on a two-day location scout, all over Southern California and into Nevada. We visited about seven different sites, including ones that we recognized from other movies. For instance, Trona Pinnacles is where Tim Burton filmed the climactic battle scene in *Planet of the Apes*. And we recognized Vasquez Rocks—a huge, craggly rock formation the size of a large office complex—from movies like *The Flintstones* and the old *Star Trek* episode ("Arena") where Captain Kirk has to fight the Gorn monster with only his wits.

We also saw some unconventional spots, such as a family-owned and operated date farm in Nevada that had a bunch of rocky terrain and would have let us shoot there really cheaply.

But we ruled out many of these places for a variety of reasons. For some locations, there was too much red tape in getting permission to film, or the locations were too small to get the variety of shots we needed. (Because our flight crew spends so much time running through terrain, we needed a lot of different terrain to shoot.)

In Barstow, California, we found these strange rock formations that looked like molten lava had dried into hard rock. I thought these would be great for *RADIUS*, but the county required too much red tape before giving us permission to film there.

I fell in love with Death Valley, although shooting there was expensive ($1,000 a day).

I had high hopes for Death Valley, because I'd found some compelling pictures of it on the Internet (http://www.nps.gov/deva) and had seen it featured in another low-budget indie film called *Six String Samurai* (http://www.sixstringsamurai.com). And, sure enough, Death Valley had two particular sites that were absolutely perfect for our needs. First, Death Valley's Golden Canyon features lightly colored, lifeless rock surrounded by sheer, steep walls. We could film our actors running through Golden Canyon from all sorts of vantage points, and the canyon walls made the characters feel small, like they might be swallowed up by the planet.

Death Valley's second allure was Zabriskie Point, which is a peak that overlooks miles of rock and canyons through the park. When I saw Zabriskie, I knew it would make a great spot for Vesay to wait for his rescue and then see the CraterMaker blast firsthand. What's more, Golden Canyon and Zabriskie were only a 15-minute drive from each other, and on a later scout, we found a third spot where we could easily shoot the flight crew's shootout with the Diamone's first twin.

Golden Canyon gave us the craggly rock walls.

Vesay climbs up to Zabriskie Point.

I fell in love with Death Valley... 63

We filmed the Diamone shootout at the start of 20 Mule Drive and found some additional epic shots along the 20 Mule dirt road.

Death Valley looked like it was custom made for *RADIUS*, and I knew we had to shoot there no matter what. Unfortunately, we paid the price for the park's photogenic qualities in three major ways:

- ◆ The closest affordable motels we could find were about a 45-minute drive to our locations. That meant we would spend an hour and a half of each day simply getting people to and from the set, which was more time than we wanted to waste on transportation.

- Death Valley has a well-deserved reputation for extreme heat, and that was a red flag that we all considered. (We did our first scout in early February, and even then the park was hot.) But at the time, we expected to shoot *RADIUS* in early April. We thought our crew could handle temperatures around 90 degrees for a few days. Little did we know, of course, that preproduction would take longer than expected, and we would end up shooting almost two months later, when temperatures climbed well into the 100s!

Yes, it was hot enough to slowly fry an egg on a rock.

- A huge national park, Death Valley gets a fair amount of interest from film productions, which means it's not cheap to film there. In the end, each day of filming cost us $1,000, broken into two separate expenses. First, it was $500 a day for the official park permit, and then $500 a day to pay for a park ranger to be present on our set, making sure that we didn't abuse the park in any way (leaving trash, blocking trails, lighting things on fire, and so on) and making sure nobody needed medical attention. And as if that wasn't enough, we also had to make a $5,000 deposit against any disasters our film might cause and prove that we had filmmaking insurance, which you can read more about in Chapter 10, "Budgeting and Scheduling."

By the way, a couple words about permits: Most public places require you to have a film permit before shooting there, but there's always the temptation to skip the permit and shoot your scenes quickly before anyone notices. This could have worked in Death Valley had we been a much smaller, less conspicuous production—that is, a couple of actors in street clothes, a video camera instead of a big film camera, and maybe one person with a small boom microphone. With this kind of slim profile, you can put your camera away if anybody walks your way and claim to be making a harmless student film. But *RADIUS* obviously couldn't be so stealthy, and we had to get a permit. Had we not, park officials could have confiscated our equipment and shut down the whole production. Keep the same fate in mind when you're planning your location strategy!

Lesson Learned

Despite the costs and pain, it's often worth bearing all those burdens to shoot in a location that will really set your film apart from the crowd. You don't have to shoot your whole film at such a spot—even a few key scenes will be enough to add some impressive production values and elevate the film.

We also picked a working cinder mine for $250 a day and got a whole new look and feel.

At $1,000 a day, Death Valley was already forcing us to spend almost twice as much as we expected on location costs. It was worth it, of course, given all its scenic locations, but we definitely couldn't afford to shoot our whole film there.

Luckily, we found a perfect complement. Only two hours outside of Los Angeles and on the way to Death Valley was an operational volcanic cinder mine called Twin Mountain Rock Venture—the kind of place that only a professional location scout is likely to know about, and thankfully, we had our line producer's friends to thank for the tip. The mine looked like Mars, thanks to all its red sand

and rock. And, like Death Valley, the mine had some key features that seemed to fit perfectly with our script—including a level clearing that ran up against a big rock wall (perfect to prop up our crashed spaceship set) and a bunch of hilly terrain that we could run our flight crew through, early on in the story.

Finding obscure locations, like a working mine, is where having a location scout can really pay off.

What's more, it was shockingly affordable to shoot at the mine—only $250 a day—because the mining company didn't have to do much to accommodate our production. (We were out of the way of the workers and heavy equipment.) Plus, I think the site's manager liked the idea of having film crews out there every once in a while, just for the fun of it. Never underestimate how much non-film people love the idea of seeing a movie being made!

And besides the mine's low cost and its vicinity to Death Valley, I loved the fact that the mine's terrain was red, instead of the more yellow color of our Death Valley locations. Had *RADIUS* featured just one kind of terrain with one kind of look, I think things would have gotten visually boring for our audience. Instead, we were able to have our flight crew move from red rolling hills to yellow canyon rock and then have Dain return to the reddish setting. Our look and feel changed every several minutes, which was really appealing to me and our director of photography, Philipp Timme.

The red, sandy hills of the mine were a great counterpoint to Death Valley's yellowish rock. Plus, the mine was a perfect setting for our crashed ship.

We made three other detailed scouts in our locations.

After we decided to shoot in Death Valley and the Twin Mountain Rock Venture, Philipp Timme (director of photography) and I visited those locations another three times, figuring out exactly where we would film each of our scenes. The idea was to be as specific as possible. We took a script and video camera with us and noted each hill, rock, or other landmark that we shot. In the end, this kind of prep work helped greatly, because when we got on the set with our cast and crew, there was no time wasted in trying to figure out where we'd set up the camera. It was already planned out, and we went straight to it.

At least, that's how things *usually* worked. The one exception was during our first day in Death Valley, where we had picked out a couple of locations about a mile or so into the rocks of Golden Canyon. When Philipp and I had scouted these spots earlier, we didn't put enough thought into how our crew would move all of its gear—heavy camera equipment, tents (for shade), chairs, water coolers, and so on—by hand into the rocks. Of course, we didn't entirely forget that the crew would have to get itself to these spots, but at the time, the distance just didn't seem like a problem. I think Philipp and I had scouted Golden Canyon so many times that we just started to take its distances for granted.

Sure enough, when crew members started making their way up into the rocks in 100 degree heat, things began to fall apart. It was taking too long to get all our gear up there, and we became worried about people dropping from heat exhaustion. So, on the spot, Phillip and I had to pick a new set of locations that were about half as far from the road. (You can see this process in the *Behind the Scenes* videos on this book's DVD.)

Lesson Learned
> When you scout a location, remember that you have to get your crew and all your gear up there, too.

For our post-CraterMaker blast scene, we found a salt flat off the highway.

Just a few minutes' drive from our cinder mine, Philipp and I noticed a huge salt flat on the side of the road. We pulled off to check it out and realized that it would make a great set for *RADIUS*' final scene, when the CraterMaker bomb has leveled everything for miles and turned it all into gray ash.

For our post-CraterMaker blast scene, we found a salt flat... 69

We underestimated the time and effort needed to get our crew and gear into the rocks.

This also ended up being the only location we shot without getting a permit. We had no idea who owned the property, and we didn't particularly want to find out. Also, the flat was about 200 yards from the highway, so we couldn't easily be seen while shooting there. Given that we only needed about 90 minutes there, we wrapped our first day of shooting by sending a small crew to the salt flat, grabbed what we needed before the sun went down, and got out quickly.

With no permit, we filmed our salt flat shots in a hurry.

Lesson Learned

Okay, you don't *always* need a permit. If you can be fast in getting your shots, roll the dice and pray for the best.

Chapter 6

Costume Design

*R*ADIUS' costume requirements called for outfitting 10 members of our downed aircrew, 2 Gemini elders, and the Diamone. This was all to take place in a couple of weeks, and for little more than $1,100.

Costume Designer Sal Salamone came from the theater world.

Sal was a friend of production designer Katherine Ferwerda, who recommended him for the job. He hadn't done costumes for a film before, but he had done lots for independent plays and musicals in Los Angeles. And that was fine by us. Most theater groups don't have money either, so we knew that Sal would be used to working with limited resources. And, sure enough, when Sal showed me pictures of work he had done in the theater world, I was amazed that he was able to create elaborate, imaginative costumes on lean budgets. In other words, he was perfect for *RADIUS*.

Sal Salamone (right) brought some serious low-budget skills to RADIUS.

Lesson Learned

Find someone who has worked on a shoestring budget before, and he'll feel right at home on your project.

I surveyed a bunch of movies for costume ideas.

I had already thought a lot about *RADIUS*' costumes before meeting Sal, so I was able to give him a pretty good idea of what I had in mind without us spending too much time working on pie-in-the-sky designs. It would have been nice to give Sal a completely blank slate to start from, but the fact was, he couldn't afford to spend too much time on the project either, so it was good that I already had some specific direction to give him. The best, most efficient way I could give him direction was to point to other costumes I had seen in movies, talk about what I liked about them, and see if that sparked ideas with Sal. I dug out a bunch of DVDs from my movie collection, rented a bunch of other movies from Blockbuster, and

I surveyed a bunch of movies for costume ideas. 73

made detailed notes about what I liked. In fact, I often took screen shots of still frames or captured video from these sources onto my computer so that I could give Sal as close of an idea as possible.

We did this concept art early on and never wavered from the basic design. I thought the tan and black uniforms would look great against a desert background.

For our soldier uniforms, I looked at costumes from a bunch of sci-fi action movies, from *Aliens* to *Starship Troopers* to *Screamers*, and also more conventional war movies, like *Patton*. In the end, I really liked the desert uniforms from a little-known war movie called *The Beast* (1988). Those inspired the uniforms of our downed flight crew.

We originally considered putting the Diamone in flowing robes, but we thought he'd look ridiculous trying to run in them. So we went with something sleeker, inspired by the costumes in *Dune*.

As for the Diamone: A lot of people think that we patterned his costume after the ones in Bryan Singer's *X-Men*. But, in fact, I hadn't seen the *X-Men* movie when I was doing my costume research. Instead, I came across the black, form-fitting desert suits worn by the characters in *Dune* (1984). I loved the look of jet black against desert terrain, so these became a model for the Diamone.

Lesson Learned

> When working on a low budget, don't try to reinvent the wheel. Look for ideas from as many other sources as you can.

Sal made our soldier's uniforms from painter's overalls and fishing vests.

We knew we wouldn't be able to rent our soldier costumes, because rental costs on eight uniforms would get high. Also, because the costumes would likely get torn up in the desert, we knew we would end up paying full price for them anyway. Sal started scoping out cheap clothing stores, like Kmart, where he could find inexpensive components to build the costumes from scratch. At a little surplus store in Hollywood, Sal found everything he needed. Cheap painter's overalls became the uniforms, black tackle jackets for fishing became flak jackets, and Sal threw in some inexpensive gloves and boots for good measure. The whole package, per soldier, came to about $60!

Sal found all the ingredients of our soldiers' uniforms in a local thrift store, right near the underwear section.

Sal's experience told him that these pieces could look great, but they didn't look so hot right away. In fact, they looked hokey. The painter's overalls were almost yellow in color, hung very stiff, and the black fishing vests were way too big. I was nervous, but Sal started to work his magic. He dyed the uniforms much darker, so they became tan rather than yellow. He also rubbed lots of oil and dirt into the uniforms, making them look like they had been through a war. And two days before production started, Sal brought the cast members in and custom-fitted each costume to the actor. End result: We had some great-looking costumes, custom designed.

Chapter 6 ♦ Costume Design

Lesson Learned

Someone who knows what he's doing will see opportunities where most people—you included—might not.

Before I okayed Sal's design, I took a "test" version to Death Valley during a location scout and tried to see how it would look against the terrain. It wasn't a pretty picture…

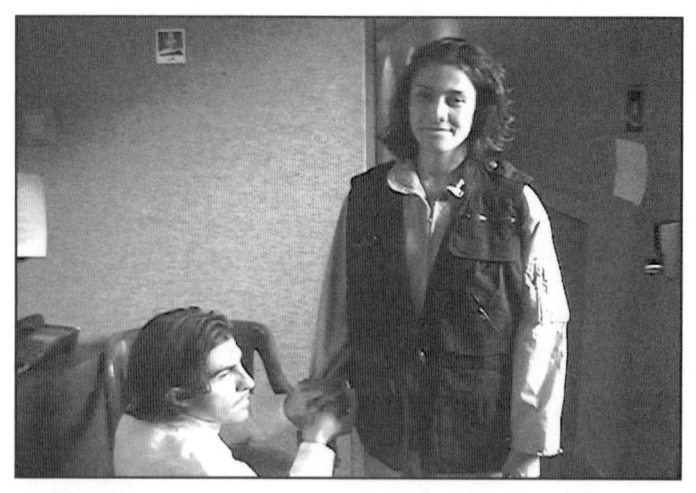

But with a little custom tailoring…

And on the frames of real actors, the uniforms looked great.

Sal made the Diamone's costume from scratch ($300).

When we were developing *RADIUS*' story, we thought about putting the Diamone in a big, flowing robe. However, as the movie's script kept getting more and more action oriented, we thought it would look pretty ridiculous to have our villain running around in that kind of thing. So we turned the Diamone's costume into a full-body suit, which was inspired by the desert suits in the old movie *Dune*, except the Diamone's costume would be sleeker and more form-fitting.

Sal had to create the suit from scratch, because you can't get this kind of thing off the rack. He showed me a bunch of potential designs, and we looked at some fabric samples—thick and thin materials, glossy and dull—but that was it. I never got to see a prototype, because we only had the time and money to make one version of the costume, and it was only ready a couple of days before shooting started. (I obviously had a lot of faith in Sal to wait this long before seeing the final costume.)

Sal took me through a wide range of possible designs and fabric options. That kind of flexibility was much appreciated.

I was thrilled with the final result. For about $300, the Diamone's costume was a miracle.

Anyway, Sal ended up making the costume with vinyl, stuffed with foam padding to bulk up the Diamone's muscles around the chest, stomach, and legs. In addition, Sal used spandex around the Diamone's joints so that actor Paul Logan could move around easily...all for a little less than $300.

The costume looked great on film—as good as anything I've seen in much more expensive films—and it really held up despite the physical beating it took in the Diamone's action scene. The one problem: Nobody envied Paul Logan when he had to wear the outfit for hours at a time in the Death Valley heat. It was so bad, in fact, that we were constantly wiping salt deposits off the suit, because Paul was sweating so much.

Costumes for the Gemini elders were distant cousins of the Diamone's costume, but because the elders would be seen through lots of visual effects, we didn't give their costumes much detail—just a simple top and some black tights.

Sal sent us a wardrobe supervisor to keep the costumes working on set.

Sal had another project to work on during our production, so he set us up with a wardrobe supervisor, Shira Harten. She came with us during principal photography. Her primary job was the care of the costumes.

Before we started production, I had honestly wondered if we needed a person on the set dedicated to costume maintenance, but it soon became quite apparent how good an idea that was. With 8 actors constantly running around in rough terrain, let's just say that Shira had plenty to keep her busy: sewing up tears, cleaning sweat and salt deposits off the costumes, cleaning up dirt stains, and then washing them in the evenings. (When actors spend 12 hours a day in their costumes, in 100 degree heat, you *definitely* want to wash them, for the crew's benefit if nothing else.) The costumes were particularly important because, thanks to our budget, we had no money for backup costumes.

Without a wardrobe supervisor, our costumes would have fallen apart.

We lost the Diamone's costume and had to make another one!

One last bit of trivia: We shot *RADIUS*' desert scenes first. Then we drove back to Los Angeles to shoot our stage scenes, including all the green screen work for the Gemini Vortex. I'm not sure how it happened, but someone packed the Diamone costume on top of one of our vans, and somewhere, somehow, it flew right off the roof during the drive through the desert.

We staged a valiant, desperate search, but we never did manage to find the Diamone costume. We knew we would have to make another version of the costume eventually, because we had come out of principal photography without all the shots we needed and

We lost the Diamone's costume and had to make another one! 81

would have to go back out to Death Valley for a few "pickup" shots at some point down the road. But there was no time leading up to our scheduled stage day, so when we filmed our interior scenes, actor Paul Logan appears bare-chested in his Vortex shots because we just didn't have the suit anymore!

Even now, years later, the Diamone's costume is said to haunt the California desert.

Chapter 7

Set Design

We had to create three major set elements for *RADIUS*: the exterior of our crashed ship, the interior of the ship's cabin, and the ship's interior cockpit. Our budget: about $3,200.

Production Designer Katherine Ferwerda went to work.

Our production designer, Katherine Ferwerda, oversaw the design for all these sets. In film, it's generally the production designer's job to work with the director and design the look of whatever you see on screen—sets, props, costumes, and so on. For *RADIUS*, Katherine focused on our sets, building many of them from scratch and resourcefully within the meager budget. At the time, Katherine did production design for other indie films and indie theater in Los Angeles, and she joined us as a favor to her friend, Line Producer Steve Stone.

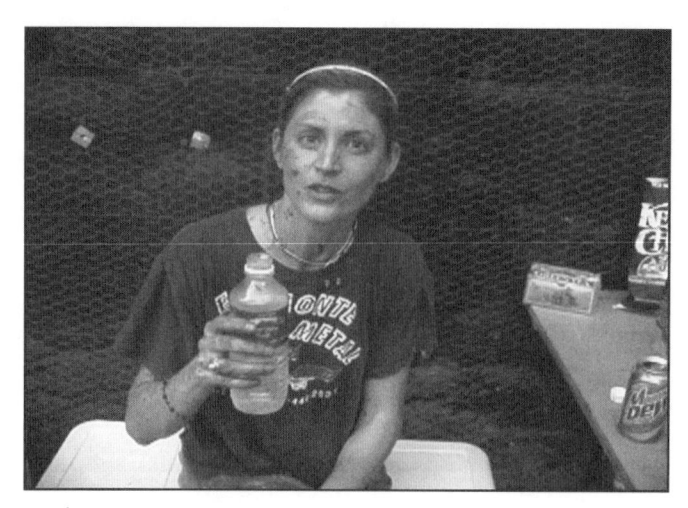

Production Designer Katherine Ferwerda.

Anyway, Katherine read the *RADIUS* script, and then we met and talked about what I had in mind for various set pieces. I'd already thought a lot about our sets as we were writing *RADIUS*' script, and I'd taken a lot of screen shots of set pieces I had seen in other movies. These included a crashed space ship in the sci-fi movie *Screamers* and various cockpits seen in movies like *Clear and Present Danger, Aliens, Armageddon,* and *The Rock*. Being able to show Katherine clear examples of things I liked helped focus her work immediately, which was essential given the slim budget she had to work with.

Katherine started visiting the many set and prop houses around Los Angeles, looking for entire set pieces or partial pieces that she could build around or extend. We'd meet sometimes to look at pictures she had taken at the warehouses, or we'd drive over together and take a look in person. But in most cases, we couldn't find much that either fit our budget or fit the story's requirements, so Katherine just bit the bullet and built most of our sets from scratch, looking for ways to stretch our dollars as far as she could.

To help Katherine handle the increased workload, Steve Stone added two other guys to the art department: Art Director Johnny Spicher and Assistant Art Director Shannon Brock.

You don't need an established, authentic "production designer" to help give your movie's sets and other elements a good look. (Besides, if you're not living in Los Angeles or New York or a few other major cities, it might be hard even to find a film production designer.) Instead, you could recruit someone with an artistic eye and some carpentry skills, and you can find such people in any number of ways. For example, a skilled carpenter might like the challenge and novelty factor of working on a film. Or you could try a painter, interior designer, landscape architect, or even someone who designs retail window displays for a living. Another option is tracking down a set designer who works with amateur theater groups in your area. There are plenty of possibilities, really.

We constructed the crashed ship exterior from scratch.

The exterior of Dain's crashed ship was the toughest set piece to build, for two reasons. First, it would be shot in open daylight, which meant that we couldn't really leave its details up to the audience's imagination, as we could with our more dimly lit interior sets. Second, the set had to be fairly big—suggesting it could carry a crew of nine—and when you're building sets, "big" is not usually synonymous with "cheap."

Fortunately, the location we scouted for Dain's crashed ship worked in our favor. It featured a sheer rock wall that we could prop our ship against, and enough gravel around to suggest that some of the ship was partially buried in the ground, making it feel bigger than the actual set piece actually was.

The crashed ship's humble beginnings.

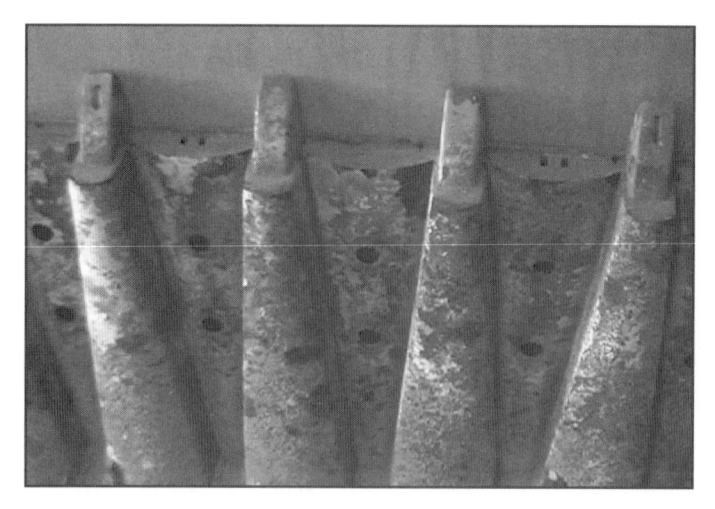

These plastic panels, when painted, looked like armor plating.

So Katherine, Johnny, and Shannon designed a ship that was custom-fitted to that location. First, they created the body of the ship by nailing together a basic frame using cheap wooden boards bought at Home Depot. Next, to make it feel like the frame was made of metal, Johnny and Shannon bought tons of cheap plastic panels, painted them metallic grey, and then mixed in a lot of dirt. When the paint dried, those plastic panels miraculously looked like rusted sheets of armor, such as you might expect to find on a war-torn ship. Finally, the trio added some cheap vacuum tubing and tons of loose wires from a salvage yard to give the ship a more busted-up feel.

Adding vacuum tubes and wires.

We constructed the crashed ship exterior from scratch.

The mine we shot at lent us an earth mover to bury the ship in a wall.

All this took about 8 hours to put together in a small studio that Johnny and Shannon worked out of, and then it took about 6 hours to reassemble and add any last details in our actual location. After the ship was assembled, the set got an additional boost from the company that owned the location. It's actually a working volcanic cinder mine, and the site manager, Aaron Franek, had a bunch of scrap metal lying around and volunteered to move it to our set. So, for free, we could suggest to the viewer that the ship had left a trail of debris as it crashed.

Finally, for a finishing touch, Line Producer Steve Stone spent $150 to hire a pyrotechnics expert to place a couple of fires and smoke bombs around the set. We only had this service for a morning, but it was enough to get the establishing shots we needed of our crashed ship on fire.

The ship in final form.

We rented a sound stage to do all our interior work.

We needed to find an indoor venue to shoot all the interior shots of Dain's ship and the green screen shots that would become our

We rented a sound stage to do all our interior work.

Gemini Vortex. Typically, films rent time on dedicated sound stages, which are big, open spaces set up specifically for shooting film, with a bunch of film-specific amenities—ceiling rigging for lights, robust electrical systems, changing rooms for actors, and thick walls so the set stays quiet while you're recording audio.

Stages, though, usually aren't cheap—for instance, a small 40 by 50-foot stage in Los Angeles might rent for $750 for a 12-hour day—so we briefly considered renting an open warehouse or garage space for a weekend and just using that as our makeshift stage. But, in the end, we went back to a genuine sound stage because we needed a lot of space to set up our cockpit and interior cabin. Line Producer Steve Stone, once again, found a great deal at a place called Santa Clarita Studios, which is about a 40-minute drive out of Los Angeles. At Santa Clarita, we paid about $500 for two days on an airplane hanger-sized sound stage—two half days for setting up and tearing down our set, and a full day for shooting all our scenes.

In hindsight, we should have paid for a little more time on the sound stage. Everything took a little longer than we expected. It started with building our sets, and then we ended up spending more than 24 hours straight in production. Still, we weren't able to get all our shots. At that point, though, we *had* to get off the stage, because another production was scheduled to use it immediately after us. The end result was that we had to spend more time, energy, and money getting pickup shots at a later date and carefully re-creating our interior sets in an improvised way. See Chapter 13, "Pickup Shots," for more.

Lesson Learned

> Schedule enough time to get your shots the first time around, because it's a big pain to go back and get them later.

The sound stage.

> **IT'S EASY TO FIND SET PIECES OR PROPS TO RENT.**
>
> You don't have to live in Los Angeles or New York to find a decent supply of set pieces or props to rent. Chances are, companies in your area rent pieces for parties, weddings, and corporate events. Have a credit card ready, which typically serves as a deposit for whatever you're going to rent.

Dim lighting and quick camera work concealed the lack of detail in our ship's cabin.

Katherine put a fair chunk of her meager production budget into creating our crashed ship's exterior, so she didn't have much leeway in making the ship's interior cabin (not including the ship's cockpit, which we treated as another set piece altogether).

The one thing in our favor was that we wanted *RADIUS* to have a dark, gritty feel. We intended to keep our set lights pretty dim and keep the camera shaking a lot, all the while cutting from one shot to the next pretty quickly. End result: We knew that the audience wouldn't get a chance to study closely what our cabin really looked like. Instead, people would just sort of take in the set's general ambiance, without focusing on any details in particular.

Dim lighting and quick camera work... 91

We had half a day to build the ship's interior cabin from start to finish. It took a few hours longer, which cut into precious shooting time the next morning.

We had a makeshift woodworking shop going on set, cutting boards to spec.

With that in mind, Katherine, Johnny, and Shannon propped up some wooden panels and painted them gray so they wouldn't reflect much light and would blend into the background of our shots. But we needed to give the cabin a *few* details so that it had some semblance of a functioning ship, and for that, we did a couple of things. First, we rented a few old, 1970s-style control panels and light boards from a local prop house (about $50 each), which, in dim light, made it seem like there were readouts and computers on the cabin walls. We also found wooden panels with precut slits. We shined our set lights through the openings, which created some nice highlights on the cabin walls and made the characters' background a little more interesting.

Art Director Johnny Spicher adds a little detail to the spartan walls.

Because we couldn't afford to add these kinds of details throughout the entire cabin, we placed the majority of them on just one side of the ship and aimed the camera that way for most of our shots.

Finally, when the ship had crashed, we got a lot of mileage just by draping cheap wires and vacuum tubes all over the place (the same ones we used on our exterior crash set). We used a little hand fog machine to give the cabin a smoky feel, and we paid our trusty pyrotechnics guy another $150 to set off a few sparks at key moments.

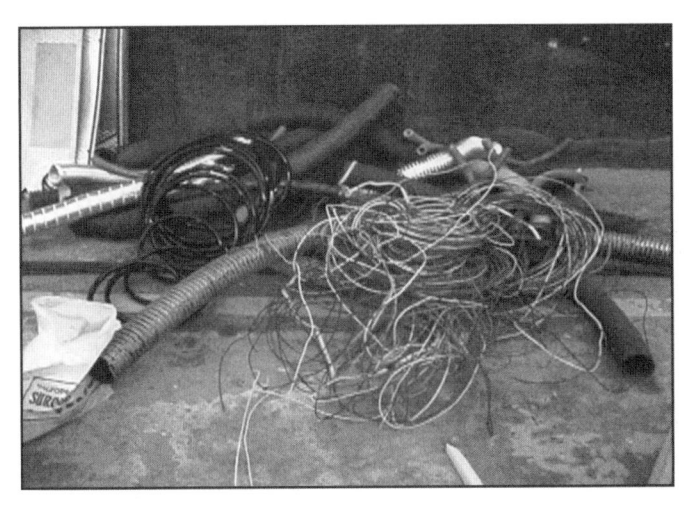

A few dollars' worth of wires and tubing from a salvage yard can go a long way.

Lesson Learned

You can hide a bare-bones set with lighting, camera work, and a couple of inexpensive detailed touches.

The cockpit was the only set piece we rented.

The ship's cockpit is the only set piece we didn't build from scratch. Instead, Katherine found it during one of her hunting expeditions at a prop warehouse in Burbank. This company put it on a truck, drove it over to our stage the day before shooting, and we just built the rest of our set around it (cost to rent for two days: about $700).

Katherine rented the cockpit because this was one set piece that needed to show off a fair amount of detail for the camera, and it would've taken too much time and money for us to build all the nice touches it already had—the glass windows, the flight sticks, the buttons and switches that light up, and so on. Even though our camera never really lingers on any of this stuff for very long—especially given the quick editing we use for the film's crash sequence—you still clearly get the sense that there's a lot of detail there, and that helps make things feel a bit more real.

94   Chapter 7 ◆ Set Design

The cockpit came ready to go.

There's no way we could have created this detail ourselves, so we rented it.

Here's how the cockpit turned out in the film.

When Katherine first took me to see the cockpit during preproduction, I thought it looked pretty cheesy and wasn't sure about it. It definitely had a 1970s feel to it, like something you might see in the old *Planet of the Apes* films, *Capricorn 1*, or something like that. But when the set is dark, all the cockpit's lights are working, the monitors are filled with graphics, and the camera's shaking like crazy... well, the cockpit definitely takes on a better feel. It worked just fine for our purposes.

By the way, the TV monitors seen in the cockpit definitely add a lot to the set piece, but they didn't come with the cockpit itself. Instead, they were another painful rental expense we had to swallow. A good friend of mine used Adobe After Effects to design all the screen graphics over a weekend, and then we recorded them onto videotape. Next, we hired a guy who's called a video playback engineer, and it was his job to modify our rented TV monitors so they showed images at 24 frames a second, instead of at TV's normal rate of roughly 30 frames a second. That put the monitors in perfect synch with our movie camera—which also runs at 24 frames a second—so we would avoid any kind of ugly stuttering effects that happen when a camera and television have different frame rates.

TVs in the cockpit had to be specially synched so that they looked good when captured on film.

Chapter 8

Prop Design

RADIUS called for a variety of props—everything from a first aid syringe for Crim to several functional guns, the scorched body parts of an aircrew member, and Dain's digital stopwatch. These props, for the most part, were the responsibility of *RADIUS*' Prop Master, a guy named Matt McGuire, who was yet another addition to our team recruited by Line Producer Steve Stone.

One of the many props used in *RADIUS*. You'd be surprised how quickly your prop count can add up.

Prop Master Matt McGuire rented and built most props.

As prop master, Matt's job was to build or rent our props, keep track of them on the set, and get them back to their owners when we were finished.

Matt enjoys one of the many gourmet meals we pampered our crew with during production.

To get started, Matt went through *RADIUS*' script and built a list of every prop called for in the story. Next, he climbed on his motorcycle and dropped in on Los Angeles' many prop houses, taking snapshots of any props that might work for the film. He showed the pictures to me before we committed to renting them.

In many cases, Matt found existing, rentable props that worked fine, such as a metallic grenade used by Crim and Dain, the handheld radio used by Vesay to call for rescue, and an LED timer for our CraterMaker bomb, which we could set to count up from any time value. (We played our footage backward to make the clock look like it was counting down.)

Props are typically rented by the day or week. We paid $50 here, $100 there for a week's worth of time. We also had to give the prop house my well-worn credit card number for insurance purposes. That way, if something happened to the prop during production—and in a couple of cases, something did—my credit card would get charged the value of the prop.

Matt built the CraterMaker from scratch.

The most important to-do on Matt's list was to find us a worthy CraterMaker bomb. Given all the bombs that make appearances in Hollywood movies, I thought we'd have no problem finding an existing prop that could fit the bill...until I really thought about the specific criteria I needed the bomb to meet:

The CraterMaker bomb had to meet a number of practical requirements, which made it hard to find an off-the-shelf prop.

- A sci-fi kind of feel
- Some height, so it wasn't too far from our characters as they stood around it
- A data entry keypad and big countdown timer that the characters could clearly see while standing over it
- Something that had a look of heaviness, but was light enough for Dai to drag it along the ground
- Clearly discernible lights on its exterior, to give visual feedback when it was armed or when its power was being drained by the Diamone

With these requirements in mind, Matt started combing various prop rental houses.

Sure enough, Matt found plenty of suitcase bombs—the kind you'd see in spy movies or carried around by terrorists—but nothing that really suited our needs. We were getting desperate with only a week to go before production, so Matt decided to create the bomb himself. Fortunately, Matt had worked as a carpenter and knew how to do that sort of thing. He sketched a couple of ideas, I approved one of them, and within a couple of days, he had built a wooden frame (total cost: about $150), with cutouts for the interior lights we needed and one on top to hold a timer mechanism that Matt had found to rent separately.

Matt and his CraterMaker in the making.

The days leading up to production were a blur, though, and I never got to see the CraterMaker finished and painted until the night before production. Its form looked good, but Matt, according to my request, tried to paint it silver for a brushed aluminum look. It was a heroic effort, but the silvery paint made our CraterMaker look like a beer keg instead of a weapon of mass destruction. The next day, our art department gave it a new paint job, using much darker paint. (You can see us on the Behind the Scenes section of the DVD, furiously spraypainting it as Catalina Larranaga waits to shoot her CraterMaker scenes.)

For the time and money we spent on the CraterMaker, I think we got pretty good results. Given the bomb's big role in the film, however, I now wish I had given Matt more resources to come up with something a little more sophisticated—something he could have fashioned using real metal, instead of a big block of painted wood. But that's how it goes…

Lesson Learned

The more people on your crew who are handy with tools, the better.

We rented seven functional guns for $400.

When we started preproduction, I expected to find gun props that had a futuristic, sci-fi look to them—not something too over the top, but definitely with a look that implied they were significantly more advanced than today's weaponry. (You can see these high-tech aspirations in the concept art we did while working on *RADIUS*' script.)

102 Chapter 8 ♦ Prop Design

Early concept art shows the sci-fi weaponry I was hoping for but ultimately couldn't get.

But, as the old saying goes: Life is what happens when you're making other plans! We searched various prop houses for guns that would fit the bill and definitely found some cool ones. In each case, though, the guns were too expensive to rent for a week for multiple actors. They were usually a few hundred dollars per gun. With seven actors needing guns, you can see how the costs would quickly add up.

Mike Tristano made an offer we couldn't refuse.

Paul Logan, who played the Diamone, kept recommending that we talk to a friend of his, Mike Tristano, who kept a significant gun collection and rented them out to filmmakers. I drove over to Mike's house, and sure enough, this guy was armed like Fort Knox. He has rented guns to numerous movie productions, including Michael Mann's *Heat*.

An AK-47. All the guns fired one round per trigger, so we used fast editing and sound effects to make them seem fully automatic.

There was one hitch: All the guns were conventional, 20th-century makes—AK-47s, Tek-9s, and so on—so they didn't quite fit into the sci-fi world that *RADIUS* called for. On the other hand, renting them from Mike offered three big advantages. First, he would rent us all the guns we needed for $400. Second, the guns could actually fire live blanks, which could make our shootouts more realistic. (We had initially planned to have a visual effects artist paint in muzzle flashes over whatever guns we found, which would have required more effects work and could have looked fake.) Third, Mike offered to send a gun safety expert to our set for a day, who would maintain the guns, load them with blanks, and supervise all the safety procedures that were necessary for working with live guns on a film. (You can see us handling these guns in the Behind the Scenes section of this book's DVD.)

This was one of those classic Sophie's Choice-like decisions that a filmmaker has to make on an indie production: whether to stick with the "artistic" vision or change it to conform to the real-world limitations of the budget. In this case, getting all that Mike was offering for was too good a deal to pass up. The penalty was that anyone who knows anything about guns will recognize conventional, 20th-century guns in our sci-fi movie. On the other hand, the majority of our viewers aren't likely to know the difference between one gun and another, so the issue is moot. (Well, that's what I keep telling myself, at least!)

By the way, you might wonder why Mike Tristano rented us his guns so affordably. Well, he already owned them, so he had two choices: either leave them sitting in his studio making no money at all, or rent them to us for what we could afford and make *some* money. This is the kind of scenario that a lot of vendors face from time to time. You might be surprised at how often others are willing to work within your budget—as long as you're not simply trying to rip them off.

Lesson Learned

Many vendors might find that it's in their best interest to cut you a deal.

When key props were stolen, we had to make our own.

We made it through principal photography with all our props intact, but we didn't have the same luck when we went to get some of the pickup shots that we didn't have time to shoot the first time around. (See Chapter 13, "Pickup Shots," for more about these extra shooting days we tagged on.)

I rented our key props again and brought them to our line producer's office. We were loading up our production van when someone stole Crim's grenade and Vesay's walkie-talkie radio, right under our noses. I'm still not sure how it happened. Our van was parked on Vine Street in Los Angeles, right outside our office (near Santa Monica Blvd.), and our production assistant left the van unattended for about 20 seconds. But that was enough time for some miscreant to walk off with two props!

Unfortunately, there was no time to properly recover from this disaster. It was Friday night, the prop company that rented us the original props was closed, and we had to hit the road for Death Valley. That left us wondering how we could replace these two key props, which would be featured prominently in the pickup shots we needed that

When key props were stolen, we had to make our own. 105

weekend and had already appeared in early shots in the film. In fact, we had only one option: to re-create the props ourselves, that evening, as we made the four-hour drive to Death Valley.

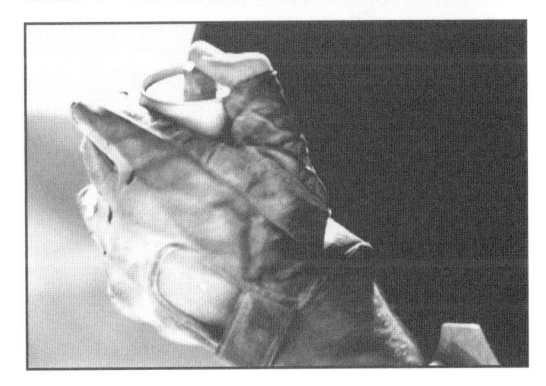

After we added our effects and some quick editing, no one seemed to notice our grenade-by-Red-Bull prop.

To re-create our grenade, we thought our best bet would be to find a soft drink can that might bear some rough resemblance to our original prop. We pulled into a roadside 7-11 and found that Red Bull soft drink cans were a pretty close match. Next, we spotted a K-Mart off the freeway and picked up some silver paint to give the Red Bull can a metallic look. Finally, when we stopped at a roadside café for dinner, we found the last piece of the grenade puzzle: the red cap from a Tabasco sauce bottle, which we glued on as the grenade's detonator button. End result: We had a grenade that roughly matched our original prop, and that's what you see in many of the shots as Crim raises his grenade within the Diamone's shield and finally detonates it. Of course, if you pay close attention, you can see both grenades in that same scene—the original and the Red Bull version—because some of the footage was shot during principal photography, and the rest was shot during our pickup weekend.

We found a similar solution for Vesay's missing radio. When we stopped at K-Mart to buy the silver paint for our Red Bull grenade, we also bought a toy walkie-talkie kit (about $7), along with some black paint. That's the radio you see when Vesay makes his rescue calls from the top of Death Valley. (Of course, we chose camera angles that barely showed the radio, never calling the audience's attention to it.)

I was paranoid that the audience would spot these inconsistencies, but after playing the edited scenes for friends and family and asking if they saw anything strange, I realized that no one noticed our fake props. They were a huge issue in my mind because I knew what to look for, but an unsuspecting audience doesn't have that predisposition. People aren't usually paying attention to such small details. They're caught up in the story, the editing, and everything else that's going on. Small inconsistencies, as long as they're not broadcast by a lingering camera, just don't register.

Lesson Learned

If you're careful, you can hide a lot of little mistakes from an audience.

When key props were stolen, we had to make our own.

Our first radio had a keypad on the front, but the toy radio from K-Mart didn't.

Chapter 9

Storyboards and Shot Lists

Storyboards are a common tool that filmmakers use to visualize how their film will look after it's shot. We created traditional storyboards for *RADIUS*, but we also shot "video storyboards." I definitely emerged from the experience with a strong preference...

We only did conventional storyboards for a couple of scenes.

When we started preproduction, I didn't have a good sense for how to use storyboards, so I unnecessarily had a storyboard artist draw a couple for *RADIUS*' scenes. Why do I say "unnecessarily"? Well, I think that conventional storyboards have a place in film production but aren't as necessary for indie films that are on a tight budget.

Storyboards let you design how each shot will look in your movie, shot by shot, scene by scene. They frame the action of a scene as the camera is supposed to capture it. There's a lot of "art" to storyboards in that a good artist will be able to compose visually interesting shots that match the emotional temperament of your scene and help keep your audience engaged. For instance, an artist might come up with the idea to capture a character's eye or mouth in an ultra-tight close-up so that the audience can clearly see any nervous twitches during a tense conversation. Or a storyboard artist might design an action sequence to use a rotated camera lens, to give the action a fresh perspective that you don't normally see.

110   Chapter 9 ♦ Storyboards and Shot Lists

A sample of how our traditional storyboards translated to film.

Anyway, we didn't need an artist to storyboard dialogue exchanges between characters, because I knew that our limited time would only let us shoot them in a straightforward way. But I did think that storyboards would be helpful for our action sequences, so I had our artist take a crack at drawing out *RADIUS*' opening crash sequence and the big crew shootout with the Diamone's first twin.

What I found tough about the storyboarding process was that our artist kept coming up with unique shot ideas, but I had no idea if we'd actually be able to implement them. We didn't have our set pieces or our locations finalized yet, and I wasn't certain what kind of specialized camera equipment (for instance, a crane or dolly shots)

We only did conventional storyboards for a couple of scenes. 111

we might have, beyond a simple tripod. So the storyboard artist could do some cool work, but it felt a little premature.

That's why I think storyboards are much more useful for productions that have a lot of money. On richer productions, a storyboard artist (or concept artist) could work from scratch to draw up some cool, pie-in-the-sky ideas. Then the production could build its sets and scout for locations that matched the storyboard artists' ideas.

In the end, I don't think doing storyboards made much of a difference.

But we didn't have that luxury on *RADIUS*. Instead, we first had to find whatever sets and locations we could actually afford on our limited budget; then we had to tailor our shots to work within whatever limits those elements imposed, instead of the other way around. Of course, after we had our sets and locations picked out, we could have started to do conventional storyboarding work. However, by that time, I realized that video storyboards would be more accurate and useful.

There was one additional case in which storyboards came in handy, and that was when we went into post production. Digital Behavior, a small company that did our computer-generated ship shots, asked for storyboards to show exactly what I wanted Dain's crashing ship to do in each shot. For Digital Behavior, it was a way to make sure that I knew what I wanted from them before they started the work so they wouldn't have to rework shots because of uncertainty on my part. In the realm of visual effects, where an entire shot is created from scratch, storyboards definitely give you valuable direction ahead of time...

Storyboarding pure visual effects shots can be helpful, because your artists can reproduce them closely and don't spend much valuable time with experimentation and trial and error.

One more thing: Before I totally swear off storyboards (at least for non-effects work), I've been meaning to try some of the storyboarding software that's been invented over the past couple of years. These applications let non-artists build storyboards from big libraries of predesigned artwork and move the storyboard's camera perspective around. A few of the packages I mean to look at further include Storyboard Quick (http://www.powerproduction.com) and Storyboard Lite (http://www.zebradevelopment.com).

Lesson Learned

> Storyboards aren't so useful until you have your locations, sets, and camera equipment in place.

Video storyboards with placeholder actors were much more useful.

For *RADIUS*' action sequences, Philipp Timme (director of photography) and I shot a series of "video storyboards," where we took some friends out to Death Valley a couple of weeks before production and actually taped them doing the same things that we wanted our real actors to do, and in the same locations.

Shooting video storyboards in our Death Valley locations gave me a hands-on feel for our shots.

You can watch a sample of these video storyboards on this book's DVD (check the Special features section). As you'll see, many of the shots we established in the storyboards ended up in the final film. Of course, the video storyboards won't win awards for acting or pretty much anything else, but they were helpful in that we could easily figure out what shots we wanted—that is, which camera angles and framing would be best—in the actual locations we'd picked. Going to Death Valley ahead of time and planning our shots right there was like having a dress rehearsal for all the camerawork we would be doing during production.

114　Chapter 9 ◆ Storyboards and Shot Lists

The upfront work of video storyboarding paid off, because by the time we returned to Death Valley with our full cast and crew, we knew exactly where we wanted the camera to go—no weighing options, no discussions. We just went straight to work without wasting any time.

Although we made some adjustments during production, many of the shots we storyboarded made it into the picture.

Of course, you can get a similar benefit by walking around a set with a director's viewfinder instead of a video camera (as you'll see directors doing in Making Of documentaries). But director's viewfinders are hundreds of dollars, and they can't record imagery! With a video camera, you can record moving action, which gives you a better sense of how your shots will look. Also, I found it really helpful to capture the videos on my computer and edit them into a rough cut of *RADIUS*' scenes. (I added a little placeholder music for extra effect.) Being able to get this kind of preview of how the real film would look isn't something that experienced directors really need, but it gave me some much-appreciated confidence that our shots would cut together pretty well.

Whatever shots we didn't storyboard, we identified on a shot list. 115

I couldn't ask our actors to go to Death Valley, and I didn't want to use them for storyboarding purposes anyway. The reason: When I was ready for the actors, I wanted to be fully prepared.

Lesson Learned

> Video storyboards let you work within your actual sets and locations. Plus, you can edit the storyboards into rough cuts of scenes to see how your shots work together.

Whatever shots we didn't storyboard, we identified on a shot list.

A *shot list* is a list of all the shots you want to get for a particular scene in your movie. And by "shot," I mean a new camera or lens setup. For instance, in our cockpit during *RADIUS'* opening crash scene, we had a handful of shots:

- A close-up of Kyle
- A close-up of Dain
- A wide shot of both Dain and Kyle in the cockpit, front on

- A shot of both Dain and Kyle, but from the cockpit's left side
- A shot of both Dain and Kyle, but from the cockpit's right side
- A close-up of Kyle's hands on his flight stick, and other flight controls
- A close-up of Dain's hands on his flight stick, and other flight controls
- A close-up of Dain's cockpit monitor

Philipp Timme and I had a similar list of shots written down for almost every scene in the film. (The exception was dialogue exchanges, which we knew would require a wide shot establishing two actors in the same frame and then close-ups for each actor.) Building this list of shots was helpful for two reasons. First, coming up with a shot list forced us to think about what we wanted a given scene to look like on film. It sparked the creative process. Second, after the shot list started taking shape, we could see whether a shot was actually feasible, given our film's schedule and budget. When it wasn't, we revised it and revised it again—eliminating shots, combining others, and so on, until we thought we had a realistic list.

The end result of all this work is that we always knew what we wanted to shoot at any moment on set and worked off a big checklist every day. It's a much better option than the alternative, which is to show up on set without a detailed plan and then just try to make things up as you go along.

Lesson Learned

> Writing a detailed shot list forces you to think carefully about the shots you want and gives you a plan to work from when you're on set.

Budgeting and Scheduling

The creative process of prepping a film for production—for instance, casting, location scouting, costume design, and so on—is a blast, but the logistical side of the preproduction process is just as important. Accurately setting your budget can mean the difference between finishing your film or completing just half of it as you raise extra cash to finally complete it. Your ability to schedule a film accurately holds the same consequences, because an accurate schedule is what lets you create and stick to a realistic budget, and vice versa.

Line Producer Steve Stone created *RADIUS'* budget.

Producer Andy Trapani and I had set our ideal budget for *RADIUS*—again, about $40,000—and it fell on Line Producer Steve Stone to figure out how we would get the film done for that amount. That's what line producers do: They budget a movie during preproduction and then keep an eye on costs as the film is being made.

Chapter 10 ◆ Budgeting and Scheduling

Steve Stone budgeted *RADIUS*, recruited crew members, and helped scout locations and find props. (He's seen here in a prop we briefly considered.)

Normally, a line producer budgets a film *before* it goes into preproduction. A producer takes a script to a line producer and asks him to come up with an accurate budget. Then the producer takes that budget to studios or financers to ask if they're willing to fund the film for that amount of money. If not, the producer might go back to the drawing board, working with the writer, attached director (if any), line producer, and perhaps other principals to figure out where they can make changes to the script to save money.

We did things a little differently on *RADIUS*. I established the budget before we wrote the film, because $40,000 was what I thought I could afford to raise myself, without great financial risk. (See Chapter 1, "Raising the Cash," for more.) Then Jon Clarke wrote the script, trying to tailor it to the budget at hand. By the time we hired Line Producer Steve Stone, we basically wanted him to figure out how to execute the script on the budget we already had.

Line Producer Steve Stone created RADIUS' budget.

Steve went over our script with a fine-toothed comb, developing an understanding for everything the script called for—locations, props, sets, the number of actors required, and so on. He also asked me a number of detailed questions about how I intended to shoot various scenes. For instance, he asked if we planned to use potentially expensive equipment, such as a dolly, for various scenes.

As Steve developed a better understanding of the script, he started building a budget. Of course, as I've mentioned elsewhere, Steve found that it was impossible to get everything we wanted done on $40,000. Our script was a bit too ambitious for that dollar neighborhood, so I ended up increasing the budget, little by little, to around $60,000 before everything was said and done.

EXPERIENCE PAYS OFF IN A LINE PRODUCER.

Not all line producers are equal. Really, anyone can build a budget by calling various vendors and asking how much such-and-such a piece of equipment will cost and then tallying all the items in a spreadsheet program. However, if you leave this job to just anybody, you're going to end up with a film that costs a lot more money than it has to.

A good line producer knows where to sniff out great deals, thanks to two qualities: past experience on other film productions, and a resourceful, dealmaker's kind of instinct. Fortunately, Steve Stone has both of these qualities. By the time we met him, he had already acted as a line producer on plenty of music videos and industrial videos around Los Angeles. (He got his start in the business as a camera technician years before.) This kind of work taught him what film productions need in the real world, and it gave him tons of contacts at vendors that rent cameras, lights, props, sets, and all other equipment. For *RADIUS*, Steve was able to go to many of those vendors—who he had frequently worked with on bigger productions—and ask them to grant *RADIUS* some favors or discounts. (The fact that we were a little indie film with only basic and short-term needs made this feasible.) Basically, Steve knew what he might be able to ask for and who might be willing to give him a deal. And, in many cases, he was successful. After all, why wouldn't a vendor want to help out a guy who brought them a lot of business in the past, especially by loaning out equipment that was needed only for short periods of time?

Steve Stone used Microsoft Excel to budget *RADIUS*.

EP Budgeting (htpp://www.entertainmentpartners.com) is well-known budgeting software that film producers use to budget all sorts of major Hollywood productions. For indie films, using EP Budgeting is like hunting a mosquito with an elephant gun. Not only does the software cost $500, but its endlessly detailed expense categories and intricate calculations are way too complicated for typical bare-budget indie films.

That's why Steve built *RADIUS*' budget with the help of a spreadsheet product called Point Zero, which he loaded into Microsoft Excel. Point Zero already had line items for just about every kind of expense that a small production might encounter. For instance, there were the obvious expenses, such as crew salaries and equipment rental costs, plus the fees you might overlook but that still add up—everything from location fees and shooting permits to rental cars, walkie-talkies, and tape dubbing fees.

Besides giving Steve tons of line item costs to consider, the Point Zero spreadsheet made it easy to quickly determine the bulk of *RADIUS*' costs, based on a few key values Steve plugged in. He would enter a day rate for various cast and crew members and key rental equipment and then a couple of values estimating each person's related costs for motels, food, and transportation. Then he would plug in the number of days our shoot would last. With those basic numbers, the Point Zero spreadsheet could instantly give Steve a ballpark idea of where our budget would end up.

Point Zero is still available (http://www.pointzerobudget.com), but it costs $395, so you might do well to consider other inexpensive film budgeting programs. (Check out the $189 Easy Budget at http://www.easy-budget.com.) But if your film is pretty straightforward, you can also build your own budgeting tools. With only a rudimentary knowledge of Microsoft Excel or another spreadsheet program, you can build a basic budget template for yourself, plug in key numbers, and see how they affect the cost of your film. Beyond the spreadsheet know-how, which you can learn in about 15 minutes by studying the program's online Help system, the budgeting process is really about anticipating smaller expenses. Obviously, you need to include primary costs for crew pay and equipment rental and location fees, but the tougher work is in catching the smaller fees that can surprise you if you don't plan in detail and that add up over time. For instance, don't forget to factor in a portable generator if you'll be setting up outdoor lights, extra hard drives to back up all the digital media you accumulate, and FedEx shipping costs that might arise.

Lesson Learned

> A producer or line producer who's already been through the filmmaking process will help you spot smaller, less obvious costs (not to mention securing better deals than you could do by yourself). But if you're budgeting things yourself, just remember that the devil's in the details. The more time you spend carefully thinking about each step in the process, the fewer surprises you'll have down the road.

Steve brought along production insurance.

Besides his many other services, Steve provided *RADIUS* with essential production insurance. This is something that a lot of first-time filmmakers aren't aware of, but it's a necessity for anything but the most off-the-radar guerrilla productions.

Just as you would buy insurance for your car or house, you can get insurance for your film. Production insurance covers a variety of things—everything from the cost of replacing damaged equipment, such as cameras or lights, to covering injuries that your cast and crew might sustain during their work, or damage to the sets and locations you're filming.

If you're working on a truly bare-bones guerrilla film, you can skip insurance. But insurance is often necessary if you want to rent expensive equipment from established vendors. For instance, although we got a great deal on our 35-mm camera system from Otto Nemetz in Los Angeles, the company wasn't about to hand over a $100,000 package until we could prove our insurance would cover its value if it got damaged. Likewise, the Screen Actors Guild requires that any production using its actors must be covered by workers' compensation insurance in case an actor is injured in the line of duty. Similarly, Death Valley National Park requires insurance for productions filmed there to cover damage to the environment.

Many things can go wrong on a film set, which is why comprehensive insurance is a good idea.

Anybody with decent credit can get production insurance on a per-film basis. Many film insurance brokers are available. One popular one in the indie community is Film Emporium, which you can check out at http://www.filmemporium.com. Insurance rates can range from several hundred dollars on up. For example, I recently called for insurance rates on a 10-day production, using about $350,000 of rented equipment in outdoor locations, with SAG actors. The insurance quote came to about $3,000, which covered the value of the film equipment, up to $1 million of workers' compensation coverage, and $1 million of vehicle liability (in case someone crashes a car while working on your production).

Of course, $3,000 sounds pretty steep for a low-budget film, but working with Steve Stone let us enjoy the benefits of insurance without actually paying for it. Steve already has his own production company called Southwest Films, which he uses to produce small jobs (such as independent music videos) on his own. Steve had already bought an annual insurance policy for Southwest Films that covered all his production work for the year. Naturally, we designed

RADIUS as a Southwest Films production, so it fell under the insurance coverage Steve had already bought, at no extra cost!

Lesson Learned

Find a producer or line producer who already has production insurance, and do your film under that insurance policy.

Assistant Director Lou Tocchet scheduled *RADIUS'* production.

About a month before production, we hired a guy named Lou Tocchet to serve as *RADIUS*' assistant director. A lot of people who don't work in the film business assume that the assistant director must be like the film director's personal assistant, or maybe a junior-style director who somehow participates in the creative process but is overseen by the senior director in charge.

Lou Tocchet built *RADIUS'* schedule on his trusty PowerBook.

But that's not actually the case. Instead, the assistant director is a key player in his own right and has entirely different responsibilities than a movie's director. The assistant director is really like an operations manager who runs the set, making sure everything and everyone is set up for each shot, ready for the director to call "Action!" Having a good assistant director on your set is essential. There are so many different people whose work needs to be coordinated, that the assistant director is the equivalent of an air traffic controller on the film set. Without him, the cast and crew end up standing around trying to get organized instead of actually shooting shots.

Anyway, because Lou would be responsible for running the set during production, he had to join our team toward the end of pre-production, planning out how we would get all our work done after we were on set.

Lou carefully went through *RADIUS*' script, and with an eye for every detail, figured out what scenes should be shot in what order, given how many different locations and how many shooting days producer Andy Trapani had given him to work with. In building this schedule, Lou created a day-by-day, often hour-by-hour breakdown of what the cast and crew would be doing—that is, who would be needed at what time in what location, along with what equipment. Lou printed a lot of different reports to help him organize the production, including a call sheet for each day, which detailed when everyone was to be on call during production. These call sheets went out to all key crew members well before production started, so that everyone could adjust their plans to follow Lou's master plan.

Lou used EP Scheduling to plan *RADIUS'* production.

Lou is a professional assistant director (one of his early gigs was as an assistant assistant director on *Titanic*), so he used professional software called EP Scheduling (http://www.entertainmentpartners.com) to organize *RADIUS*. EP Scheduling runs on Macs and PCs and offers a bunch of tools that help assistant directors and producers schedule the nitty-gritty of a production. For starters, the software features templates that help estimate the time that various tasks take, based on the complexity of those tasks (the number of crew members involved, the kind of equipment you have, and the types of shooting locations). It can also automatically "ripple" any changes you make through the rest of your schedule. For instance, if you double the time required to shoot a scene, you'll quickly see how that can impact the rest of your schedule, even accounting for details such as the times that certain locations are available to your production, or how schedule changes might affect overtime hours for your cast and crew.

But EP Scheduling costs $499. It's really designed for scheduling major film productions, so it's clearly overkill for what most guerrilla filmmakers need. If you're making a film on a shoestring, you'll certainly want to schedule it as meticulously as possible, because working to a prearranged plan helps you squeeze every bit of efficiency out of the precious time you have on set. Don't go easy on the scheduling just because you don't have a specialized scheduling tool. Instead, spend plenty of time thinking through exactly how you'll spend each production day. Consider how long the following will take crew members:

- Get organized in the morning
- Move from one location to the next
- Change costumes
- Set up lights
- Eat lunch

After finishing *RADIUS*' principal photography, we still needed to spend a few days getting pickup shots, and I ended up scheduling some of these days myself to save money. Our cast and crew were smaller on these days, and our equipment needs were lighter. However, there was still a considerable amount of planning needed, and I did it all by making a detailed list in Microsoft Excel, thinking carefully about the time each step would take.

Lou called a final meeting with all key team members.

Three days before production, Lou called in all the key crew members for a final preproduction meeting. Besides Lou and me, attendees included the following people:

- Line Producer Steve Stone
- Producer Andy Trapani
- Visual Effects Supervisor Adam Howard
- Visual Effects Producer Kelly Granite

- Director of Photography Philipp Timme
- Gaffer Mark Brinegar
- Key Grip David Hadsel
- Production Designer Katherine Ferwerda
- Art Director Johnny Spicher
- Wardrobe Supervisor Shira Harten
- Prop Master Matt McGuire
- Makeup Artist Jennifer Darany
- Sound Recordist John Taylor
- Script Supervisor Veronique Fletcher

Although many of us had met each other separately, this was the first and last opportunity that the team would have to meet as a group before we were actually on the set. It was also a final chance to make sure that nobody had any last-minute questions about the script or any other issues we would be dealing with on the set.

Lou led the entire group page by page though the script, interjecting helpful information that people might need to know and giving anybody a chance to stop the reading with a question. For instance, Makeup Artist Jennifer Darany wanted to know if Dain's bullet wound (after being shot by the Diamone) would be visible on camera, because that would require some unique makeup effects she would have to be prepared for. Likewise, Dave Hadsel, our key grip, wanted to know how far away we would be shooting from the parking lots of our locations so that he would know how far his grips would be carrying gear to set.

It took about 2 hours for us to make it through the 30-page script and answer everyone's questions. With that, Lou reminded everyone when and where we would be leaving for set the day before shooting. That essentially marked the end of *RADIUS*' preproduction.

PART 2

PRODUCTION

CHAPTER 11

ON THE SET

Finally! After almost 4 months of preproduction, we were ready to shoot *RADIUS*! We had 12 actors lined up and a crew that, at its height, would top off at around 26 people. And we had scheduled a 6-day shoot, working 12-hour days, that entailed the following:

- 2 days at a working volcanic cinder mine in Ridgecrest, California, to film anything in red terrain—the crashed ship, our running air crew, and the Diamone and Dain's final standoff over the CraterMaker bomb
- 3 days in Death Valley to film anything in yellow terrain—lots of running scenes, the crew shootout with the Diamone, and Vesay's rescue
- 1 day on a sound stage to shoot all our interior scenes of the ship's cockpit, cabin, and green screen shots for the Gemini Vortex

We usually had a crew of 26 people.

During principal photography, we usually worked with a crew of 26 people. The exception to this was days when we didn't need to shoot set pieces, in which case our art department stayed home. On those days, our crew was 23 people.

Figuring out how many crew members we would need required walking a fine line between our usual penny-pinching ways and the desire to be as productive on set as possible. Obviously, we wanted to keep our crew's headcount low, because every additional body on set meant spending more cash on crew pay, food, and lodging. In addition, it was tempting to pare down our crew to the bare bones. We knew that during long stretches of any given day, some crew members would end up just sitting around, not out of laziness, but simply because there would be nothing for them to do.

At the same time, we had to consider the benefits of having enough crew members available so that we could instantly address any need we had on set. In other words, it could be worth having someone sitting around being unproductive for a couple of hours a day if it meant that he could immediately be productive when we really needed him. That would let us avoid productivity bottlenecks on set and keep us filming our shots as quickly as possible.

The cast and crew of *RADIUS*.

We settled on a crew of 26 people. Following are the crew positions we took with us on production and each position's core responsibilities:

We usually had a crew of 26 people. 131

Director	Leads the creative efforts of the film production, including actors' performances, shot selection, and art design (sets, props, costumes, and so on).
Producer	Keeps an eye on mounting costs and scheduling issues. Is the person responsible for going to the director and saying, "We need to start making some compromises to stay on schedule and budget." Also is available as a strategic problem-solver on set.
Line Producer (LP)	Like the producer, the LP is a member of "senior management" on the set. During production, the LP also watches costs, communicates with vendors (for instance, arranges to buy more film or other supplies when needed), arranges to return rented equipment on time, and lets the producer know where the production stands regarding the budget.
Production Manager	Works for the LP and is responsible for managing the production's money. That includes paying cast, crew, and vendors when needed and keeping track of financial records.
Assistant Director (AD)	The AD runs the set according to a predetermined schedule, making sure all the actors, crew, and equipment are ready when needed, and moving the whole production so we stay on track. If the director is a movie's CEO (Chief Executive Officer), the AD is the set's COO (Chief Operating Officer).
Second Assistant Director	Helps the AD keep the set working smoothly. Often is in charge of physically rounding up people when needed—waking them up in the morning, getting them back after lunch, and so on.
Third Assistant Director	Another assistant for the AD.
Production Assistants	Often work for the AD or producers and are generally around to run errands, relay messages, and so on. We had two production assistants during principal photography.

Director of Photography	The DP is the guy who's responsible for capturing the movie on film and making sure it looks great. (In *RADIUS'* case, the DP doubled as a cameraman.) See Chapter 12, "Cinematography," for more on this crucial role.
First Assistant Cameraman	Sets the camera's focus, changes lenses, and otherwise maintains the camera.
Second Assistant Cameraman	Records technical information about each shot filmed, changes the camera's film magazines, and otherwise assists the first assistant cameraman in maintaining the camera.
Gaffer	Works for the DP and is in charge of setting up whatever lighting the DP calls for.
Key Grip	Works for the DP and is in charge of setting up any camera-related equipment needed (for instance, dolly tracks, a camera crane, and so on).
Grips	Work for the key grip and assist in setting up camera equipment. They're called *grips* because they're often gripping various gear. We had two grips during principal photography.
Prop Master	Keeps track of all props on the set and makes sure they're ready to go when needed.
Wardrobe Supervisor	Helps actors get into costume, keeps costumes clean (or dirty) as needed, and repairs inevitable tears or other "wardrobe malfunctions."
Makeup Artist	Applies makeup to the crew and creates makeup effects such as bruises and blood.
Script Supervisor	Makes sure that everything described in the script—from lines of dialogue to character actions to props that are called for—is actually filmed. The script supervisor also worries about *continuity*, or making sure a detail you see in one scene—such as the location of Dain's bruises, the bandage that Crim is seen wrapping around his leg, or the order that our fleeing crew members run in—is shown the same way in other shots and scenes.

...ist	Runs the portable, battery-powered sound recording deck that captures dialogue and other on-set sound. Monitors the audio as it's being recorded, making sure it's not distorted or otherwise marred.
Boom Operator	Holds the microphone at the end of a long *boom*, or flexible pole. Usually hangs the boom microphone over actors' heads, just out of the camera frame. With a pair of headphones, the boom operator also monitors the quality of the audio that the microphone is recording.
Visual Effects Supervisor	Makes sure that various elements of the shots we film in production (that is, camera angles, camera movement, actor choreography, and so on) will work with what our visual effects artists will need later on.
Production Designer	Supervises the construction of outdoor and indoor set pieces and maintains the sets as the crew works with them. As with the rest of the art team, our production designer went home on days when we weren't shooting with set pieces.
Art Director	Works with the production designer to assemble set pieces.
Assistant Art Director	Builds set pieces.

Lou made sure everyone was awake and ready to go.

The night before a shooting day, Assistant Director Lou Tocchet would let everyone know our call time for the next morning—that is, what time to be on call in the parking lot of our motel, ready to go to set.

We usually had a call time of 6:30 a.m., which meant that around 5:45 a.m., Lou would send his production assistants through the motel to knock on doors and make sure people were up in time to get a little breakfast beforehand. Those production assistants would also slip a copy of the day's call sheet under everyone's door. The *call sheet* would list the schedule for the day so that everyone could get a bird's-eye view of what we would be doing and who would be needed where and when.

Each morning at roughly 6:30 a.m., a ragtag collection of cars, passenger vans, a motor home, and an equipment truck or two would hit the road, moving everything and everyone to set. After our caravan arrived at a location, it was Lou's job to start organizing everything. For starters, he would need to figure out where to park all our vehicles so we would have the easiest access to our set but wouldn't interfere with the traffic flow of the location. (He would also consult with Director of Photography Philipp Timme to make sure the parked vehicles wouldn't be visible to our camera.) If we were shooting at a location for the first time, Lou would meet with a location representative (such as the park ranger in Death Valley), who would fill Lou in on any particular rules that our crew would have to follow on the property.

In the desert, it wasn't too hard to find good parking. For productions in a more urban environment, parking can become a huge headache for the assistant director and producers to manage.

With the vehicles parked, Lou would call a quick all-company meeting and give our assembled cast and crew an overview of the whole day—what scenes we would be shooting, where we would be shooting them, and any other specifics they had to know. Then Lou would explain the details of the first shot we would start the day with, and everyone would break and start preparing for it.

Lou made sure everyone was awake and ready to go. 135

Assistant Director Lou Tocchet gives the team his plan.

Let the unloading begin.

Hauling gear back and forth each day was just one of the pleasures of shooting in the middle of nowhere.

Preparations included the following:

- Any actors required would get into costume and go through their makeup work.
- The camera and sound crew would start moving their equipment to our first shooting location and get set up.
- Grips and production assistants would move the endless gear we needed (chairs, tents, snacks, ice chests of bottled drinks, and so on) to set.

- Philipp Timme and I would review our location and talk about any last details of camera placement that we needed to work out.

Shooting our scenes involved a lot of preparation time.

After our team arrived at a location, it usually took around 45 to 60 minutes to get our camera set up, get actors through makeup and into costume, and get everyone else ready to film our first shot.

When everyone was ready, the first thing we did was *block* the scene we were about to film, which meant working out where and how the actors would physically move in relation to the camera's position. Blocking was quick and easy for some scenes—for instance, we might have simply told our actors to run from point A to point B, right through our camera frame. Other scenes required more elaborate blocking. Consider the scene in which our fleeing aircrew catches up with Dain and Crim. This scene required a lot of choreography, where we had to figure out each of these things:

- Where the aircrew would stop when they finally see Dain and Crim
- Where they would move when Dain punches Vesay
- When they would pull their guns
- Where each cast member would fall when the Diamone shows up unnoticed and sends an energy blast that way

We worked out all these details by blocking the scene, which answered questions of choreography and served as a detailed rehearsal for the actors. You can see us blocking the aircrew scene in the Behind the Scenes section of this book's DVD.

Blocking a scene, such as Dain's confrontation with Vesay, takes time upfront, but after everyone knows what he's doing, you can film a scene's shots in quick order.

After we finished blocking a scene, we were ready to shoot. Even that act involved a number of different steps, all orchestrated by Lou. First, Lou would call out and ask if everyone was ready. For instance, he would ask the following:

- Did the wardrobe supervisor or makeup artist need to apply any last touchups?
- Did the actors know what they were going to be doing?
- Did I have any last-minute comments for the actors?
- Were the camera guys ready to go?

Shooting our scenes involved a lot of preparation time. 139

Makeup artist Jennifer Darany was available to constantly reapply makeup that our actors sweated off in the heat.

Wardrobe Supervisor Shira Harten had to stitch Paul Logan in and out of his suit multiple times per day. Maintaining soldiers' costumes also kept her busy.

Assuming Lou got a quick affirmative answer from everyone, he would call, "Quiet on the set" and then tell Sound Recordist John Taylor, to "Roll sound!" (meaning to start recording). When John responded that he was rolling, Lou would say, "Roll camera!" Then the camera operator, Philipp Timme, would start running the camera. After a second or so, Philipp would say "Speed," meaning the camera's film mechanism was running at full speed (24 frames a second), which was also a cue for Tommy, our second assistant cameraman, to get out of the camera's frame. She had been holding a camera slate—otherwise known as "clapper"—in front of the camera. (The slate noted the scene we were shooting and some other technical information. It also electronically synched our camera and sound equipment so that video and audio could easily be synched together when we went to edit the film.) As soon as Tommy was safely out of the camera frame, Philipp would say "Set," meaning that he and the camera were ready to go. Finally, hearing that the camera was set, I would call "Action!" We would shoot the scene, and I would call "Cut!" when we had gotten the footage we wanted.

The set.

After cutting, Lou would ask the camera and sound guys if the take was good for them, meaning there were no technical problems, no botched camera movement or focus issues, and so on. Then I would decide whether to do another take of the same shot or move on to something new.

Shooting our scenes involved a lot of preparation time. 141

Jeremy Brill developed some good upper-body strength holding the boom mike day in and day out.

We recorded set audio to these 60-minute DAT tapes.

Even if a shot is perfectly executed by the camera guys, the actors, and everyone else, film productions do at least two takes of just about everything in case there's a technical problem (bad light exposure, a hair in the film gate, and so on) with the original take that's discovered after the fact or there's some subtle, undesirable detail that no one noticed while filming. For instance, suppose that an actor's eye flutters a bit from dust in the air. That's the kind of minute detail that can go unnoticed until you look at the processed film, sometimes days later. But for *RADIUS*, we had to be sparing with our film stock, so we generally did two takes only for important dialogue exchanges.

If Lou determined that the shot worked for everyone (director, camera team, sound guys, and so on), we would move on. That often meant filming the same scene from a different camera angle or a different lens (for instance, to get a wide shot and then a close-up of the story's events). Lou would then organize everyone and everything for the next shot. He would make sure that the cast and crew knew what we would be shooting next. Then he would give the camera guys time to prepare the camera and me time to talk to the actors. He would also ask the makeup artist and wardrobe supervisor to check their work and do any necessary touchups. Then he would call for any other services we needed from other crew members (water bottles, umbrellas for shade, and so on).

That's the process we used to shoot the film. We would just repeat it throughout the day, logging shot after shot, scene after scene.

By the way, here's a quick trick we used to make production easier for everybody. Go to Kinko's and print miniature copies of your script (reduced to maybe 50 percent of the original size, and physically trimmed down to that size). Give these mini-scripts to your crew members so that they can easily reference the script when they need it. (The miniature size lets people keep the script in their pockets.)

Shooting our scenes involved a lot of preparation time. 143

Script Supervisor Veronique Fletcher watched us film each scene carefully, making sure we didn't accidentally veer from the written script. When we had to make on-set script changes for various reasons, she kept detailed notes as to what we changed.

WHAT MAKES A GOOD ASSISTANT DIRECTOR?

Your productivity on set can easily be made or broken by the effectiveness of your assistant director. Fortunately, Assistant Director Lou Tocchet had all the right qualities that a good assistant director should have: He was a detail-oriented planner, but he also was able to think quickly on his feet. In addition, he commanded respect from the crew and could be an authoritative figure when he had to be, but he managed to do so without ruffling feathers or hurting crew morale with a harsh manner. If you're doing a film, I highly recommend that you find an assistant director with similar qualities. That way, you can worry exclusively about the creative issues of your production and leave the rest to the assistant director.

WE SHOT IN 120-DEGREE WEATHER.

The heat of the desert, particularly Death Valley, became an incredible burden for our production. When we were scheduling *RADIUS* in preproduction, we originally expected to shoot the film in late March or early April. However, our preproduction work took longer than expected, so we kept moving our shooting dates forward into late April and then finally late May/June. Given the late shoot date, we expected our desert locations to be hot, but we had checked with weather services and knew that the worst temperatures weren't expected until a week or two *after* we would be finished filming. But as luck would have it, our team happened to drive into the desert just as an unforeseen heat wave settled in, and we faced temperatures several degrees hotter than expected. The end result: It ranged between 100–110 degrees while we were shooting scenes at the cinder mine in Ridgecrest, California, and it got as high as 120 degrees in Death Valley. Most of our crew had never been in heat like this, much less *worked* in it. The extreme temperatures took their toll in a variety of ways.

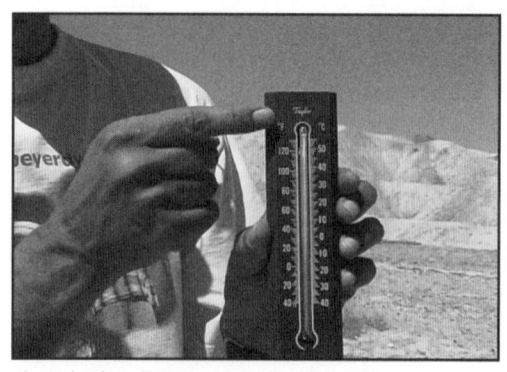

They don't call it Death Valley for nothing.

We dealt with a number of setbacks on the set.

One of the many givens about indie filmmaking is that despite your best efforts, things go wrong, and you'll have to figure out how to deal with these hitches on the spot. Following are some of the unexpected headaches we ran into on the *RADIUS* set:

- A couple of our team members suffered heat exhaustion in Death Valley and had to be taken out of the lineup for an hour or so at a time.

The heat was tough on everybody, but the actors bore the brunt of it.

- We slowed down our overall pace in the desert heat, trying not to overexert ourselves and take anyone out of the game entirely. Camera moves and setups went slower, and we gave actors breaks between shots to get in the shade and cool off.

- Some of our gear stopped working. For instance, our sound recording deck went out for an hour or so (we had to revive it in an air-conditioned van), and on another day, the electronics in our 35-mm camera went out, wasting two hours of precious time as we tried to repair it.

- We went through the original budget of bottled liquids (water and Gatorades) we had bought for the crew within our first 3 days of shooting. We had to spend considerably more money buying out the stocks of any markets we found in the Death Valley area.

- Our gun props could shoot live blanks, but they often jammed because sand and dust kept getting into their chambers, despite our best efforts to keep them clean. Dain's Tek-9 gun was a particular problem child, and we wasted time and film trying to get a few usable shots of it firing properly. (Even then, we had to give it some more muzzle flashes in post production, to make it look like it was firing faster.)

All the muzzle flashes you see in the film were added by a visual effects artist.

- It took longer than expected for our crew to move large amounts of gear far into the rocks and hills of some of our locations. We tried to be realistic in estimating the time all this would take, but it still took longer.
- After spending 5 days in extreme heat and tough terrain, we were looking forward to doing our last day of filming on a cool, easily accessible sound stage. But even that work became an ordeal. First, it took our art department longer than expected to assemble our ship's cockpit and cabin sets, which meant we started shooting our scenes later than we had hoped. Plus, the volume of shots we had to cover—from cockpit shots to cabin shots (both in the air and post-crash) to green screen shots for our Gemini Vortex characters—turned out to be a little too ambitious given the time at hand.
- In the last few hours of our stage day, a crew member suffered an epileptic seizure, and we had to call an ambulance. Obviously, our crew's safety came first, but it's just another example of how things happen that you can't anticipate, and that took a toll on our ability to get all of our planned shots that day.

And we rolled with the punches when we could.

We tried to be flexible and deal with all the unforeseen problems as they came. During our first day in Death Valley, it became obvious that Philipp Timme and I had picked a bunch of locations in Death Valley's Golden Canyon that were too hard for our crew to reach. These locations required walking almost a mile with heavy gear in the extreme heat, and a crew member had already fainted from heat exhaustion. After a quick conference with Producer Andy Trapani and Assistant Director Lou Tocchet, we decided we would have to give up all those locations we had carefully picked weeks earlier and come up with new ones that were closer to the road. Because we needed to find new locations as we shot, Lou's call sheet for the day (his schedule) went out the window. He didn't know which scenes we would be shooting, where, or in what order. He just had to work out these details on the fly, as Philipp and I tried to identify new spots in Golden Canyon to shoot.

Director of Photography Philipp Timme, Assistant Director Lou Tocchet, and I worked out a new shot list and schedule on the fly during our first day in Death Valley.

As time marched on during production and we realized we were falling behind, we made a lot of other adjustments. One effective exercise was looking for multiple camera shots that we could combine into a fewer number of shots. A perfect example of this is the hand-to-hand fight scene between the Diamone and Dain, as Dain tries to protect the CraterMaker bomb. Going into production, we expected this scene to be an elaborate fight, which actor Paul Logan (the Diamone) had choreographed ahead of time. We had rehearsed a number of fight moves with Paul and actress Catalina Larranaga (Dain) before the shoot. We had plans for Dain to throw a lot of choreographed punches and use props such as a smoldering metal pipe to defend herself. However, we were running behind that day, and we had to eliminate most of the cool choreography Paul had planned for the sequence. Instead of more than a dozen or so shots we were planning, we had to settle for about six handheld shots showing the Diamone beating the daylights out of Dain, with little resistance from her. It was a painful sacrifice to make for all of us—especially Paul. However, our compromise let us get the shots we really needed in a couple of hours and then move on.

And we rolled with the punches when we could. 149

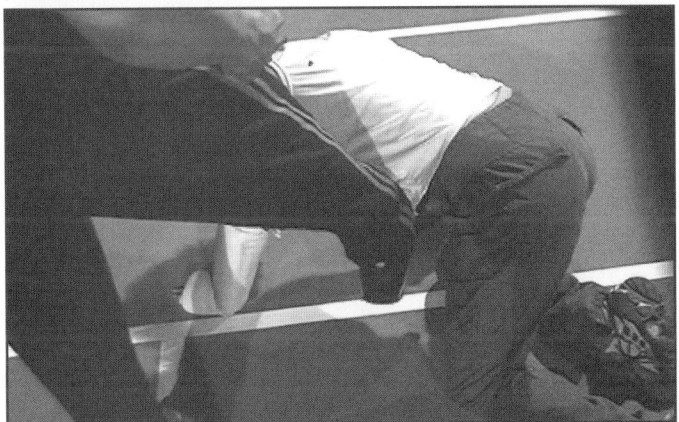

If only we could have used some of Paul Logan's more elaborate choreography, which we rehearsed on a tennis court a couple nights before production. At least we managed to film the basics of his designs, though.

Likewise, in a few instances, we had to cut out small scenes from our script. For instance, we had a scene in which a fleeing aircrew member falls behind the rest of the group, gets lost, and becomes the Diamone's first casualty. Shortly after, the lagging Dain and Crim pass by the same spot and find the crew member's smoldering remains. We were fully intending to shoot these shots, but with time running out on the scheduled shoot day, we had to improvise. To compensate, we had the lagging aircrew member catch up with the rest of his group. Then we just killed him off with another crew member later on.

We filmed this crew member (played by Carlton Bruce) falling behind, but we ran out of time to shoot the rest of his related scenes. The most painful part about this scenario is telling an actor that you have to cut down his camera time.

Another example: When Dain's ship is crashing, we had written in a moment in which one of the air crew members can't get off the floor and into his seat because of the ship's turbulence. Crim, played by Matt McCoy, sees this from his own seat and thinks about getting up to help the flailing crew member, but he can't quite bring himself to risk his own safety. When the ship finally crashes, the seatless crew member is killed, and Crim feels guilty. I really liked this sequence because it gave Crim's character a little more depth and played into his decision to sacrifice himself later on in the story. But with time short during our 24-hour stage day, we had to ditch the scene.

You can watch us grapple with a lot of these issues in the Behind the Scenes videos found on this book's DVD.

> **Lesson Learned**
>
> The best-laid plans of mice and men go awry, so you have to be ready to quickly size up the effect on your product and make quick adjustments to your plans. Be ready to prioritize your goals without sentimentality. Consider this: Do you really need a certain shot or scene, or will your audience not know what it's missing?

Amazingly, cast and crew morale stayed high.

Despite all the setbacks we encountered, our cast and crew handled all the stress of the production extremely well. Given long hours, the extreme heat, a constant pressure to stay on schedule, and the fact that most people were making $100 a day (if that), you would think that we would have had a mutiny on our hands, but that wasn't the case. In fact, we had a pretty happy, productive team throughout the production, and I chalk that up to a few key factors.

Cast and crew alike raved about the luxurious accommodations we were able to provide on set.

Chapter 11 ♦ On the Set

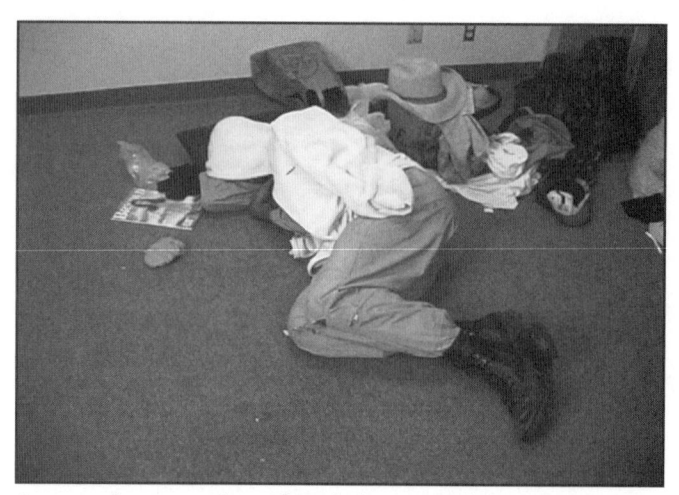

Cast members sometimes slept during our 24-hour stage day. It takes a special group of people to take this kind of thing in stride.

We lucked out by recruiting level-headed, well-meaning, hardworking people. Many of them already knew each other, which gave our crew a tight-knit feel from the start. (See Chapter 4, "Crewing Up," on how we found our crew.) If we had even a couple of "bad apples"—cynics, whiners, prima donnas, and so on—they easily could have poisoned the morale of everyone else, and who knows what would have happened to our production when things got tough.

Another factor that motivated the team was personal pride. I can tell you, there were a couple of moments where even I felt like hanging my head in defeat and just escaping the nightmare. (And this was *my* film—I had the greatest stake in it!) But at those moments, I remember noticing that Philipp Timme and his camera crew were right there, getting ready for the next shot, and the actors were present, waiting for direction. The fact that these other people weren't crumbling at that particular moment gave me strength. If nothing else, my pride required me to keep going and not break down in front of my teammates. I suspect that most people had moments like that; taken together, they helped the team move forward.

After a couple of days, the tough shoot really started to bond the team. Most of the obstacles became subjects of jokes—the cheesy motel accommodations, the boxed lunches, the absurd heat, the rough terrain, the Death Valley park rangers who thought we were crazy, and so on. When we achieved a little success—such as a good-looking, well-executed shot—it was something to be proud of. We had earned the success through hard work.

Despite the stress of the shoot, we managed to have fun working with each other.

I don't mean to imply that there was never friction within the team, because there was. The day before production started, Directory of Photography Philipp Timme and Assistant Director Lou Tocchet got into a yelling match over various schedule issues, and Line Producer Steve Stone and I snapped at each other over the delays on our sound stage. There were other small flare-ups and complaints among people during the shoot, of course, but they all passed quickly and never threatened the overall harmony and stability of the production.

In short, because everyone was sharing the hardships equally, we had a common experience to rally around, and it brought people together. I'd hate to see what a prima donna star, with her plush trailer and surrounding entourage of fawning assistants, does to crew morale on bigger-budget film sets.

Lesson Learned

> I'd hate to do a film in which everything was easy and comfortable. People stay more focused, engaged, and happy if they're faced with a challenge rather than a walk in the park. Give people something that's outside of their normal experience and comfort zone, and most will be glad to rise to the occasion.

WE HAD OTHER LOGISTICS TO FIGURE OUT, TOO.

Lodging. As I mentioned earlier in this book, when we were in the first few weeks of preproduction, I had floated the idea of skipping the motel and putting the team in sleeping bags and tents to save money on accommodations. However, that notion was nixed by our producers about as quickly as it escaped my lips. Instead, Line Producer Steve Stone tracked down an affordable motel at each of our major locations and put up the team, two to a room. It's a good thing we didn't try the camping option, because people would have physically fallen apart after a day or so.

Meals. We kept people fed a number of ways. For starters, we always had a snack table on set, stocked with cheap foods we could afford or find at our location—everything from potato chips to granola bars, and plenty of water and Gatorade. For major meals, Steve Stone took a number of different approaches. Our Death Valley motel had a small coffee shop, so Steve cut a deal for the kitchen to cook up a buffet breakfast and dinner for us each day. But when we weren't at our Death Valley motel, breakfast consisted of a table of donuts, bagels, coffee, and juice, and dinners were served at a greasy spoon roadside diner. For lunches, Steve found a local catering company at each location to come in and serve the team a hot meal on set. I thought this food was great, because my culinary tastes are pretty simple. (I'm fine with a cold turkey sandwich for lunch, and I'm one of those people who thinks those Budget Gourmet microwave dinners are pretty tasty.) Some crew members were tougher critics.

Amazingly, cast and crew morale stayed high. 155

Stocked with only the finest foods, our trusty snack table kept crew members going throughout the day.

Prop Master Matt McCoy scrutinizes a piece of ham from his box lunch.

Transportation. Steve rented a few passenger vans out of Los Angeles so that most of our cast and crew could leave their cars at home. He also rented an RV motor home. This type of transportation gave crew members a slightly air-conditioned retreat when they needed it and the only available bathroom at some locations.

CHAPTER 12

CINEMATOGRAPHY

Having a compelling script, cast, sets, and whatever else will only go so far if your film footage doesn't actually look good. That's why I put a great emphasis on *RADIUS'* cinematography—finding the right person to shoot *RADIUS*, and then scraping up the cash to afford a good camera system and some additional equipment that would give *RADIUS* some reasonable production values.

RADIUS was shot by Philipp Timme.

One of the luckiest breaks we got on *RADIUS* was finding Philipp Timme to be our director of photography (DP). As our DP, Philipp was the guy responsible for making *RADIUS* look as good as possible from a cinematic standpoint—in other words, doing everything from designing the lighting of all our shots to picking the appropriate lenses for particular shots to identifying what camera equipment we would need on set and then operating the camera. And he did all this with little money and a pretty short shooting schedule.

Philipp Timme was a dynamo, working 12- to 14-hour days in extreme heat. He was that famous German work ethic, in the flesh, and a huge factor in us surviving the shoot.

Philipp and I worked closely together from the start. We chose our locations together and talked about how our sets should be designed to support the kind of lighting we wanted. We shot video storyboards in Death Valley to become familiar with the settings we were going to work in (see Chapter 9, "Storyboards and Shot Lists"), and we came up with a full shot list for all the major scenes in the movie. That way, we knew exactly what we wanted to shoot before filming began.

We found Philipp online.

We met Philipp completely by chance, without introductions through mutual friends, references, or any other kind of connections. Early in preproduction, Producer Andy Trapani posted an ad for a DP on a Web site called Cinematographer.com, and Philipp was one of about two dozen people who responded by e-mail. When Andy saw Philipp's online resume, he was pretty sure that Philipp wouldn't work out, because he seemed overqualified for our short film. The first thing that caught Andy's eye was that Philipp had worked as the Visual Effects DP on major Hollywood films including *Armageddon*, *Dante's Peak*, and *Independence Day*, where he lit and shot live-action models like *Independence Day's* exploding White House.

Right away, Andy told Philipp that we couldn't pay much, but Philipp seemed kind of intrigued by our plans. He came in to meet us and we all hit it off. Plus, his demo reel showed that he was a perfect match for *RADIUS*; he had been a DP on other independent films and some German television shows, and he clearly had experience designing nice lighting on fairly small budgets. But apart from loving his demo reel, I found that Philipp and I simply clicked. He was really easy to talk to, open to ideas and collaboration, and most importantly, he was willing to explain his craft to me. At the time, I knew next to nothing about cinematography, and I really wanted to come out of *RADIUS* with at least a basic understanding of what went into shooting a film. It was a big plus when I saw that Philipp was enthusiastic about being a part-time teacher.

Philipp and I worked together like partners. I can't imagine a film production really succeeding if the director and the DP aren't in synch.

Philipp ended up joining us for a grand total of $500—not much, but he wasn't working at the moment, and he liked the idea of shooting an ambitious little sci-fi film over a handful of days. After Philipp came on board, he brought a lot of other crew members he knew along with him—the first and second assistant cameraman, the gaffer (who typically rigs the lights on a set), and the key grip (who sets up any equipment the camera guys need, such as a dolly or camera crane). This saved us a lot of effort because we didn't have to recruit these positions ourselves, and it also did wonders for the harmony of our set, having so many people who had worked with each other before.

We shot on 35-mm film, not digital.

Digital video cameras have become the tool of choice for many low-budget filmmakers, but we strayed away from digital for a number of reasons:

1. At the time, HD (High Definition) camera systems were relatively new, untested, and very expensive to rent. They were being used by George Lucas and a few other brave and well-funded filmmakers, but that was about it.

2. Video cameras that shot in the MiniDV format (called "DV" from here on out) were much easier to come by, but the image quality of their footage clearly shouted "cheap video camera!" (These were the days before more competent DV cameras that could shoot at 24 frames per second, and in widescreen aspect ratios.) As I've said many times before, I wanted *RADIUS* to have a professional feel and not have to make excuses for poor image quality. That meant DV cameras were out of the question.

3. Surprisingly, we could shoot on film fairly cheaply. There are an abundance of 35-mm cameras in the Los Angeles area, because 35 mm has been the standard for decades. That meant our chances were pretty good for finding good deals on 35-mm equipment, if we knew where to look, and Line Producer Steve Stone did indeed know where to look! He had done a lot of business with a big rental company called Otto Nemenz in Hollywood, and was able to rent a 35-mm camera package, with lenses, at $500 for about 10 days of use (although only 6 days were sequential).

Lesson Learned

> You would be surprised what you can get when your crew has a good relationship with a vendor who has a surplus of equipment on hand.

We shot on 35-mm film, not digital.

Going with a 35-mm film camera gave us a great look but also came with plenty of tradeoffs during production.

We were able to save some money buying our Kodak film (5245 ASA 50 for daylight shooting, and 5293 ASA 200 for interior work) as *recans* or *short ends*. Most indie filmmakers who have worked with film are well acquainted with these terms, because they refer to what is essentially "used" film. Bigger, richer productions often buy brand new film but don't end up shooting all of it. So these productions sell back their pieces of unexposed film to companies like Dr. Raw Stock (http://www.thedrgroup.com) in Los Angeles, which then tests the film for any obvious defects and then sells it at a pretty steep discount. So, where a popular Kodak film might cost 58 cents per foot in brand new 400-foot loads, a recan version of the same film would go for only 38 cents. And a short end version of the same stock (short ends are unusually short rolls, such as 200 feet) could go for just 15 cents a foot!

Of course, there are other costs involved with shooting film, such as the time on set to repeatedly change the camera's film magazines (our magazines held 400 feet of film at a time, which translates to roughly 4 minutes of footage, versus the 60 minutes of a typical videotape), not to mention the costs to develop the film, transfer it to videotape, and possibly hire a negative cutter to assemble the film negative according to your film's final edit. (See Chapter 14, "Film

Editing," for more about this process.) But given that we wanted a "film-like" image quality, we really had no alternative at the time.

Lesson Learned

> You can minimize the costs of shooting on film in some respects—for instance, by buying used film—but not others.

We used an Arriflex 35-mm camera, with sound.

We rented two different 35-mm cameras from Otto Nemenz. During principal photography, we rented an Arriflex BL-4s, which is a workhorse model that's also suitable for sound recording. (The camera itself doesn't record sound, but its mechanical operation has to be quiet enough not to register on your sound equipment.) A couple of months after principal photography, we had to go back out and film some additional shots that we didn't get the first time around. For these, we used an Arriflex 3 camera, which was not appropriate for sound work because it made quite a racket while operating. (That was okay, though, because we didn't need to record sound for these extra pickup shots.)

You don't exactly travel lightly with a 35-mm camera system.

We used an Arriflex 35-mm camera, with sound.

If you spend just a few minutes on the set, you quickly realize that a film camera is nothing like a video camera. In fact, it's a monster that demands to be fed and pampered constantly, and it's often the biggest factor in determining how quickly you can get your shots.

For starters, our camera system—camera, film magazines, lenses, batteries, and so on—came packed in about a dozen industrial-strength cases, and just getting all this stuff out of a van and onto our set was a time-consuming struggle. (Getting the camera set up and running smoothly was the job of our first and second cameramen, Jim Jost and Tommy Izumi.)

First assistant cameraman Jim Jost services the beast.

Operating the camera was also pretty complicated. Every time I looked over at the camera crew, they were fiddling with the camera—adjusting some doodad on the thing, cleaning out dust, changing lenses, changing film magazines, you name it.

Jim Jost and second assistant cameraman Tommy Izumi had the pleasure of getting the camera on set and into position. They pushed this camera cart almost a half mile into the rocks on one occasion.

We had a lens for every season.

A major difference between a 35-mm camera and a video camera is its lens system. Typically, a video camera has a built-in zoom lens that covers, say, a 10x magnification range. Some cameras—like the Canon XL-2—let you change lenses on the camera, but generally, video filmmakers stick with the lens on the camera and simply zoom it in and out with the press of a button.

We had a lens for every season. 165

Lenses big and small.

Our 35-mm camera came with about a dozen different lenses, and we constantly changed them to frame shots in different ways and get other optical effects. We *did* have a zoom lens, but it was huge. (It looked like a small cannon.) We used the zoom lens for a few scenes, but it was generally too unwieldy for our shot work, especially handheld shots.

166   Chapter 12 ◆ Cinematography

The zoom lens you see here would let us get close to a subject like Dain and then quickly zoom out by a factor of 10 times magnification to get a wide shot of the same scene.

For the most part, we used prime lenses with the camera. If you've ever done 35-mm still photography, you're probably familiar with primes. A *prime* covers only a single focal length—for instance, 35 mm, 50 mm, or 100 mm—so it's much smaller than a zoom lens. A prime also offers sharper image quality because it's honed for one purpose. We used about 10 different prime lenses during production, from an ultra-wide angle to long telephoto and just about everything in between.

Having this kind of range gave Philipp plenty of options for shooting a particular shot, without having to take the time to physically move the camera. At the same time, it seemed to take about 5 or 10 minutes each time we changed a lens, because the former lens needed to be stored safely away, the camera's innards had to be checked for dust, and the new lens had to be attached and focused. (I talk about focusing issues in a moment.)

We used a wide-angle lens to make settings feel bigger than they really were.

168　Chapter 12 ◆ Cinematography

Long lenses can have a narrow range of focus, or depth of field. In this shot, Crim is in focus, but the background and foreground elements are not, which helps keep the audience's eye on Crim.

We used even longer lenses to get fairly close to an actor, like Mike Yavnieli here, even though our camera team was far away.

Working with a 35-mm camera brought with it some headaches.

Besides the time it took to work with our lenses, focusing the Arriflex camera was a challenge. Unlike video cameras, these cameras have no auto-focus system, and the camera operator who's looking through the camera's eye piece—in our case, Philipp Timme—can't concentrate on manually focusing the camera on whatever he's filming, given all the other things he has to worry about. These "other things" include keeping actors in the camera frame, looking out for a stray boom microphone that may accidentally bob in and out of the picture, and so on. (In addition, it can be hard to see if a scene is perfectly in focus when looking through a small view finder.) So for each shot we filmed, the first assistant cameraman, Jim Jost, would have to do two things. First, he would get out a tape measure and actually measure the distance from the camera to the subject. Second, using a chart he had memorized, he set the camera's focus wheel to the appropriate position, given the particular lens we were using and the camera's distance from the subject. We repeated this measuring process endlessly for any new shot in which our actors had moved, requiring a new measurement.

We would measure the distance to the subject and then adjust the camera's focus wheel according to that measurement and the lens we were using.

Things got even more complicated when a scene called for an actor to move around while on camera, such as when Dain stood up and walked over to face Vesay as they argued about going back to the CraterMaker bomb. As the actor walked from point A to point B, we had to take time to set physical marks for each place the actor moved. (We usually dropped a stone or a piece of wood on the ground out of the camera frame to mark a position.) Then we got out the old tape ruler again and measured the camera's distance to each mark. As we filmed the actor moving from one mark to another, the assistant cameraman also moved that focus wheel to keep everything in focus.

Dain gets on her feet and walks toward Vesay in a single shot...

Working with a 35-mm camera brought with it some headaches. 171

...so we had to place multiple marks along her path (Tommy drops a stone at one) and focus the camera to each mark ahead of time.

As you can imagine, coordinating and rehearsing an actor's moves with the camera team took precious time on set. Also, it was sometimes hard to keep focus in certain scenes where there was a lot of movement going on. For instance, the Diamone's running shots were tough to keep sharp when he was running straight at the camera. Jim Jost would lay down multiple focus marks along the Diamone's path, and as actor Paul Logan ran forward, Jim would have to smoothly move the camera's focus wheel in synch with Paul's position. Because Jim couldn't see whether he was in focus, he would have to be really confident that his focus wheel was at the right place at the right time, as Paul was running. Just to be sure, we would do a couple of different takes for those tricky running shots.

Jim wasn't sure he caught the Diamone in focus during our first take of this shot, so we tried again. As you can see, the second take was indeed sharper than the first.

Note: It wasn't necessary to set focus marks for all cases in which an actor was moving on camera. For instance, when the Diamone was beating up Dain at the end of the film, the actors moved around a moderate amount, but Philipp chose to use a wide-angle lens, which basically kept them in focus within a margin of several feet. It's when you use longer lenses, which tend to throw backgrounds out of focus to emphasize your foreground subject, that you most need to worry about focus issues.

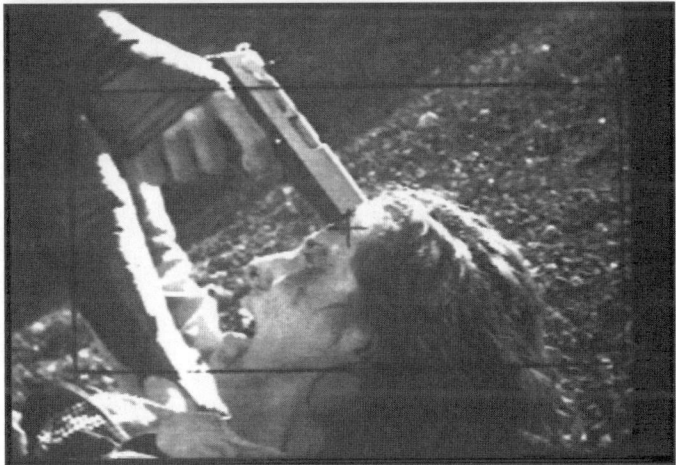

Working with a 35-mm camera brought with it some headaches. 173

I could see what the camera operator saw thanks to this handheld wireless Sony monitor. There's a wireless transmitter attached to the camera, and it sends a black-and-white image to the Sony, so I could see how Philipp was framing our shots.

Some other complications that came from using a 35-mm camera included the fact that the film magazines we used with these cameras could hold only about 4 minutes' worth of film (yes, only 4 minutes per 400-foot roll of film), so our camera guys needed to change them pretty often. And after nearly every shot we filmed (not a take of a shot, but each new shot), we would have to check the camera to make sure no dirt or hair had wound up in the film gate. If you're on a movie set, you'll constantly hear the assistant

Chapter 12 ♦ Cinematography

director or some other crew member say "checking the gate, checking the gate," which means the camera guys are checking the camera for anything that might have marred the last shot. When you're sure the gate is clean, you can move on.

Each film magazine on the camera carried about 4 minutes of film, so Second Assistant Cameraman Tommy Izumi had to change the magazines frequently.

Anyway, by now you understand all the major steps involved in using a film camera on set. Having played around with my digital video camera, this process seemed foreign and counterproductive to me, but that's basically how movies are made with 35-mm film cameras. It definitely takes a toll on your ability to shoot fast, and most 35-mm camera crews require at least three people: the camera operator; the first assistant cameraman (who worries about focus issues and cleans the camera); and the second assistant cameraman, who changes and manages the camera's film magazines, writes down each shot recorded along with some technical information, and generally assists the first cameraman where needed. Shooting with a video camera, you could probably get away with one person operating and maintaining the camera from start to finish.

Lesson Learned

Besides dollars, the cost of shooting on film is all the time needed to operate your camera.

It does take the camera team some time to do its thing, but it doesn't slow you down quite as much as you would think. You often have plenty to do in the meantime, such as talk about performances with your actors, reapply makeup, adjust your lighting, and whatever else.

We sometimes went handheld for convenience or energy.

We used a lot of different equipment either to steady the camera while we were shooting or to give a smooth sense of movement. But my favorite option was going handheld with the camera, which we did for a lot of *RADIUS*' quick, action-oriented shots. Philipp might not agree with me, because he was the one who had to bear the weight of a 45-pound camera in his arms or up on his shoulder. Physical strain aside, though, going handheld offered a couple of great benefits:

- Shooting handheld went quickly because Philipp could cover a lot of different shots in a single take, just by pointing the camera in a different direction. For instance, when Dain shot Kyle over the CraterMaker bomb, Philipp just quickly moved the camera from one crew member to another, recording their reactions to the event. It would have taken a lot longer to get all this different coverage if we had the camera mounted on a tripod or any other piece of equipment. We also went handheld for scenes where the Diamone twin was beating the daylights out of Dain. Again, with all the movement of the actors, it would have been harder to capture this sequence from a fixed position, but it was relatively easy with a handheld camera.

Lesson Learned

If you're in a hurry, just go handheld and film your movie.

♦ The other nice thing about going handheld is that you get a natural, organic movement to your footage, which can give scenes a bit more energy and tension. For instance, we went handheld to film the shots of Dain and Crim finally being reunited with their aircrew. When Dain decked Vesay and everyone drew guns, the organic movement of the camera helped the scene feel a little unsettled, and that was the mood we wanted.

Handholding the camera let us cover a lot of different shots quickly. Just keep the camera rolling, and point it at different actors.

We sometimes went handheld for convenience or energy. 177

These shots of Crim and Dain taking cover from the Diamone were shot on a steady tripod. We added a little camera movement to the shots by smoothly gliding the camera on the tripod's head, but I wish we had gone handheld to give the actors a little more desperate energy.

Lesson Learned

Use a handheld camera if you want to add some energy or an unsettled, realistic quality of movement to your footage.

The tripod is the most basic camera equipment.

We used a tripod for shots in which we wanted to keep the camera either utterly still or give it a smooth, controlled, steady movement. For instance, we used a tripod to track our aircrew members as they ran by or for a quiet conversation between Dain and Crim, where you can see the camera subtly move to follow our actors in their close-up shots.

With the camera on a tripod, Philipp could smoothly track these runners as they went by.

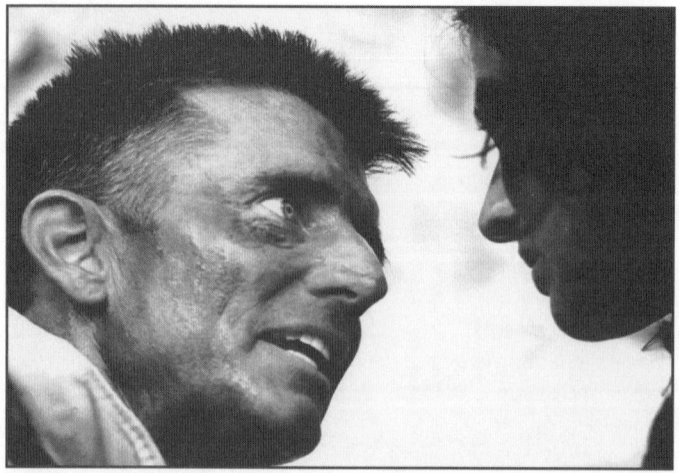

Framing Crim and Dain in tight close-up, Philipp was able to subtly move the camera on its tripod as the actors shifted back and forth during their conversation.

The tripod is the most basic camera equipment.   179

Filming the CraterMaker's bomb timer.

The only drawback to the tripod was the time required to get it into position for a shot. We would move the tripod, and when we were shooting outdoors on sand or uneven rock, it would take a couple minutes to make sure the tripod and camera were secure on the ground and not lopsided. Because we were doing a lot of different shots and covering a lot of angles, repeating this process began to burn some valuable time. We would try to minimize this wasted time where we could. For instance, in our running shots, we would set up the tripod once and then film the actors running toward the camera and then away from the camera. Then we would do the same thing with different lenses. The result was that we got a lot of different footage from one tripod position. Still, sometimes we couldn't achieve this kind of efficiency from one tripod position and had to take the time to move the tripod and get it all set up.

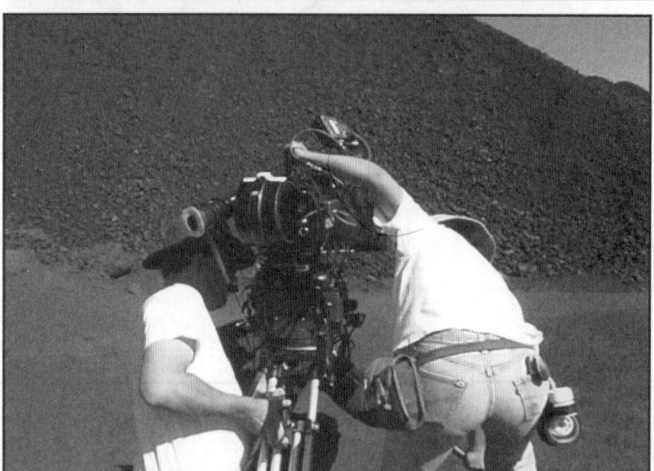

Moving the camera and tripod and then getting them level on uneven ground took time.

The dolly and crane gave us smooth movement.

We also tried to use some slightly more exotic camera equipment, here and there, that would let us take more interesting shots and add a little more production value to *RADIUS*. For starters, we put the

The dolly and crane gave us smooth movement. 181

camera on a dolly, which was pushed along tracks that our key grip and his team of two grips had set up ahead of time. The effect was that the camera could smoothly glide through space and reveal the world as it moved along. (For instance, we used a dolly to slowly reveal the flaming wreckage of Dain's crashed ship, early in the movie.)

We also used a dolly to slowly push in on Vesay's face as he watched the CraterMaker blast come at him. We couldn't have gotten this smooth, subtle effect any other way than to physically move the camera along dolly tracks. (The effect would have appeared differently had we just used a zoom lens to slowly zoom in on Vesay.)

The dolly let us slowly reveal the extent of the ship's wreckage.

182   Chapter 12 ♦ Cinematography

Likewise, we used the dolly to follow behind Vesay as he ran and then slowly reveal his setting as he radioed for help.

Before shooting *RADIUS*, I had heard other indie filmmakers talk about how impractical dollies were, because it takes so long to set up the dolly's tracks and make sure they're level so that the dolly has a smooth ride. It's true that setting up all that track took time, but our key grip and his team of two grips did this work while we were shooting other scenes, so the setup time didn't really slow down our production. We set up dolly tracks on three occasions during the shoot, and I don't remember ever waiting around for the grips to get the dolly ready. Of course, having a dolly required us to have a bigger crew. Without it, we might not have needed two additional grips on set, but overall, I'd say it was a worthwhile expense for what the dolly gave to *RADIUS*.

Setting up the dolly didn't affect our shooting pace, but what did take time was coordinating the dolly's movement with what our actors were doing. Sometimes we moved the dolly too fast or too slow, and it could be tricky to coordinate the actors' movements with what our dolly was doing. End result: We had to rehearse our dolly moves many times for all but the simplest shots, and we probably doubled or occasionally tripled our shooting time to work out all this stuff and allow for extra takes.

The dolly and crane gave us smooth movement.

In this shot, Dain walked one way and the dolly moved the other. It sounds easy, but it required a few rehearsals and takes to get things just right.

Lesson Learned

> A dolly adds some production value to your film, but you pay the price in the time you have to spend rehearsing dolly moves with your cast and crew.

When we wanted to add movement to shots but it was impractical to set up a dolly (for instance, when actors had to run many yards at a time), we put the camera in the back of a flatbed truck or van and drove along beside our actors. Sometimes, with a smooth road, the results were pretty good. (We would generally also use a wide-angle lens for these shots, because the wider angle tends to minimize camera movement.) In other cases, the footage looked pretty bumpy because our pickup truck was rolling over uneven sand and rocks. Even then, our film editor, Ann Trulove, was able to use at least a portion of these shots.

Lesson Learned

> In an action movie, where you're constantly cutting from one shot to another, you only need a couple seconds of steady footage to edit into your film. Nobody has to know that the rest of the shot looked pretty horrible.

184   Chapter 12 ♦ Cinematography

We could get long, single shots of Vesay running, thanks to our handy pickup truck.

> **YOU CAN USE CHEAP DOLLY SUBSTITUTES IF NECESSARY.**
>
> Don't have money for a dolly? If you're shooting on a smooth, fairly level surface, try using a wheelchair or an office chair on wheels as a cheap substitute. Or, if practical, use a slow-moving car. Also, try to use a wide-angle lens to minimize the effect of any bumps that might jar the camera while you're shooting.

The dolly and crane gave us smooth movement.   185

As *RADIUS'* key grip, Dave Hadsell was responsible for building any equipment that the camera guys needed. He had a couple of grips working with him to build our dolly tracks, camera crane, and such.

Renting all our camera equipment—the dolly, the crane, and the ladder pod—wasn't nearly as expensive as I thought it would be. For instance, Line Producer Steve Stone dug into his bag of contacts and found a great deal on this grip truck, which cost about $600 to rent for the whole shoot and was filled with just about everything we needed.

We used other "exotic" camera equipment.

We also used a big camera crane arm, which we could roll on dolly tracks or keep stationary, but the important thing was that it let Philipp smoothly move the camera up and down. Unfortunately, although we planned to use the crane a fair amount, we ran out of time on set, so the only shot we got that really showed off our fancy crane ended up being the shot of Diamone after he had obliterated a crew member. The crane moved from high above his head to shoulder level in the same shot. Not a great return on investment!

We used our crane to track Crim as he walked toward the Diamone, but its effects were barely noticeable.

We used other "exotic" camera equipment. 187

The crane let us start a shot high above the Diamone's head and then end it at shoulder level. This was the only shot in the film where we got our money's worth out of this piece of equipment.

We also set up a ladder pod, which is like a three-legged ladder. It allowed us to get the camera off the ground every once in a while and give the audience some variety in terms of their perspective on the action. We only set it up four times in the whole movie, but these shots were enough to let us change our perspective in a few key scenes. They helped keep things a bit more visually interesting.

The ladder pod let us shoot some scenes from a fresh perspective.

Again, setting up both the crane and the ladder pod never seemed to take up shooting time, because we scheduled our shots so that our key grip, Dave Hadsell, could set up the fancy equipment while we were off doing other things.

We used different approaches to light *RADIUS*.

We shot *RADIUS* both indoors and outdoors, which meant we had to take different approaches to lighting our scenes.

We shot outdoors for the vast majority of the production. I thought this was a smart goal to have for an indie production because we wouldn't have to bother renting expensive lighting equipment, hauling it around, or wasting time rigging it up. I was right about that; while we were shooting in the desert, the most sophisticated lighting equipment we used was a white reflector board that our gaffer, Mark Brinegar, held off camera and aimed at our actors. The white reflector bounced a little additional sunlight (called *fill light*) onto the actors' faces and lessened the difference between the lit and unlit sides of their faces. It also softened any harsh shadows. For instance, eye sockets can cast deep, ugly shadows on an actor's face; these go away with a little fill light.

Gaffer Mark Brinegar takes a light meter reading.

Lighting outdoor scenes required only a simple reflector or two, which took no time to set up.

Relying only on daylight can also have some drawbacks, which stem from the fact that natural light is constantly changing. Here are some factors that filmmakers have to deal with when shooting outdoors:

- There's a big difference between the light on an overcast day versus a sunny one. On our last day in Death Valley, it grew overcast and started to rain lightly. (Of course, it was still over 100 degrees; we didn't get a break in that department.) We were shooting the scene where Dain and Crim are reunited with their aircrew and Dain punches Vesay.

We used different approaches to light *RADIUS*.

The cloud-blocked sun was casting a soft, even, shadowless light. The rest of the movie had been shot during sunny conditions, where the actors were clearly in bright light, and the environment had strong shadows. We had to bite the bullet and film the scene anyway. If you pay attention, though, you can tell those shots have a different lighting quality to them. Fortunately, we were able to minimize the difference during the color correction process in post production. (See Chapter 14, "Film Editing," for more details.) Color correction can't work miracles—that is, it can't make an actor appear like he's in bright sunlight when he's really under an overcast sky. But we used correction to brighten the highlights in those overcast shots and better match the cloudy shots to the bright, glowing highlights in the rest of our footage.

To see how color correction helped cover up our lighting problems, see the appropriate movie under the Special Features section of this book's DVD.

We filmed the Diamone in bright sunlight in this shot. Notice the strong, direct light on his cheek and the shadows on his nose.

The sun was hidden in the clouds by the time we filmed this shot, so the Diamone's face is evenly illuminated, with no shadows. Fortunately, we used color correction to make the highlights in both sunny and overcast shots glow white, which helped to minimize the difference.

- The color cast by sunlight changes throughout the day. In the morning and at dusk, light has a golden or orangish color to it, but it lacks that color quality in the middle of the day. We definitely filmed some shots that had different color qualities to them, but color correction techniques went far in changing the golden color of light and matching it better to the rest of our shots.
- Shadows can move over the course of the day. If you're filming a scene that takes all day in the same location, you'll have to be careful so that your audience doesn't notice different shadows from shot to shot.

We used different approaches to light *RADIUS*. 193

We filmed this shot at midday. The sun was directly overhead, casting no shadows on the ground.

A few hours later, you could see shadows making their way across the ground. We still used this shot, though, because we thought most audience members wouldn't have time to notice the shadows.

After a while, shadows were even more apparent. This time, our actors were clearly in shadow, and we couldn't use the shot.

- Daylight eventually goes away! We ran out of daylight on a number of days. For instance, when we filmed Dain and the Diamone after the CraterMaker blast, we got to our salt flat location later than expected and literally raced through our shots as the sun set behind the nearby mountains. Trust me: If you want to see people get jittery on a movie set, just watch them try to get key shots while the sun goes down! (In fact, you can see us getting these shots in the Behind the Scenes section of this book's DVD.) In this particular case, our shots miraculously turned out alright and weren't underexposed. The scene's lighting had a noticeably softer quality than you see in the rest of the film, but that actually suited the storyline because the CraterMaker blast clearly affected the environment. A couple of other days, though, we shot scenes that we just couldn't use in the film. They turned out to look too different from the rest of our shots.

Mark Brinegar used a small, battery-powered light when the sun was setting on our salt flat set.

There are definitely some penalties for shooting in daylight. Given all these gotchas, I developed a newfound appreciation for shooting indoors, where we had to provide our own lighting. On stage, Philipp Timme explained to Gaffer Mark Brinegar how he wanted to light the sets and actors, and Mark would figure out which lights to use and then set them up and operate them. (That's the gaffer's job: to

We used different approaches to light *RADIUS*. 195

execute the lighting required for a scene. The gaffer is helped by a team of electricians working under him.) Of course, you have to have access to lighting equipment, and in our case, Mark Brinegar lent us some of his own, and Line Producer Steve Stone lined up the rest at a good discount. Plus, you need to have a few extra hands around to rig your lights and keep an eye on them, not to mention the time to set them up (which could otherwise be used to shoot). I was surprised at how fast Mark and his team changed lights around and got them ready for various shots. If you have a crew that can take a no-nonsense approach to lighting—making it practical and making it look good, without treating each frame like a Rembrandt painting—you can move pretty quickly.

Setting up our lights took a lot more time and manpower during our stage day. Whereas Mark Brinegar worked alone in the desert, he had a crew of three lighting technicians to help rig lights on stage.

We typically used 1K and 2K fresnel lights but created light flashes for our cockpit shots with a Lightning Strike, which is a huge, 70K light that acts like an oversized flash bulb.

We placed gels over our lights to add some color. We used blue gels while Dain's ship was in flight, orange gels for when the ship was entering the planet's atmosphere, and red gels for the crashed ship's emergency lighting system.

Lesson Learned

> Nothing is ever easy with lighting. Shooting outdoors is fast and cheap, but you can get burned by the ever-changing sun and unpredictable weather. On a stage, you have full control, but the equipment, crew, and time necessary to light sets properly can add up.

Shooting with a digital video camera has several advantages.

Chances are, most indie filmmakers today are going to shoot their films with digital video cameras. Film looks absolutely great and can give your movie a little extra prestige, though, because you're using the same format that's used by major movies and TV shows. You should at least *consider* shooting on 16-mm or 35-mm film, but to do this cheaply, you'll have to line up a lot of favors and find a crew that's film savvy. If that's not in the cards, digital video is your answer. There are a few different formats in the digital world to choose from, as detailed in the following sections.

MiniDV video cameras usually don't offer the quality that other cameras do.

MiniDV cameras are on the lowest rung of the digital video ladder. These cameras generally shoot on a tape format called MiniDV (DV for short) and cost between a few hundred and several thousand dollars. Video shot on DV cameras (I'll call it "DV video" from here on) is a standard-definition format. This means that a frame of video generally uses a resolution of 720 horizontal pixels by 480 vertical pixels on NTSC video equipment found in North America. (On European equipment, which uses the PAL standard instead of NTSC, that pixel resolution is 720x576).

It used to be that you could clearly tell that a movie was shot on DV video because it had an obvious "video" look to it. The look wasn't flattering, if you were comparing it to film. Now, though, DV cameras have adopted a few new technologies that improve their image quality and get a little closer to film. For the most part, you can still tell you're looking at video, but it's more agreeable. For instance, cameras like Canon's XL-2 and Panasonic's DVX100 can shoot DV video at 24 frames per second (fps) instead of the typical 29.97 fps of other DV cameras. 24 fps is the same frame rate that film uses, and it gives your imagery more of a "cinematic" look. (I'm not going to try to describe what that is, but most audiences prefer it.) These next-generation DV cameras also let you shoot video in a 16:9 aspect ratio, which more closely matches the widescreen ratio that people are used to seeing in mainstream movies (as opposed to the 4:3 ratio used for TV programming).

Shooting on DV has some problems.

A distinguishing feature of DV cameras is that the video they record to tape is compressed (just as a JPG picture you might e-mail to friends is compressed). DV video uses a 5:1 compression ratio, so an hour of video requires only about 12.5 gigabytes (GB) of data instead of more than 60 GB per hour for uncompressed video. That compression makes it possible to store an hour of video on a small MiniDV tape and to edit it on a computer without super-big or super-fast hard drives or other high-powered gear. (The fact that you can edit DV video so easily on a low-end laptop is a tribute to that compression.)

But DV's compression can cause artifacts (little imperfections) in your footage, and its compression leads to other complications. For instance, it's hard to precisely remove actors from greens or blue-screen backgrounds, in case your film includes effects (although you can still get acceptable results if you're not a perfectionist). What's more, DV's compression limits the color data recorded in the video. Colors will still look pretty accurate, but the loss of data limits your ability to significantly tweak colors in post production (for instance, to create a highly stylized look in a music video, or to correct for poor lighting setups).

DV's low, standard-definition resolution (720x480 pixels) and its compression are two reasons why DV is not considered a "professional" format. But really, who cares? Thanks to today's better DV cameras, the format still looks pretty good, and even bare-bones filmmakers can afford to shoot in DV. If your film has a good story, good acting, decent lighting, and interesting shot composition, most audiences will care less about the camera you used and more about your movie's content.

Honestly, if DV has a so-so reputation in the movie world, it's because many DV movies shot by amateur filmmakers also have cheesy acting, poor cinematography, bad sound, and so on. DV ends up being guilty by association, but it's an unfair charge, and there's no reason you can't steer clear of it. Just remember how many other films have succeeded despite being shot on DV: *28 Days Later*, *Pieces of April*, *Open Water*, and *The Blair Witch Project* all come to mind.

HD cameras are the latest craze.

HD video is a hot topic with filmmakers these days. Consumer (or at least "prosumer") HD cameras are on the scene, and editing software from big players like Apple, Avid, and Adobe all work with HD video. Even Apple's super simple iMovie proudly shouts HD compatibility.

So what's the big deal with HD? Well, whereas standard definition video uses a resolution of 720x480 pixels, HD video has a resolution of either 1280x720 pixels (this HD format is called 720p), or 1920x1080 pixels (called either 1080i or 1080p, depending on whether the video is interlaced or progressive-scan). This high resolution gives your video a much sharper picture and lets it maintain respectable detail even when it's projected on a huge TV or a theatrical screen. (Standard definition video would start to look more pixilated and blurry, just as a low-resolution still photograph looks when blown up to poster size.) Plus, HD cameras can usually shoot at a film-like 24 fps frame rate and use a 16:9 widescreen aspect ratio.

Of course, there are many different HD camera models that shoot different kinds of HD video. On the low end of the scale, cameras such as Sony's HDR-FX1 (street price: about $3,700) and JVC's JY-HD10U (about $2,500) shoot an HD video format called HDV and record the imagery to the same little MiniDV tapes that DV cameras use. HDV cameras have caused a lot of excitement because they're relatively cheap as far as HD cameras go, but that low price comes with some liabilities. For one, the video is compressed even more than DV video. In fact, HDV uses the same compression technology that's used to compress video on DVD disks. The video still looks sharp, but you can see artifacts or other weird effects if you move the camera around quickly while filming, and there's little latitude for color corrections. Also, the camera lenses used by HDV cameras aren't first-rate, which somewhat lessens the sharpness you gain from HD's higher resolution. Finally, the camera's internal CCD chips, which convert imagery into digital 0s and 1s, reduce the sharpness of video as it's recorded to tape.

You can correct all these issues with a more advanced HD camera. Better models use high-quality, interchangeable lenses and more capable CCD chips, and employ much less compression when recording footage to tape. But, of course, the better cameras also cost an arm and a leg, starting in the tens of thousands of dollars, on up to $100,000 and beyond.

Obviously, no indie filmmaker can afford such a beast of a camera, so you'll have to rent it, which isn't cheap either. What's more, you'll need a high-powered computer to capture and edit the camera's little-compressed HD video. (It needs to be one with a fast CPU or two and tons of hard drive space, because capturing a minute of HD without compression requires almost 10 gigabytes of storage.)

Note that as this book was about to go to press, Panasonic announced the development of a new kind of HD camera called the AG-HVX200. At about $6,000, this camera shoots as high as 1080p (24 frames per second), and it uses compression that's much less extreme than that of HDV cameras, without all the drawbacks that come from such heavy compression (and yet, you can edit the HVX's less-compressed footage without an industrial-strength computer). Scheduled to be released at the end of 2005, the HVX could make HD shooting much more feasible for mere mortal filmmakers.

It's difficult to distribute your film in HD format.

All other issues aside, there's one key gotcha to consider if you're dreaming of shooting in HD. I hate to spoil the fantasy (and I fantasize about HD as much as the next guy), but HD video is not really appropriate for many low-budget, indie filmmakers. Although you can shoot HD fairly affordably (thanks to HDV cameras at least) and even edit it now, it's much tougher to distribute your film to audiences in the HD format. Here are a few things to consider:

- If your film is going to be distributed over the Internet, HD's high-resolution benefits are a moot point. Your film will have to be downsized to play in a small video window so that it can be downloaded over the Internet fairly quickly.

- If you plan to submit your film to festivals, keep in mind that many festivals are only set up to project movies from standard definition videotapes or DVDs. Having an HD version of your film will be pretty irrelevant, because you'll have to downsize it to a standard-definition format, at least for the next couple of years.

- Likewise, many people today don't yet have HD TV sets, so they won't be able to view the HD video you shot in its super-crisp form. Instead, you'll have to down-convert your HD video to a standard definition VHS videotape or DVD so that people can play it on their standard definition TV sets.

♦ Even people who have HD TV sets won't be able to fully appreciate your HD content. That's because most people's HD sets are attached to a DVD player that can only play DVDs containing standard definition video. At the end of 2005, a new wave of DVD players that can play disks with HD-encoded video will hit the market. (There are two competing formats you'll probably hear about: Blu-Ray and HD-DVD. Anyone remember the Beta versus VHS wars?) Finally, people will be able to play DVDs that offer genuine HD video that they can enjoy on their HD sets. Still, it will be years before you'll find these HD DVD players in an appreciable number of living rooms.

On the other hand, shooting a film in HD makes sense in a couple of scenarios. For instance, if you hope to sell your film to a cable TV network, many networks are beginning to broadcast HD material to HD TVs and want to acquire more content in that form. Another benefit of HD: If you want to project your film in a commercial movie theater, you'll appreciate having shot at HD's higher resolution. Most theaters still use conventional film projectors, and you'll have to make a transfer of your HD tape to film. A handful of theaters actually have high-resolution digital projectors installed, which play films from digital files. Either way, if your film ends up projected on a big screen, it will look a lot sharper if it's coming from high-resolution footage instead of a lower-resolution source (like standard definition footage).

But let's be realistic. Selling a film to a cable network or showing it in a movie theater will not be a top priority for many indie filmmakers, let alone guerrilla filmmakers. A top priority for many of us is simply getting our films made! For this group, shooting in HD sounds sexy, but it just isn't practical until more film festivals and end users can play HD content in all its glory. My guess is that it will be at least 2007 or 2008 before HD really hits a critical mass.

Lesson Learned

> For now, it's better to work in the standard definition world, where the camera gear is relatively cheap, and a wide audience can easily appreciate all the work you've done.

Chapter 13

Pickup Shots

This chapter covers a topic I hope you'll never have to deal with as a filmmaker: the pickup shot. What's a pickup shot? Well, it's basically footage that you have to go back and "pick up" after principal photography. In *RADIUS*' case, we had a fair amount of pickup footage to get.

We finished principal photography missing many shots.

As I explained in Chapter 11, "On the Set," our crew ran into a few problems that slowed us down and caused us to fall behind schedule. The following list details some of these problems:

- The temperatures in Death Valley rose as high as 120 degrees Fahrenheit, which significantly slowed our crew's work pace.
- It took longer than we thought to physically move all our crew's gear to some hard-to-reach locations, far into the desert rocks.
- When shooting on stage, it took longer than we thought to finish building our ship's interior set, which in turn delayed the start of filming.
- We were probably overly optimistic in building our master shot list, given the number of crew members we had and the time we scheduled to get those shots.

Chapter 13 ◆ Pickup Shots

- We had a couple of other unforeseen problems. For instance, a crew member suffered an epileptic seizure during the last few hours of our stage day, causing us to lose about an hour of shooting time. (That doesn't sound like a lot, but that hour would have been enough to get some key shots while we still had our sets up and ready to shoot.)

The heat of the desert forced everyone to slow way down. Had it not been so hot, I think we would have gotten all our shots the first time around.

Of course, we tried to compensate for these delays as we went. For instance, we greatly simplified the hand-to-hand combat between Dain and the Diamone so that we could shoot their fight more quickly. We skipped short scenes that weren't key to the story, and in general, we looked for ways to combine multiple shots.

Still, the cumulative result of all these little setbacks was that we ended our six days of principal photography with roughly 75% of the shots we actually needed. That meant we had to schedule another few days of shooting for some later date.

Doing pickup shots can be risky.

Since shooting *RADIUS*, I've learned how common it is for mainstream Hollywood productions to go back for pickup shots. Maybe the filmmakers run out of time before they get all their shots. (In many cases, actors immediately move on to other projects, so there's no opportunity to extend the movie's shooting schedule at the end of production.) Just as often, the movie is edited and test screened, and then the film's studio or producers decide that it needs additional footage to be successful.

Pickup shots are generally accepted and even expected on bigger productions, but let me assure you that they can be a major pain for small, indie films to deal with. Avoid them at all costs!

Here's the gist of the problem: When a film finishes up principal photography, everyone and everything (props, sets, costumes, and so on) go their separate ways, and it becomes time consuming and potentially expensive to reassemble all these elements later. It's like you have to start from scratch again, with no momentum behind you. Getting pickup shots also calls for you to redo work you've already done, because you need to get permissions for sets again, rerent props, schedule cast and crew availability, and so on. Also, the more time that goes by between principal photography and your pickup shots, the greater the chance that you won't be able to re-create some aspect of your original footage. (For instance, a prop or set piece might no longer be available.)

Following are some of the problems we ran into as we tried to get our pickup shots two or three months after principal photography.

Reassembling the cast and crew was a pain.

Just scheduling a time when all our cast and crew could work again became a pain in the neck. Here are some examples:

- Our director of photography, Philipp Timme, started a 4-week feature film shoot shortly after filming *RADIUS*, and he took his whole camera crew with him.
- Our visual effects supervisor, Adam Howard, was working on a tight deadline for another film, so he wasn't available for a number of weeks.
- Likewise, actor Catalina Larranaga had booked a 2-week vacation to Italy, and actors Paul Logan and Matt McCoy were off shooting other projects.

Suffice it to say, finding a few days to get everyone back together became a huge scheduling challenge. There were so many variables that I created a database on my computer to plug in possible shoot dates and quickly determine if everyone would be available. Still, for a couple of months after shooting, I could never find an opportunity to bring our core cast and crew together at the same time.

In fact, I got so desperate that I decided to use a different director of photography and camera crew because Philipp was the only piece of the puzzle that I couldn't lock in on a certain weekend. But that, of course, raised some other nerve-wracking questions—for instance, would the new DP and his crew be any good? Of course, I had found this guy through a good reference, but you can never be sure until you really work with someone. Would the camera team be able to work as quickly as Philipp's team did? Would I be able to communicate well with them? In the end, this "second-unit" team turned out fine, but going into our first pickup day with a totally new camera team added to my stress level instead of reducing it.

We tried to keep our pickup crew to a minimum: a 3-person camera team, a gaffer, a key grip, a makeup artist, a wardrobe supervisor, and a production assistant was about as lean as we got. At most, we added an assistant director and a couple of additional grips.

Our cast was changing!

Besides simply getting our cast members back out for more shots, we had to deal with the fact that their physical appearance had changed since principal production. Fortunately, nobody gained 50 pounds or anything quite so dramatic, but actor Matt McCoy (Crim) had let his hair grow noticeably longer since his buzzcut days with us in Death Valley, and he couldn't cut it because he had starting work on yet another film. Likewise, actor Paul Logan (the Diamone) had cut his hair shorter for another film and let the black hair dye he had used as the Diamone thin out.

Ultimately, changing hair lengths was something we managed to deal with. Crim's longer hair wasn't very noticeable because it appeared only in visual effects shots when he was surrounded by the Diamone's shield. And Paul Logan's shorter hair wasn't so drastic that most audience members would notice it.

So we were lucky, but you can see how, as time goes by, everyday changes in your cast's appearance can really cause problems when you go back to film them later. What if Paul Logan couldn't dye his hair black again because he had another film coming up? What if Matt McCoy had grown a beard that he couldn't shave, instead of just longer hair? What if someone had been struck by lightning or fallen into a vat of acid? All unlikely, sure, but these just underscore how vulnerable a film production is as time goes on.

You can clearly see the difference between Crim's hair in original footage and later pickup shots. Thankfully, fast-paced film editing and visual effects from the Diamone's shield made it hard to notice.

We had to re-create some costumes and props.

Another challenge was reassembling costumes, props, and set pieces that our pickup shots called for. Case in point: As I mentioned in Chapter 6, "Costume Design," we lost the Diamone's original costume right at the end of principal photography, as our crew drove back home from Death Valley. Our wardrobe department was able to create a new costume for actor Paul Logan, but it wasn't a perfect match with the original—for instance, the new costume's neckline was lower, eliminating the mock-turtleneck look of his first suit. It's a difference that most audience members probably don't notice as they watch the film, but *I* sure notice it, and it drives me crazy!

You can see the Diamone's shorter hair and lower neckline in these before and after pictures.

We also had to rent some key props again, including the grenade that Crim detonates inside the Diamone's shield, the radio that Vesay uses to call for a rescue ship, and the timer and keypad for our Crater-Maker bomb. (We owned the CraterMaker body outright, because we had built it ourselves.) It was a pain to go out and rent each of these pieces again. The prop rental shop that provided our CraterMaker timer actually rented it to another production one weekend, and that forced me to reschedule an entire pickup day. It's maddening to spend so much time lining everything else up, only to find that you can't move forward because of one cheap prop!

But even when we could get all our props together, new headaches cropped up. On our last pickup day, for instance, I had rerented the big gun that Dain uses to shoot the Diamone as he's disarming the CraterMaker bomb. Those scenes of Dain shooting the Diamone were a big item on our agenda for that day, but I forgot that we would also need Dain's smaller Tek-9 gun—the one she uses throughout most of the film—for a couple of running shots we planned to get. In the end, we had to film those running shots as she carried the bigger gun, even though she wasn't supposed to have it yet in the story!

As Dain runs back to her crashed ship, she's seen with her standard Tek-9 gun...

…but that gun was unavailable for her pickup shots, so we used this thicker, shotgun-like model (even though she's not supposed to find it until she's arrived at the crashed ship).

Another example: We rerented our grenade and radio props, but they were stolen from our crew van as we were getting ready to drive to Death Valley for Vesay's pickup shots. (See Chapter 8, "Prop Design," for more.) Later that evening, we had to create new props from a Red Bull can and a toy radio.

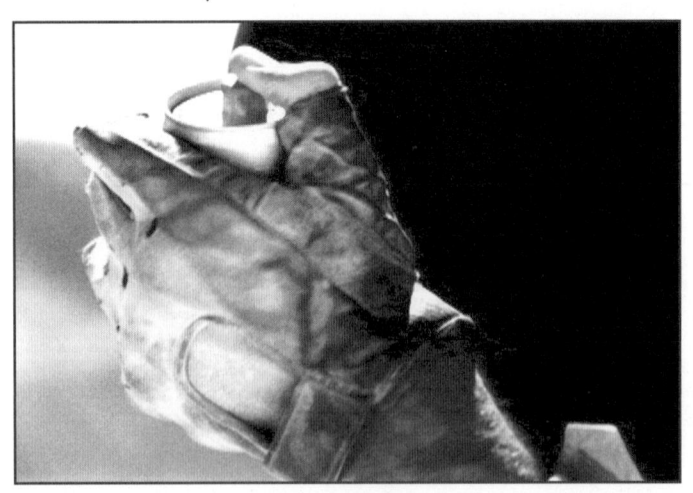

We had to make this replacement grenade out of a Red Bull can, with a cap from a Tabasco sauce bottle as the detonator.

Our original sets were gone.

We also had to go back to the two main locations where we shot *RADIUS*—Death Valley and the volcanic cinder mine—and ask for permission to film there. Fortunately, the guys at the mine agreed to let us shoot there for free for a day, but Death Valley National Park required another $1,000 per day. (There's no negotiating with the government, I found.)

Besides the cost of renting those locations again and driving our crew out there, there was another obstacle to deal with. We had to get footage that involved the Diamone and Dain fighting around Dain's crashed space ship—that is, the Diamone standing over the bomb to disarm it, Dain blasting him with a big energy gun, and the two of them invoking their Gemini powers and fighting hand to hand. The problem was, we had long since dismantled the set piece of Dain's crashed ship, and we couldn't afford to reassemble it just for a few select shots. That meant we had to carefully frame all our pickup shots away from where the crashed ship should have been. We got away with it in the end, but it took time for us to plan out exactly where we could point the camera and where we couldn't.

To match the real smoke that appeared in our original footage, we had a production assistant kick up dirt. On film, it looked a lot like smoke.

A bigger challenge was shooting pickup shots of Dain arming the CraterMaker bomb while inside the cabin of her crashed ship, which takes place early in the film. Because the setting is the interior of a ship, surrounding the actors, we couldn't just point the camera somewhere else (and obviously, we couldn't afford to rebuild the set on a sound stage). Instead, we had to meticulously re-create isolated parts of the ship in the kitchen of our line producer's office, and that's something I'll detail for you in a moment.

These examples just serve to press home my point: Getting pickup shots after principal photography can entail lots of headaches and redoing of work you've already done.

Note: For all the complications created by getting pickup shots, I suppose there were two benefits to the whole process. First, *RADIUS* Film Editor Ann Trulove was able to edit a rough cut of our film together with only the original footage we had. With that rough edit, we could tell exactly what new shots we needed, because they were custom tailored to fit into Ann's specific edit. That let us waste no time in shooting extra material when we finally did go out for the pickup shots. Had I simply shot this material during principal photography, I would have wasted a little more film and time to get those shots, because I would not have had such a pinpoint accurate understanding of what I really needed.

The second benefit to the pickup shots process was that I had to personally do most of the work to organize our new shoots—that is, I rented and picked up the props, scheduled our cast and crew, secured location permissions, worked out new shot lists, and created the production schedule needed for shooting. (During principal photography, other people handled most of this.) It was a great hands-on experience, and by our last pickup day, I felt like I could plan out a day or two of shooting with great accuracy.

Lesson Learned

Do everything you can to get all of your shots during principal photography. The best defense: Try to schedule some margin for error into your production schedule so that you have leeway to make up for unforeseen delays. Of course, most people do try to build some padding into their schedules anyway (we did), but even that padding might turn out to be insufficient. If that's the case on your production, do everything you can to extend your shooting schedule if you don't have all your shots yet. As budget-strapped as we were and as tired as our crew was from six hard days of filming, I wish we had simply appended another couple of days to our original shooting schedule and gotten the needed shots while we still had a crew, actors, and everything else on hand. Doing so would have saved a lot of time and money in the long run.

To spend as little money as possible, we used a different kind of Arriflex 35-mm camera for our pickup shots. It was so loud that we couldn't record sound with it.

In most cases, our pickup shots didn't require sound anyway, but when they did (such as Vesay's radioing for rescue), we simply dubbed in dialogue later on. (See Chapter 17, "Post-Production Sound," for more.)

The CraterMaker arming scene was a particularly complicated pickup shot.

One thing I can say for doing pickup shots: If you're willing to go through the hassle, you would be surprised at how cleverly planned and executed pickups can plug some serious holes in your film.

Case in point: As I said earlier, we had to walk off of our rented sound stage without some key shots showing the CraterMaker bomb being armed and characters' reactions to it. To be sure that I really needed these shots, I asked our film editor, Ann Trulove, to edit the CraterMaker arming scene with just the footage we originally shot on stage. And sure enough, just as I suspected, the edited scene was pretty pathetic. Problems included the following:

- We never got shots of Dain beginning to arm the Crater-Maker (that is, setting her watch and typing a keycode into the bomb's numeric keypad), so the audience got little sense of what she was about to do.
- We had only a single shot of the CraterMaker turning on, which wasn't very dramatic.
- We also didn't have any shots of the CraterMaker's clock beginning to count down from its 30-minute timer.
- Finally, we had no appreciable reactions from crew members as Dain arms the bomb and it begins ticking down.

In other words, without any of these shots, Dain's act of arming the CraterMaker was a total non-event, even though it was supposed to be a big moment that really sets *RADIUS*' whole story in motion. (You can see a version of this anemic scene in the Behind the Scenes section of this book's DVD.)

We clearly needed to get some new footage to beef up this scene. The problem was that these new shots took place within the cramped set of our crashed spaceship—a set that had long been dismantled and couldn't be reassembled. In fact, we didn't have the money to rent a sound stage; the best we could manage was to borrow the small kitchenette in Line Producer Steve Stone's office. It was no bigger than the kitchen area of a typical studio apartment, but Philipp Timme, our director of photography, thought that if we cleverly decorated a couple of walls in the kitchen, kept the lights dim, and framed the camera tightly on our actors and the CraterMaker bomb, we would be able to match the look of the original shots we filmed on our big stage.

Here's exactly what we did:

1. I set up a VCR in Steve's office, where we could play a copy of *RADIUS*' original footage. We used this footage as a reference so that we could match its lighting and the camera angles we had used when we were on the stage.
2. We started building our "set" by laying down a few panels of rubber flooring—the same kind we used on our original set to cover its floor. That way, no one would ever see the office's carpet.

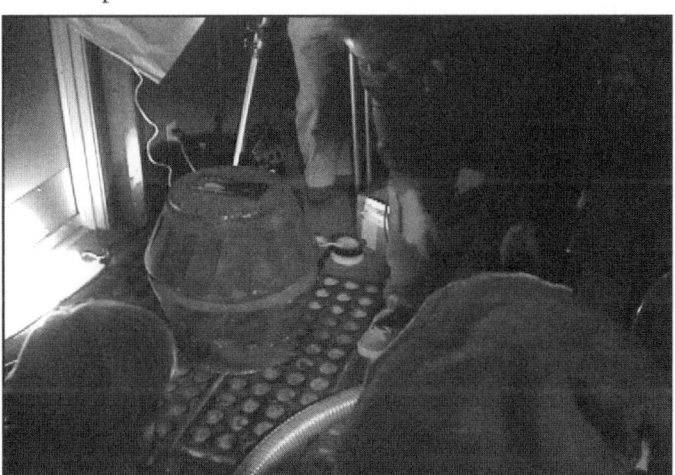

Carefully arranging our "set"...

3. We also got the same kind of jumbled wires and vacuum tubes we used on the original crashed ship set and draped those on the walls and around the CraterMaker bomb. Seeing these same elements in the pickup shots would help tie those shots to our original material.
4. We brought in just a couple of small lights and wrapped them with the same red gels we used on our original set. That way, the lighting of our new shots matched the old ones.

5. We also blew cigarette smoke into the new shots so that we could match the smoke we had had on our original stage.
6. We brought in actor Catalina Larranaga ("Dain"), fit her into the hallway, and kept the camera tight on her as she armed the CraterMaker.
7. Catalina had to leave for an audition before we filmed all her shots, but we noticed that our production assistant, John Iskander, had the same kind of skin tone as Catalina, so he ended up acting as a hand model for her. Anything you see in the actual film where Dain sets her watch or presses buttons on the CraterMaker's keypad is actually John.
8. We brought in actor Michael Yavnieli ("Vesay") and got some great slow-motion shots showing him reacting to the CraterMaker's arming.
9. While we had all our gear at the office, we also grabbed tons of shots of the CraterMaker bomb lighting up and its timer counting down.

That's it! By dimming the lights, carefully placing a few key props, and keeping our camera tightly framed, we were able to get our shots in a pretty ridiculous setting.

To see how all these new shots integrated with the rest of the footage that we got on the original set, see the Behind the Scenes movie for this scene on this book's DVD. I've superimposed the word "kitchen" on all the newer shots that we filmed in that little kitchen. You can see how many pickup shots made it into the film and how they really saved the scene.

Lesson Learned

> You would be surprised how you can fake an elaborate set by cleverly arranging some lights and a few props and keeping the camera tightly framed.

The CraterMaker arming scene was... 217

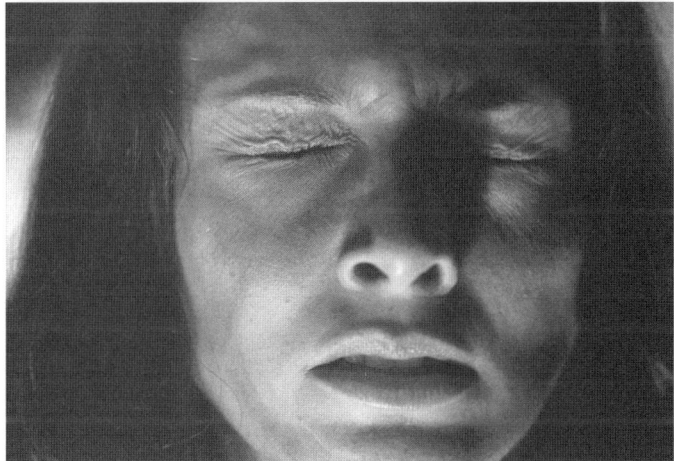

A sample of shots we filmed in the kitchen.

WE LEARNED SOME TIPS FOR BETTER PICKUPS.

Regardless of how hard you try, you'll sometimes find that pickup shots are necessary. Following are some tips for making them go as easily as possible:

Take reference shots of actor's makeup and costumes.
We had to get our actors (Dain, the Diamone, Vesay, and so on) looking as they did during principal photography. For instance, we had to make sure that Dain and Vesay had the same bruises and dirt patches on their faces as they did in their original shots. To help maintain this kind of continuity, have someone like a makeup artist or costume designer take pictures of your actors at different stages of your film. That way, you can use the pictures for guidance when you need to re-create the same look.

(continued on next page)

> **WE LEARNED SOME TIPS FOR BETTER PICKUPS.**
>
> *(continued on next page)*
>
> **Build a notebook of shots you have to match.**
> A lot of the pickup shots we were doing had to be precise, because they had to be edited together seamlessly with earlier footage we had shot. For instance, we filmed some shots of the Diamone disarming the CraterMaker bomb during principal photography, but we also needed some pickup shots within that same scene. We wanted the pickup shots to use the same camera angles and be framed the same way as our original footage. To make sure that our pickup shots perfectly matched the original shots, I used my video editing software, Final Cut Pro, to take still pictures of each original shot we wanted to match. Then I used Microsoft PowerPoint to arrange those pictures in a standard 8.5x11-inch layout. I went to Kinko's to print the pages on a color printer and bind them together as a booklet. I took that booklet to the set and stuffed it in my back pocket so that I could pull it out as a quick visual reference when our director of photography, Philipp Timme, was framing his new shots.

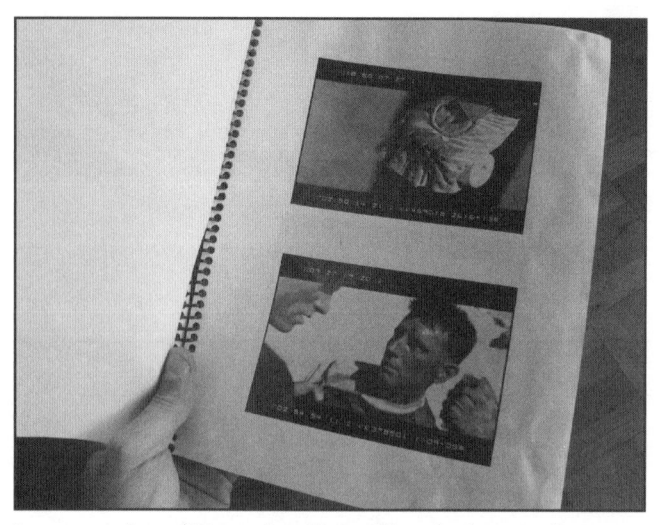

It cost me about $12 to print this booklet of reference shots at Kinko's.

The CraterMaker arming scene was... 219

TAKE ALONG A VIDEOTAPE OF YOUR FILM.

Sometimes a pickup shot would have to match original footage that had movement in it (where an actor or the camera was moving). I wanted to show our cameraman how the camera moved in the original shot or show the actors how they moved in their original performance. To do so, I used my editing software, Final Cut Pro, to record a rough cut of *RADIUS* to a MiniDV tape. Then I took my small MiniDV camera (and a fully charged battery) along with me to set, and I stuffed the camera in the deep pockets of my shorts. Whenever I wanted to show someone moving footage from the film, I just pulled out the camera, flipped open its little viewscreen, and played the scene right there, on the spot.

My Sony DCR-PC5 camera (since replaced by better models) let us watch our original footage on set.

PART 3

POST-PRODUCTION

Chapter 14

Film Editing

We shot about 5 hours of film while making *RADIUS*, and it was the job of our editor, Ann Trulove, to boil down those 5 hours to about 33 minutes of edited footage.

Editor Ann Trulove had plenty of experience.

We were really lucky to hook up with Ann, because she had a lot of in-the-trenches editing experience. She had edited a few indie feature films that got distribution and press attention, including Penelope Spheeris' music documentary *Decline of Western Civilization Part III*, and *Bad Seed* starring Luke Wilson and Dennis Farina. Plus, Ann worked as an assistant editor on major Hollywood films like *Reindeer Games*, *The Virgin Suicides*, and *Wayne's World*. (She's since worked on other major releases, such as *Team America*.)

Editor Ann Trulove at her Avid workstation.

We found Ann through Producer Andy Trapani. Andy's first feature, called *True Rights*, was edited by Ann, so the two of them got to know each other while working on that indie project. Andy thought Ann would be interested in editing an action movie, which she hadn't done before. Ann came on board for a fee of $1,000.

> **IT'S BEST NOT TO BE YOUR OWN EDITOR.**
>
> These days, everybody can run editing software on his computer, so you might consider editing your own film. That's definitely a reasonable idea, but I also urge you to at least consider bringing another person on board to do the editing. The reason: You'll already be super close to your film and will probably have a clear idea of how you want your scenes edited together. But having someone else do the cutting can bring a fresh perspective to telling your story. Chances are, that person will see some possibilities or alternatives that you never imagined. You can, of course, give your editor direction and make sure you get an edit you're happy with. But having that fresh eye can lead to some pleasant surprises and a better film than you imagined.

I definitely enjoyed collaborating with another person. Editing a film yourself can be a lonely experience, and you'll miss the benefit of someone else's fresh perspective.

First, we had to convert our film footage to videotape.

When you shoot on film, you have a few extra hoops to jump through before your footage is ready for digital editing. For starters, all the film negative that we shot had to be developed, just like you have to develop film you might shoot with an old point-and-shoot camera. We ended up developing the film at a Los Angeles-based company called FotoKem, which is well known to indie filmmakers around Los Angeles. Total cost: about $1,700.

Second, we took the developed film negative to a post production services company and used a process known as *telecine* to have the negative's footage recorded to Beta SP videotapes. (We also had our production audiotapes on hand; we added our dialogue to the videos so that video and audio were in synch.) These videotapes are known as *dailies* in the film business. (On major film productions, the day's footage is often converted to tape and reviewed by the director, producer, and other key team members—hence the term *dailies*.)

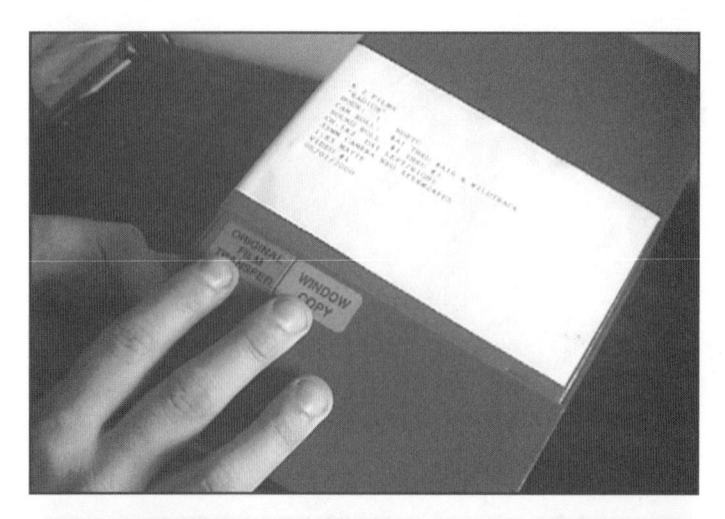

Our film footage was converted to these Beta SP tapes. If we did it all over again, I'd have the footage converted to much cheaper and smaller DV tapes or HDV tapes (an affordable High Definition format).

Note: Again, film processing and telecine conversion isn't necessary if you shoot your movie digitally—whether you're shooting on DV video from a consumer camera or HD video on pro-level gear. But, of course, we shot on 35-mm film. We wanted *RADIUS* to look as professional as possible and use a format that most Hollywood productions were using.

We digitized the taped footage into our Avid editing system.

Finally, Ann took our handful of Beta SP tapes and brought them to our Avid Media Composer workstation. (I'll talk more about the Avid later in this chapter.) The Avid was hooked to a Beta SP tape deck, and Ann used that deck to play each tape and digitize its footage to the Avid's hard drive.

One thing about the footage that Ann digitized: It's purely placeholder footage, used for editing, but not for assembling the final "master" of our film. Why? Well, for starters, those Beta SP tapes that carried the footage aren't known for their high quality. Beta SP is an analog format, and although it's certainly better than, say, VHS, it doesn't preserve image sharpness and color fidelity like a pure digital format can. Second, during the telecine process, we didn't bother to color-correct our film footage as we were recording it to our Beta SP tapes. (You typically adjust colors of your film before it's ready for final distribution. See this chapter's later sections for more information.) Finally, the Avid we used to edit *RADIUS* was definitely a low-end model, and it couldn't digitize footage without compressing it fairly heavily. By compressing the footage, the editor can store more of it on the hard drive, but the compression hurts image quality.

None of this really mattered, though. We simply needed decent-though-not-perfect footage for editing purposes, and we would deal with assembling better-looking footage after we had "locked" our final edit. (Again, more on that later in this chapter.)

This footage is taken from our dailies tapes. The image quality isn't great, but it was fine for editing purposes.

Working from the script, Ann built each scene shot by shot.

When you're editing, you're essentially telling a story by choosing how to arrange the footage you've shot for a given scene. For instance, in *RADIUS*' shootout with the first Diamone twin, we filmed the action, from start to finish, using a total of 15 different shots:

- Wide angle of Crim, Dain, and Vesay firing from behind
- Wide angle of Crim, Dain, and Vesay firing from the front
- Dain firing from behind
- Crim firing from behind
- Vesay firing from the side
- Dain firing from the front
- Crim firing from the front
- Vesay firing from the front
- Crew #4 firing in a wide shot, from the front
- Crew #4 firing in a close-up, from the front
- Ultra-wide angle of the Diamone taking fire
- Wide angle of the Diamone taking fire
- Medium angle of the Diamone taking fire
- Close-up, from the side, of the Diamone taking fire
- Medium shot from the side of the Diamone taking Crew #4's fire

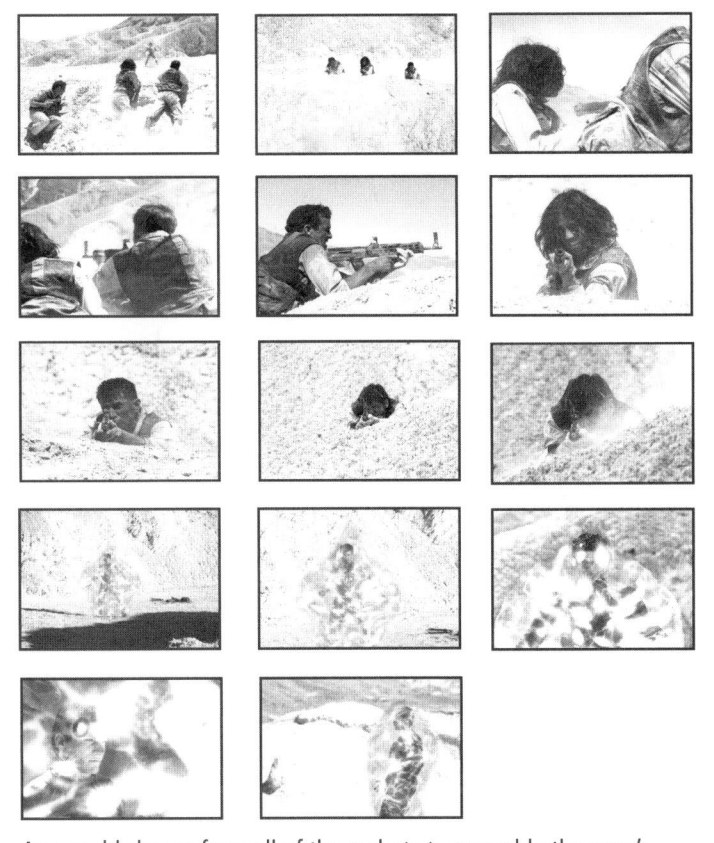

Ann could choose from all of these shots to assemble the crew's shootout with the Diamone.

Ann started building a scene, deciding which shots to use and how to cut back and forth between them all. When she finished editing a scene, I'd come in, we'd talk about the edit, and she'd usually make some adjustments. We went through the whole film that way.

We had lots of coverage for some scenes, but others had virtually none.

All these different shot angles that you see in the same scene, by the way, are called *coverage*. The action is *covered* from lots of different angles or views. Editors like to have lots of coverage because it gives

230   Chapter 14 ◆ Film Editing

them more creative possibilities to tell their story, and it lets them cut around problems in certain shots. For instance, when Dain and Crim are reunited with their fleeing crew, Death Valley's wind kept blowing Dain's hair in her face, so you couldn't even see her lips moving. Fortunately, we had other shots of this scene that we could cut to, like a wide shot of the whole crew, or a close-up of another character. Before Dain's hair becomes unbearable in her close-up, Ann simply cuts to another shot. That's how having ample coverage can help you solve lots of problems as you edit your film.

When Dain's hair kept blowing in her face…

…we could cut to a wider shot where her hair wasn't a problem anymore, or…

...to a shot of another crew member. That's the security that coverage buys you.

When we were filming action scenes like *RADIUS*' opening crash or the crew's big shootout with the Diamone twin, I tried to capture the action from as many angles as our time and budget would allow. Action scenes generally need lots of coverage so that you can quickly cut from one shot to the next and keep the scene feeling fast and exciting. But for slower scenes, such as a quiet conversation between Crim and Dain, we filmed little—just a close-up of Crim, a close-up of Dain, and a wide shot of the two of them.

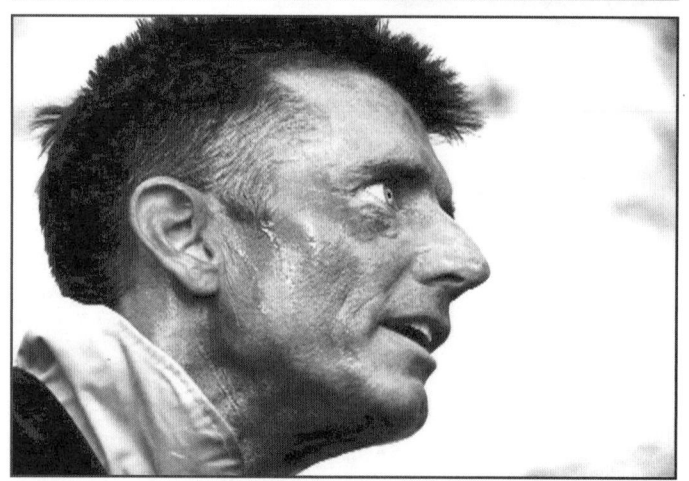

If it wasn't an action scene, we gave it only basic coverage—for instance, a wide shot establishing both actors in the scene, and then a close-up for each as they delivered their lines.

On our 24-hour stage day, when we were running seriously behind schedule, we got even less coverage. For instance, in the scene where Dain shoots Kyle as he tries to disarm the CraterMaker bomb, we filmed Dain's gunshot and the aircrew's reactions in one continuous shot. (Philipp Timme, our director of photography, just kept the camera rolling and pointed it at different actors.) This was the only shot angle we had for the entire aircrew, and then we had one additional shot for Dain. Having only two shots for an entire scene doesn't give the editor much to work with or make her too happy, but sometimes that's the way it goes, and you just have to work with what you have.

Lesson Learned

> Do everything you can to avoid one-shot coverage for a scene. Being able to cut away from your main shot gives you some creative flexibility, not to mention some emergency fallback options.

Unfortunately, it took us more than 4 months to edit our 30-minute film.

Normally, it shouldn't take so long to edit a 30-minute film. In fact, before production, we estimated a timetable of more like 2–3 weeks to edit a rough cut, and maybe another month to polish off the final edit. But alas, that was not to be for a couple of reasons.

First, before Ann could finish the final edit, I still had to film a significant number of shots that we ran out of time for during principal photography. Ann spent a couple of weeks building a rough cut of the film without these shots so that I could determine exactly what shots I still needed to get after I went back out into the field. But it took about 5 or 6 weeks for me to get our cast and crew together for all of those pickup shots, which obviously delayed Ann in getting a complete edit of the film squared away. In Chapter 13, "Pickup Shots," I talk about the harm it did to grab so many pickup shots after principal photography. In short, it triggered a domino effect of delays throughout the rest of the project.

Ann had originally planned to edit *RADIUS* over a roughly 6-week time frame, but when that time passed and *RADIUS* was still not close to done, she accepted an editing job on an NBC miniseries called *In His Life: The John Lennon Story*. While that job ramped up slowly, it still cut into the time Ann had to edit *RADIUS*. That project eventually monopolized all her time for more than a month.

Finally, the Avid editing system we used was being rented to us cheaply by a friend, but there was a catch: We could only use it during off-hours, such as weekends, weekday mornings, or nights. Eventually, our friend had to rent the workstation to more paying clients, and our work window got paired down even further—it was only open from 3 a.m. to 10 a.m. in the morning! Obviously, between the limited time we had on our Avid and Ann's limited time to work, our editing progress slowed to a crawl. Desperate, Ann recruited a friend of hers, Dan Brazelton, to work with me on those late-night shifts, and for about 2 weeks, Dan and I started tweaking scenes at 3 in the morning, finally finishing the edit. Note: This issue of our editing system's availability would have been a moot point had we used an editor like Final Cut Pro. See my thoughts on Avid versus Final Cut Pro later in this chapter.

> **Lesson Learned**
>
> Do everything you can to make sure you have easy, unregulated access to your editing equipment, not to mention your editor! Without it, things can slow to a crawl.

We edited on an Avid, but I would use Final Cut Pro now.

We used an Avid system to edit *RADIUS*, which surprises a lot of people who know me, because I swear by Apple's Final Cut Pro. But when we were editing *RADIUS* in 2001/2002, Final Cut Pro wasn't as established or mature as it is now. At that time, Avid had a near-monopoly in Hollywood, most professional editors knew only the Avid, and there was a lot of skepticism that a $1,000 editor from Apple—one that initially was intended for editing DV video—could really work as a professional tool. Also, at that time, Final Cut Pro didn't have the feature set for editing video that would ultimately

We edited on an Avid, but I would use Final Cut Pro now. 235

go back to the film world. That is, it couldn't generate a list of film frames for a negative cutter to splice together, and that was an important requirement for us. (Read more about negative cutting later in this chapter.)

Old habits die hard. Even now, Avid is the preferred tool for mainstream Hollywood editors, but Final Cut Pro is coming on strong.

We used an entry-level Avid Media Composer (which was based on an old PowerMac 9600), but there was a catch. At that time, Avids weren't exactly affordable; not only did they require a Mac or PC computer, but they also required a bunch of proprietary hardware and software that pushed the system's prices up to several thousands of dollars (or even tens of thousands of dollars). So in those days, most editors didn't have their own editing systems. Instead, a filmmaker would usually have to hire his project's editor and then secure an Avid edit bay. This bay is basically an editing system set up at a post production company, which rents by the hour or day. That's what we had to do for *RADIUS*. Fortunately, our Line Producer, Steve Stone, had a friend who agreed to let us use his Avid to edit the film for only $300. But the flipside to that deal was that we only had sporadic access to the edit bay (as I mentioned earlier in this chapter), and that really hurt our ability to edit the film in a timely manner.

Chapter 14 ◆ Film Editing

Anyway, Final Cut Pro began to change the editing landscape. For only $1,000, it delivered tons of professional editing tools—arguably more than Avid's offerings that cost many times more—and it also ran on everyday Macs without the need for additional proprietary hardware. Suddenly, editors could afford to build their own editing systems, and the need to rent time on Avids, at least for basic editing, became a thing of the past.

I edited more than four hours of the *Making Of* video using Final Cut Pro running on an Apple PowerBook. You could edit just about anything on even a lowly Apple iBook.

Of course, Avid has had to adjust its business model over the past few years, and it has launched lower-priced products designed to stop Final Cut Pro from eating Avid's lunch. But Final Cut Pro is still the best value for indie filmmaking, bar none. Feature for feature, it's as good as Avid's best offerings, it still costs only $1,000, and it also includes lots of other useful software for scoring music, designing cool title sequences, and compressing video for DVDs and the Internet. And it still runs great on just about every Mac around, including all manner of laptops and even Apple's low-end Mac mini.

Final Cut Pro is also leading the charge into HD (High Definition) video, which many indie filmmakers will start shooting in the next few years. When viewed on an HD TV set, HD video looks a lot sharper than typical DV video, and HD can be used as a substitute for real film, in case you're doing a movie that might ultimately be projected in a theater. Apple has been aggressive in building HD compatibility into Final Cut Pro, and you can build an HD editing system around Final Cut Pro much cheaper than you can with an Avid or any other editing software that I'm aware of.

Lesson Learned

> Final Cut Pro has a distinguished track record of delivering the most features hand in hand with the cheapest price. Avid doesn't, which is why I feel a lot more comfortable building my expertise around Apple's product.

> **IT'S GOOD TO LEARN HOW TO EDIT YOUR FILM.**
>
> Even if you don't edit your own film, I *highly* recommend teaching yourself how to edit for the following reasons:
>
> ♦ When you start to think like an editor, it makes you a better director, because you're more aware of the shots you'll need to get during your film's shoot.
>
> ♦ When you're in post production, you'll be able to do experimental edits with your footage to show your editor what you had in mind for a scene.
>
> ♦ At some point, you might want to edit your own film (or trailers, or whatever else), and the more experience you've built up, the better.
>
> ♦ Editing is a lot fun. When I edit, the hours seem to fly by.

Learn editing basics with Final Cut Pro.

Of course, editing can seem pretty complicated to the uninitiated, especially when you look at the interface for advanced editors like Final Cut Pro or Avid's Xpress products. Fortunately, that's all a mirage. Editing is actually pretty straightforward, and you can learn the basics—enough to edit your own film—by spending about 30 minutes with the software's manual or online tutorials.

Chapter 14 ♦ Film Editing

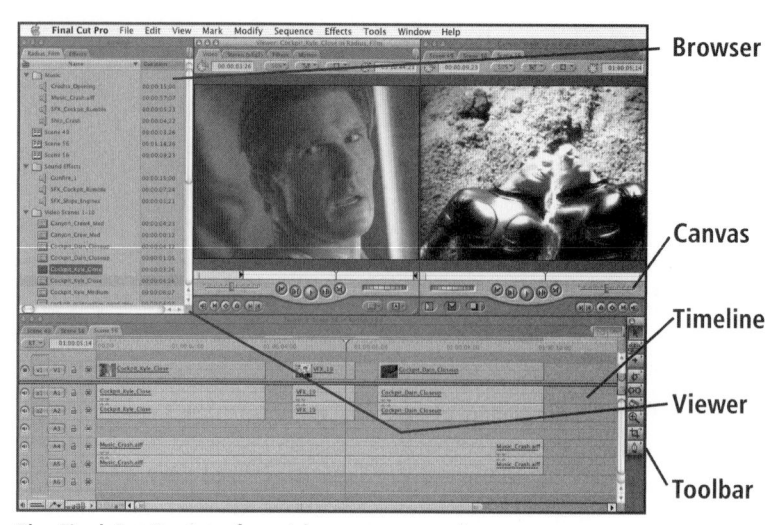

The Final Cut Pro interface. It's pretty easy, after you get to know it.

To demystify the editing process, check out the interface for Final Cut Pro, which, in my opinion, is the best editor around for indie filmmakers. Here are the major components of Final Cut Pro and how they work together. (Even if you don't use Final Cut Pro, most editing programs work fundamentally the same way.)

The Browser keeps media clips organized.

The Browser is the central storage depot for all the media clips (video, audio, or still pics) used in your Final Cut Pro project. You can get media clips into the Browser by importing them from your hard drive or by capturing video from a video camera or deck that's attached to your Mac. It's all pretty straightforward.

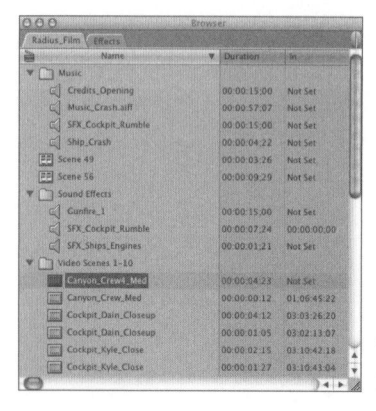

The Browser helps you organize your media clips.

The Viewer plays a media clip.

After you have media clips in the Browser, you can use the Viewer window to watch and listen to them before you move them to Final Cut Pro's Timeline (more on the Timeline in a moment). Besides playing clips, you can use the Viewer to edit clips in a basic way by setting *In* and *Out points*, which let you isolate only the part of a clip that you're interested in. To set an In point, just press I on the keyboard at the first frame you want to keep, and then press O (for Out point) on the last frame you want to keep.

Through the Viewer, you can watch, listen to, and edit your media clips.

Use the Timeline to arrange clips in time.

The Timeline window lets you arrange *when* your media clips play in time. (You can click and drag a clip from the browser or Viewer directly to the Timeline.) Stretching across the top of the Timeline is a bar that has notches and numbers, which looks like a ruler. But those numbers aren't measurements of distance; they're measurements of time, increasing from left to right (for example, 5 seconds, 10 seconds, 15 seconds, and so on). To edit, you can simply drag your media clips to the Timeline (solid-colored rectangles represent clips on the Timeline) and position them under a time value. That's exactly where, in time, the clips play in your story.

240   Chapter 14 ♦ Film Editing

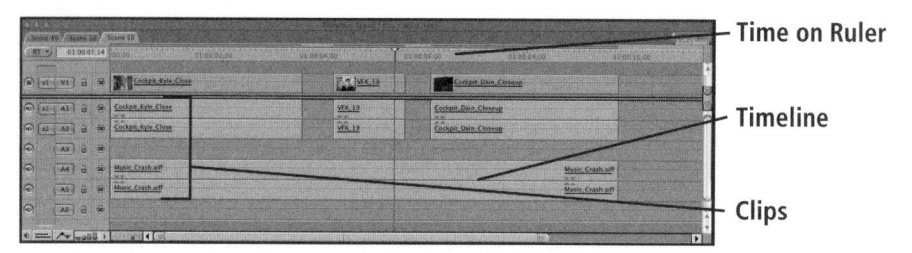

Time on Ruler

Timeline

Clips

The Timeline allows you to arrange when your clips play.

Another feature to note about the Timeline is that it's divided into rows, which are called *tracks*. Tracks make it possible to stack media clips on top of each other, so that they play at the same time. For instance, if you want dialogue clips, music clips, and sound effects clips to play at the same time, you would drag those clips under the same time value on the Timeline, but on different tracks. (You can easily create new tracks, too.)

The Tool palette allows you to edit your clips in various ways.

After you have moved media clips to the Timeline, you can edit them—that is, make them longer or shorter, cut them into smaller pieces, and rearrange them until they tell your story. Enter Final Cut Pro's Tool palette, which offers a host of tools that you can use to edit your clips in all sorts of ways. Honestly, you could edit an entire film with just one tool—Final Cut Pro's basic selection arrow tool—but as you get more experience, you'll learn how to use some of the other tools to edit more efficiently.

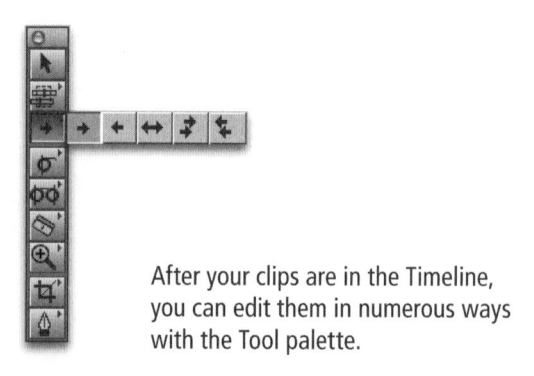

After your clips are in the Timeline, you can edit them in numerous ways with the Tool palette.

The Canvas plays your whole movie.

The Canvas is where you watch your movie in progress as you've arranged it on the Timeline. You can easily play, fast forward, pause, and rewind by clicking some intuitive buttons or pressing keys on your keyboard.

The Canvas allows you to play, fast forward, pause, and rewind your movie.

MAC VERSUS PC

Engaging in the Mac versus PC debate is a great American pastime, so let me state my position unequivocally. In my opinion, the Mac is an appreciably better computer for indie filmmakers and editors. I could write an entire book backing up this argument, but let me touch on the highlights, as I see them.

- The Mac can run Apple's Final Cut Pro, but the PC can't. Sure, there are other capable editors for the PC, including Adobe's Premiere Pro and Avid's Xpress DV or Xpress Pro. But none of these programs delivers the blend of power, low price, ease of use, and compatibility with all sorts of different video formats that filmmakers might need to work with (DV, HD, film, and so on).

(continued on next page)

Mac Versus PC

(continued from previous page)

- Besides making a world-class editor, Apple makes a ton of other top-flight digital production tools that go hand in hand with editing and film production in general. A great example is DVD Studio Pro, which lets you author and encode DVDs with the same kind of professional features (subtitles, commentary tracks, hidden Easter eggs, and so on) that you find in commercial Hollywood DVDs. Apple also makes Logic, which is one of the music industry's leading composition and sound editing packages. Or, take Apple's Shake, which is a top-tier visual effects compositor used for the effects in major movies like *Lord of the Rings*. There are plenty of other examples, but the point is this: Apple has all of these best-of-breed media products, and Apple's engineers are constantly making them work better together. Apple merges their interfaces so that what you know in one program can help you in another. (For instance, if you know Final Cut Pro, you can learn the basics of DVD Studio Pro in a few minutes.)

- If you're just getting started, Apple also has an award-winning collection of entry-level media applications that you can use as stepping stones to the more professional programs. For instance, you can edit your first movies with iMovie and burn them to DVDs with iDVD. In some cases, Apple even makes mid-level software like Final Cut Express and Logic Express, which offer many pro-level features but cost just a couple hundred dollars. (The Express programs also use the same interface as their more sophisticated cousins, making it easy to step up when you're ready.)

- Finally, the Mac's overall operating system—OS X—is a lot more intuitive than Microsoft Windows, not to mention immune to all the Windows viruses and spyware that plague the PC world.

OS X is powerful, intuitive, stable, and virus-free.

> Anyway, I'm not saying that the Mac is the only option for indie filmmakers. If you already have a PC, you can certainly find capable tools to edit and otherwise produce your films. And yes, PCs are usually about 10% or 15% cheaper for comparable hardware. But Apple has had a laser-like focus on media production for many years, and that shows in the quality of its applications, not to mention the elegance of its overall hardware and operating system. So if you have a chance to start from scratch, the Mac is the way to go.

When we finished the edit, we "locked" it.

When we finished editing *RADIUS*, we had a "locked" picture, which meant we wouldn't change the length of the film or any of its shots anymore (despite the constant temptations to go back and fiddle with it over time). This unchanging, locked nature is important going forward, because we were going to send the edited film to other people, such as a music composer, sound designers, and effects artists, and much of their work would rely on shots maintaining their original length. For instance, composer Jeremy Zuckerman would time his music to specific events in the picture. If, later on, we tried to change our edit because we thought we could tighten it further or improve it in any other way, the music would become out of synch and require Jeremy to go back and readjust his score, which would have been a major hassle.

Given the volume of music, sound work, and visual effects done for *RADIUS*, we couldn't afford to ask people to go back and redo work simply because we changed the edit. So after the edit was locked, it stayed that way.

We still needed to reassemble the edit with higher-quality footage.

After more than 4 months of work, we were ready to call *RADIUS'* edit "locked," but we weren't out of the woods yet. If you remember from the beginning of this chapter, the footage we built the edit around wasn't high quality. It wasn't color-corrected, and it was recorded to analog Beta SP tapes; it also was heavily compressed by the Avid editing system we used.

But now that we knew exactly what footage our edit called for, we were ready to reassemble the entire film with the best images possible—with uncompressed, color-corrected footage recorded to high-end digital Beta tapes (the standard tape format for broadcast television—good enough for us).

We hired a negative cutter to assemble the keeper shots from *RADIUS'* negative.

The first step in this process was to return to our original film negative, all of which we had telecined to Beta SP tapes at the beginning of the editorial process. This time, though, we didn't want to work with our entire negative, which included all the footage that we filmed during production. Instead, we only wanted the shots that *RADIUS*' final edit used. We hired a Los Angeles-based company called Computamatch to go through our 5 hours of negative footage, cut the keeper shots out of the negative, and paste them together to run in sequence.

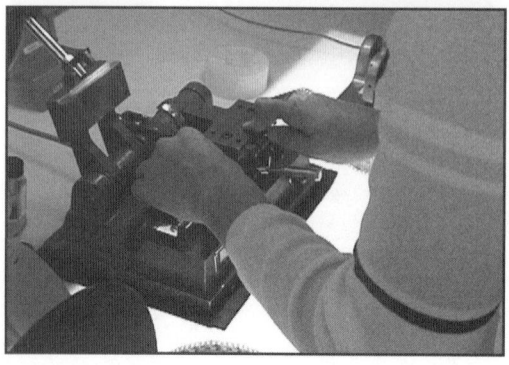

We literally had to cut our film negative and glue various pieces together. That's downright barbarism in today's digital world, and I look forward to avoiding it on my next film.

Most feature films are shot on film, edited digitally, and then their final edit is assembled, shot by shot, by a negative cutter. After the producers have this assembled negative (which can also include visual effects shots that are designed on computers but recorded to film frames), they have it converted to a "positive" film print. Then they make hundreds or thousands of copies of that master, shipping each one to a movie theater for projection.

Our reasons for cutting the negative were a little different. I didn't expect *RADIUS* to be projected in theaters on conventional film projectors. As I've said elsewhere, I was expecting *RADIUS* to be seen on television—either via DVD, cable TV, or maybe video projection at an occasional film festival. (Many festivals now accept submissions on video instead of film.)

But the next step in our editorial process was to color-correct our footage (see the next section). It's a pretty expensive process, and it goes a lot quicker if you have less footage to work with. Cutting our negative down to a smaller, more manageable size cost us $1,000, which was a good deal. We weren't looking for fast turnaround and could wait a few weeks for the work to be finished, instead of a few days. In the long run, cutting the negative saved us some money by cutting our costs in color correction.

By the way, you might wonder how a negative cutter can make super-accurate cuts to a small film negative. Obviously, being off by even a single frame spells disaster, because it throws your picture out of synch with the film's sound and music. But the process is pretty straightforward. Our Avid editing system generated a list of frame numbers to cut and film reels on which to find those frames. Those numbers coincided with numbers that were recorded on each frame of the film's negative. The negative cutter simply worked off the Avid's "negative cut list" and cut where it said to cut.

The cut negative went to a color timer.

After Computamatch had assembled our negative, I took it to a post production company called Pacific Data Post, which is where we did our color correction (also known as *color timing*). This process was basically a repeat of the telecine work we did at the start of our editorial adventures. Basically, Pacific Data Post placed our assembled negative in a machine called a Spirit, which read the film and converted it to a video signal that we could tweak.

In many cases, color correction is used in subtle ways. Let's say that you're shooting outdoors, and over the course of the day, the sun's color temperature changes and gives different shots different color hues. (Shots recorded later in the day, as the sun goes down, would have a more golden tint than shots from the middle of the day.) At any rate, color correction can make these color differences less noticeable.

But color correction can also be about style. For instance, when you see a slick TV commercial or music video, and the imagery has an unusual look—maybe it's super saturated, or it's got a blue or tobacco tint to it—that's also the work of color correction.

We used color correction aggressively, trying to give *RADIUS* a visual style that you don't see every day. Philipp Timme (our director of photography) and I sat with colorist Paul Lear and experimented with a bunch of different color options for the film. Eventually, we settled on a blown-out quality, where all the highlights in the image seemed to glow. (To see what I mean, check out the before and after shots shown in the Color Correction movie found in the Special Features section of this book's DVD.) I really liked the effect, not only because it looked cool, but also because it supported the idea that our aircrew had crashed on a hot, alien, inhospitable planet.

Paul added this effect to all our shots and carefully matched each adjacent shot so that the effect was consistent throughout the film. He also recorded these final color-corrected shots to Digital Betacam videotapes (commonly called "Digibeta"), which offer high image sharpness and color fidelity.

We did our final assembly on a top-tier Avid.

After we had color-corrected our footage and recorded it to Digital Betacam tapes, we retired our film negative for good. From then on, we worked with the footage on those videotapes.

We did our final assembly on a top-tier Avid. 247

We called the Digibeta tapes back into service on two more occasions before we had a high-quality master tape ready to go. First, many of our shots called for visual effects, which meant I had to get those shots to our effects artists. I rented a couple of hours on a high-end Avid editing system that could capture the video from my Digibeta tape and save the images as uncompressed QuickTime video files. (Remember: The low-end Avid we used for editing couldn't capture video without heavily compressing it.) I saved these files onto a portable FireWire hard drive and either hand-carried or mailed that drive to our various effects artists so that they could work with our final, color-corrected footage.

A Digital Betacam tape deck costs tens of thousands of dollars. I once again had to reach into my pocket and scrape up some change for a few hours' rental.

When our effects guys finished their shots, I rented time on that high-end Avid again. But this time, I loaded each finished QuickTime effects shot into the Avid and then recorded the shots to *RADIUS*' Digibeta master tape. You can actually insert shots right onto the tape, replacing existing, pre-effects footage with the new shots. After I added all our effects shots into the *RADIUS* edit, we finally had our final master tape, which was ready for duplication to videotape, DVD, or any other format.

We weighed the difference between film and video.

Shooting with a digital video camera, you can save time and money by skipping the steps of film processing, telecine, and negative cutting. Also, most editing programs—such as Final Cut Pro, Avid Xpress, and Adobe's Premiere Pro—offer color-correction tools. Although digital video might not have the same latitude for extreme color correction that film does, you'll still have a fair amount of flexibility working in the digital world.

Why did we bother shooting on film, when it involved so many costly, time-consuming steps? Well, it all boiled down to achieving as high a degree of image quality as possible. We decided to shoot on 35-mm film so that *RADIUS* would look professional, and so we could proudly say that we used the same format as major Hollywood films. But, of course, that meant we would have to process film, telecine it, and then ultimately convert the color-corrected images to top-tier tape formats, such as Digibeta. Then we would have to rent time on high-end editing systems that would not further compress the Digibeta's imagery.

Shooting with a film camera made sense at the time (and still does for bigger-budget productions), but it required us to jump through a lot of hoops while editing and assembling the movie.

We weighed the difference between film and video. 249

Shooting with digital video would have required compromises that I wasn't willing to make. Had we shot *RADIUS* on a DV camera (even a pro-level camera, such as the Canon XL-1, which was king of the hill at that time), our footage would have had more of a "video" look, and the images would have been instantly compressed. (DV video uses 5:1 compression, which loses some image quality and latitude for doing color correction.) Of course, since shooting *RADIUS*, some commercial films have used DV video successfully (Danny Boyle's *28 Days Later* comes to mind), but getting those results took a lot of technical experimentation and post-production magic that probably would have required as much effort and money as *RADIUS'* film route.

You might wonder why we didn't decide to shoot on HD video, then, because top HD formats offer much sharper, crisper images than DV and use much lighter image compression because they record video to tape. The problem was that at the time, professional HD video cameras were phenomenally expensive to rent. (We wouldn't have gotten the great deal that we got on our 35-mm film camera). Plus, computer systems that could edit and color-correct HD video were rare and expensive to rent. Of course, as I write this in 2005, working with various HD formats has become much more affordable. The cameras are still expensive to rent, but the computers that can work with HD are more easily found, and software like Final Cut Pro has many HD-friendly features built in.

Had we filmed *RADIUS* in the 2005–2006 time frame, we probably would have either shot in HD or converted our film to HD video in one feel swoop and left it in that format for the rest of the editorial process.

Lesson Learned

> HD video gives indie filmmakers a format with image quality that's not as good as film but is much better than today's DV video. Plus, HD skips all the post-production headaches of the film world. That's good enough for me.

Chapter 15

Visual Effects

RADIUS features more than 150 visual effects shots, which we accomplished on a budget of about $9,000. Some effects are 100% computer-generated, such as our shots of Dain's crashing ship, but most effects in the film are layered (that is, composited) on top of live-action footage we had taken on location or combined with shots we did in front of a green screen.

Most of the effects, are, of course, pretty obvious. You clearly know you're seeing a visual effect, such as when Dain fires an energy gun or the CraterMaker blasts through a canyon range. Other effects are more subtle. For instance, when we tried to get a shot of Dain's first twin lying dead on the ground (after being shot by the Diamone), actress Catalina Larranaga couldn't stop blinking because of all the dust in the air. The solution: We had to digitally remove her blinks so that she really looked dead.

We found Visual Effects Supervisor Adam Howard through a reference.

When we started preproduction for *RADIUS*, we knew that we would have a lot of visual effects to create, but we weren't exactly sure how we would get them all done. We thought we might find a small company or even a single artist who needed to build up his demo reel (basically, the portfolio of work that artists use to sell their services) and would be interested in taking on *RADIUS* and making it a showcase for his work.

Adam Howard, visual effects supervisor.

Producer Andy Trapani made a lot of inquiries, most of which weren't looking too promising, but then we got a lucky break. We had just hired our director of photography, Philipp Timme, and Philipp referred us to a guy named Adam Howard, whom he had worked with before. Adam had a great résumé. He had worked as the visual effects compositing supervisor on *Armageddon*, won an Emmy for his compositing work on *Star Trek: The Next Generation*, and had done additional hands-on effects work for major films like *Titanic*, *Contact*, and others. Best of all, Adam seemed interested in getting involved with an indie sci-fi film and liked the idea of working again with Philipp on a short project.

Adam suggested a brilliant plan to get our effects done cheaply…

When Andy told Adam about *RADIUS*, Adam had a great idea for how to get all our effects done quickly and cheaply. First, he would come on board as our visual effects supervisor and do some of *RADIUS*' most ambitious shots himself. What's more, Adam had a relationship with a small post-production company that could supply us with the high-end computer systems that Adam was used to working with (usually based on expensive SGI computers running expensive compositing software called Flame and Inferno, from a company called Discreet). In exchange for this free time on the effects workstations, Adam would give hands-on training to a group of young, relatively inexperienced artists that the company was assembling, hoping eventually to use this team to go after visual effects work on TV commercials and other shows. Adam's training, of course, would have the artists working on real shots for a real movie—*RADIUS*.

It was truly an inspired idea, figuring out how to get things done with little money involved and where everyone came out ahead. The visual effects company would get hands-on, first-rate training for its artists from a visual effects pro, and in return, we'd get a small team of enthusiastic artists working for free on *RADIUS*' effects, under Adam's watchful eye. Given this arrangement, we thought we'd be done with our effects in 4–6 weeks tops. We hired Adam for $2,000; he also brought in his wife, Kelly Granite, as visual effects producer, to help us schedule our effects work.

Adam helped us frame our shots for the effects to be added later on and oversaw all our green screen work.

At any rate, having Adam on board gave me a nice feeling of security, starting in preproduction. No longer did our effects seem like this huge, daunting mountain of work. Instead, we had a professional on the case, guiding and reassuring us that what we were trying to pull off was indeed doable. In that vein, Adam helped us hone our script, figuring out what kinds of effects we should write in—that is, what effects could look pretty good but wouldn't take too much time and effort to pull off. Adam also joined us on our set, making sure that what we did with the camera and our actors would work with what the effects guys needed later on.

Lesson Learned
> You don't have to know much about visual effects production to make a visual effects-oriented film. You just need to find someone who does and who can guide you through the process.

…but disaster struck our brilliant plan.

Sadly, a couple of unfortunate events conspired to sink our plans for getting *RADIUS*' effects done quickly and cheaply. Namely, the post-production company we had allied with started having financial difficulties.

We learned of this just after we finished principal photography, so we tried to edit as many effects-dependent scenes as we could with the footage we had already shot. Our editor, Ann Trulove, was able to finish some short but key effects scenes, like the Gemini Vortex and shots of the Diamone splitting into two, and we rushed that edited footage to Adam so that he could start working on *something*. But we didn't have other scenes ready for the junior effects artists. Besides, the post-production company started to reconsider its plan to get into the visual effects business. Not that any of that really mattered, though, because about 6 weeks after production, the company was out of business.

In the end, Adam managed to finish our shots of the Diamone emerging from the mountainside and splitting in two. But that was it. All we had to show for our plan was four completed effects shots, with more than 150 left to go. We had lost the expensive equipment that Adam intended to work on and the team of junior artists who were going to work under his direction. In other words, it was like watching the *Titanic* go down and managing to save just a few deck chairs.

Lesson Learned

> Don't count your chickens until they hatch. The road to hell is paved with good intentions. Whatever can go wrong will.

It was time to switch to plan B.

I took a few days to mourn our loss. Then I swallowed hard and faced the unknown: how to get a large number of effects done on as low a budget as possible. Normally, this would be the job of a film's producer and visual effects supervisor, but by this time, Andy Trapani and Adam Howard had to move on to other things. (You can only do so much for a couple thousand dollars.) Even though they always lent a hand at critical junctures, I had to handle the day-to-day management of the film and any heavy lifting.

It would have been nice to find a single, convenient source for all our effects work—as we originally had—but that didn't look likely, given the amount of work that had to be done and the budget I thought we could scrape together. Still, I tried to come up with some unconventional possibilities. For instance, I phoned a handful of California-based art schools that also had strong computer programs—schools like San Francisco's Academy of Art and Los Angeles' Cal Arts—looking for an instructor who might want to have students work on *RADIUS* as a real-world exercise. I piqued some interest in this idea, but it became clear that such a deal would take months to iron out and wasn't practical given *RADIUS*' timetable.

Therefore, it looked like our best bet was a divide-and-conquer approach—in other words, piecing together a team of individual freelance artists who would be interested in becoming involved.

256　Chapter 15 ◆ Visual Effects

> **IT TAKES TIME TO GET SHOTS READY FOR VISUAL EFFECTS.**
>
> Just getting to the point where we could start working on our effects required multiple steps:
>
> 1. First, Editor Ann Trulove had to finish editing the film so that we knew exactly what shots would need effects work, out of the hours of footage we shot on set.
>
> 2. A negative cutter had to find only those select, effects-destined shots out of hundreds of feet of film negative and then splice them together, one after another.
>
> 3. Those pieces of negative went on to our color timer, who then changed the color of the footage to suit the style we wanted. Then he recorded that treated footage to high-quality Digital Betacam tapes.
>
> 4. We used a high-end editing system to capture the images from our Digital Beta tape and save it as uncompressed video files in the QuickTime format. Those files were saved to a portable hard drive, which I used to transport to each of our effects guys. Finally, the artists were ready to go.

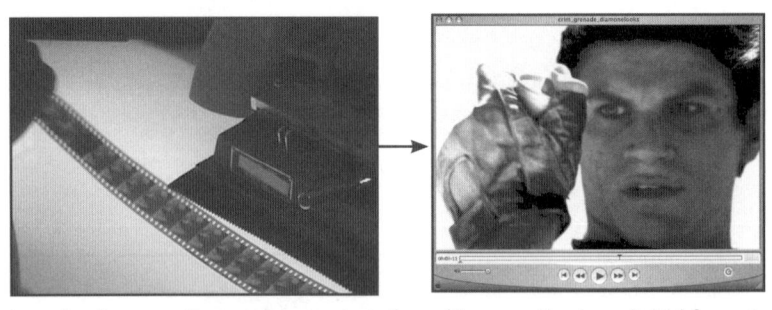

It took a few months to take our shots from film negative to a digital format.

I recruited a handful of freelance artists.

Adam, Andy, and I put out the word to friends and colleagues, letting people know we were looking for artists who might be interested in contributing a few shots to an ambitious sci-fi short film. (We emphasized that it wouldn't be a big time commitment.) I also went to Web sites such as VFX Pro (http://www.vfxpro.com) and Craigslist (http://www.craigslist.com) and placed online ads for artists, stressing that applicants needed to have their own hardware and software (preferably Adobe After Effects). I also flatly stated that we couldn't pay a lot of money, but that *RADIUS* was a good opportunity for artists looking to add some professional-looking shots to their portfolio.

Lesson Learned

> It's better to be up front with people about what they're getting into. The last thing you need is someone whom you coax and cajole onto your project but ultimately won't be content doing the work.

Over a month or so, we found a number of leads that panned out, including these:

- **Robb Hart.** A professional compositor who had done a ton of work for TV commercials (mostly color-correcting and superimposing product shots over video) and liked the idea of doing a few shots on a narrative film.
- **Atomic Imaging.** This was a post-production company in Chicago that did a lot of computer animation for trial lawyers and liked the idea of one of their artists—a guy named Don Quinn—getting some different experience.
- **Michael Bogen.** A beginning compositor who served as a grip during RADIUS' production and wanted to start building an effects reel for himself.
- **John Ellis.** An effects artist who was between projects and had some time on his hands.

Artist John Ellis worked efficiently using Macs with G3 and slow G4 processors. Don't think you need robust hardware to tackle visual effects. Just about any computer from the past couple of years can do the trick.

To make the most of these guys' time, we divided the workload so that each artist could focus on a group of similar effects. For instance, one artist worked only on bullet impacts on the Diamone's shield, while another did all our 3D ship shots. Another did the Diamone's hand glows and their effects, while another did anything involving green screen work, such as for our Gemini Vortex.

As I spoke to potential artists, one of the first questions they asked was what resolution they would have to use to render their effects shots. For instance, would I want the shots at NTSC's 720×486 pixel resolution, or a higher resolution, such as HD's 1920×1080? This was actually an important issue, because higher resolution effects take much more time to render on the artists' computers and require a lot more attention to detail. (Because fine details show up a lot more clearly at higher resolution, the designers actually have to be mindful of those details!) The fact that we expected Radius to play only on TVs meant that we could settle for NTSC-resolution effects, which made us more attractive to artists who might be willing to work on our low budgets.

Getting the process started took some organizational skills.

As I said, it fell on me to manage the workflow and process with all our artists. To get started, I went through the entire film and gave each visual effects shot a sequential number. For instance, *RADIUS*' first effect shot was Dain's video letter, so I numbered that VFX001. (I numbered the next effects shot after that VFX002, and so on.) To make it easy to remember which shot was which, I used Final Cut Pro to superimpose each shot number over a video of the entire film. That way, you could clearly see each shot's label as it played in the film. Then I compressed this version of the film into a small QuickTime movie and gave it to our artists so that they could clearly see which shot was which.

Getting the process started took some organizational skills. 259

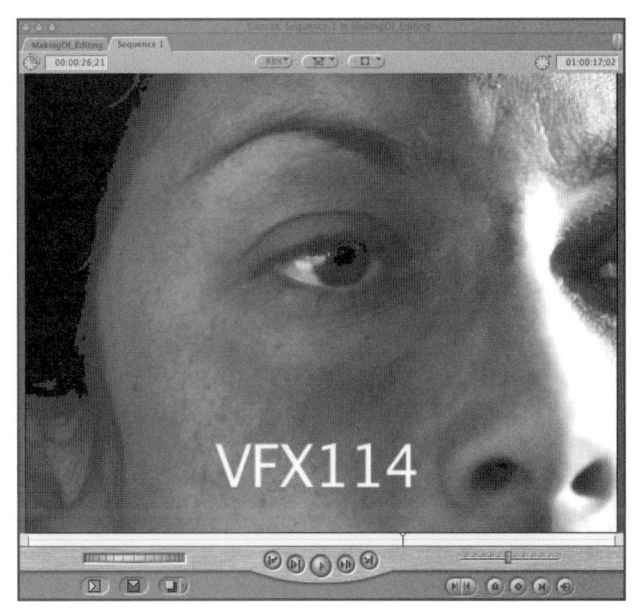

Numbering each shot in sequential order helped a lot.

Next, I used Microsoft Excel to create a table of all the effects shot numbers, along with a written description of what each shot required. This table also went to the artists. That way, they could start each shot by reading a clear, written description of what was called for. (Of course, we talked about all this, too, but I always find that giving people written instructions helps reinforce the details they need to keep track of.)

Note: Over time, my Excel table evolved into a helpful tool for keeping track of all the steps our effects shots had to go through before making it into the film. Eventually, I created columns to indicate a number of factors, including these:

- Whether the design work on the shot was done
- Whether the artist had submitted the final, uncompressed shot to me (as opposed to a compressed shot sent via the Internet)
- Whether I had properly labeled the shot and moved it to its proper folder on my effects hard drive and on a backup hard drive

- Whether the shot had been cut into the master copy of the film (meaning I'd never have to think about it again)

Without such a list, managing all these shots would have driven me crazy!

Our visual effects gear included inexpensive Macs and PCs, Maya, and After Effects.

Most of our artists used everyday Macintoshes and the occasional PC to create our effects. The guys relied heavily on two programs: Alias' Maya (http://www.alias.com/maya) and Adobe's After Effects (http://www.adobe.com).

We used Maya to create and render 3D models, such as Dain's crashing ship and Vesay's rescue ship. Another 3D model we created for the film was the Diamone's energy shield and its pulsing energy glow. We also used Maya to create 3D particle effects. For instance, when Crim detonates his grenade in the Diamone's shield, the swirling energy caught inside the shield is a particle system created in Maya. Maya particles also created the energy blast from Dain's gun (when shooting the Diamone) and the CraterMaker's blast wave that obliterates our Death Valley canyons.

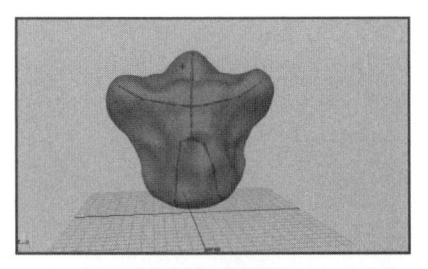

Alias' Maya created our 3D ship models and the Diamone's shield. It also handled particle effects, such as the energy blast from Dain's gun.

We used Adobe After Effects to composite all the different effects elements into our live action footage. *Compositing* means adding different elements, layer after layer, to build a shot, otherwise known as a *composite*. For instance, although we created the Diamone's 3D shield in Maya, we superimposed it over the Diamone's film footage using After Effects. We also used After Effects to position bullet impacts over that. Occasionally, we used After Effects to add glowing energy to the Diamone's hands. After Effects can also do 3D particle effects—like the swirling grenade fire in the Diamone's shield—but our artist, Don Quinn, seemed to prefer using Maya.

262   Chapter 15 ◆ Visual Effects

We composited any effects created in Maya over our live action footage in After Effects.

Big Hollywood productions use Maya, but it's also fairly affordable (about $2,000 to start with, up to about $6,000) for common folk. Any artist who is serious about doing visual effects will probably have it or something like it. Other alternatives include Discreet's 3ds max (http://www.discreet.com) and LightWave (www.newtek.com). As for compositing tools, Hollywood effects artists typically don't use After Effects. It's too generic and was made to do too many things besides just compositing. (For example, it has plenty of features for doing sophisticated font animation.) But that's what makes it popular with freelancers and independents—it does so many things respectably well, and it costs between $700 and $1,000. That might sound expensive, of course, but compared to the cost of higher-end compositing tools—for instance, Apple's Shake costs $3,000 —After Effects is a good deal.

We set initial deadlines, and then we set them again. And again.

I started to build a schedule for the artists' work. I'd always ask the artist, "When do you think you can get this done?", and then we would enter a date into yet another column of my Excel table. After years of working in video games and as a writer, my experience told me that you should always set deadlines for your work, even if you know they're rough and subject to change. Deadlines help convey a sense of timeliness and give some structure to all the things you're trying to accomplish. But I can honestly say in hindsight that trying to set deadlines and predict when our effects work would be finished was just a fool's errand, thanks to a combination of a few things:

- First, we underestimated the time it would take to truly polish off each shot. Getting a shot to, say, 85 percent of what I expected always went quickly, but that last 15 percent involved unforeseen details that always seemed to take longer than planned. For example, placing bullet impacts on the Diamone's shield went quickly, but then we discovered that we needed to manually rearrange a lot of them so that they didn't obscure the actors' faces or Crim's hidden grenade. That's the kind of detail that doesn't really occur to you when you're estimating how long the shots will take to finish, yet it has to be addressed.

- Sometimes I asked for shots to be reworked because they needed to be better. Other times, an artist created a shot with some cool, unexpected detail, and we both got excited and decided to rework other shots to include the detail. For example, artist Robb Hart's first stab at our Vortex used a blue color palette and felt like a kind of water-based energy. I liked the effect and could have used it as is, but then Robb said, "Hmmm, what if we added some color and a few other layers to this?" The result was an effect we liked even more and that we ultimately used in the film. But that change meant that we had to go back and add the new elements to numerous shots we had already worked on.

Things went more slowly than we expected, and given the relatively large number of shots we had to work on, the delays accumulated. But what really killed our schedule was the same problem we encountered with our music and sound design work: When our artists got busy with real, paying work, they had to put *RADIUS* on hold. For example, there was a 5-week stretch where Atomic Imaging's Don Quinn couldn't get work done because he kept getting pulled to do rush jobs for court cases. (Atomic Imaging was earning more money for a single court animation than we were paying for dozens of shots, so you can see why.)

We had plenty of delays in addition to these—a week here, a couple weeks there—with our other artists, but in most cases, I understood that the artists were at least sincere in trying to get back to their work on *RADIUS* when they could and finish their shots with as much quality as they could muster. Given that sincerity, you can't blame someone for making a living, especially when he's essentially doing you a big favor by working on a tight budget to begin with.

There was only one exception to that experience, actually. A now-defunct company was doing all the 3D shots of Dain's crashing ship at the beginning of the movie. This company was really just a two-man operation, and the partners started squabbling, and one left the company. The remaining partner then told me that he was out of money and either needed more cash for his work on *RADIUS* or needed a lot more time to finish his shots. Obviously, I wasn't going to pay more money, so I could do nothing but wait an additional 2 months for this guy to finish the last of his shots. By the end, getting him to work on *RADIUS* was like squeezing blood from a turnip—he seemed to find every excuse as to why he couldn't finish a shot, I constantly had to hound him, and our relationship became very strained. You can always tell when someone's making a sincere effort to follow through and when he's just being a flake. This guy was a flake whose mind had just moved on to other things.

Although I finally got the last of our shots from him, some of them didn't have the quality I was hoping for. That still pains me, because I think our ship shots could have been among the most exciting effects in the film!

That's how things go sometimes. When you're working with a low budget, this kind of scenario is always a risk, and I'm just glad that our ship shots were the only instance on the entire film when someone really flaked on us and stopped caring about his work.

In any event, these various delays made a joke out of any kind of "schedule" I was trying to plan or deadlines we were trying to meet. It wasn't long before I gave up trying to schedule things and was just happy when someone found time to work on our shots.

By the way, these effects delays also had a ripple effect on our sound design work. On several occasions, our sound designers had free time, but I didn't have new effects shots to give them. By the time I had new effects shots ready, the sound guys had been pulled onto another pressing project and couldn't work for a while. Frustrating? You bet. However, there's really nothing you can do about it except cultivate a Zen-like detachment (and I've never been good at Zen-like detachment).

Lesson Learned

> It's hard to keep a schedule when people are working at bargain-basement rates. What you can't give your team in dollars usually comes out in terms of time.

Green screen work allowed us to isolate a character or prop for use in a different background.

Green screen work is at the heart of visual effects production, and these days, even movie fans, much less aspiring filmmakers, know why it's important. When you film an actor (or any prop or set piece) in front of a green screen, you can isolate that actor from the green background and composite him into another background. What many people don't know is how easy it is to do this green screen work. You can use a dedicated effects program like Adobe After Effects to composite green screen shots together, but the basic functionality might be built directly into your video editing program. Here are some essential tips for doing your own green screen work, including an example of how to quickly isolate your subject from green screen footage using Apple's Final Cut Express and Pro programs. (If you've read Chapter 14, "Film Editing," you know that Final Cut is my favorite editor.)

Get yourself a green screen.

You can buy green screens from photography shops or online. (Try http://www.chroma-key.com, or do a Google search for "green screen sale.") The screens come in lots of different sizes and materials, but a full body screen could typically go for about $100, and a kit with screen and stands (which hold the screen up) could cost about $200. You could even build your own screen cheaply by buying smooth cardboard and some green screen paint. (Not any green will do. Once again, a Google search for "green screen paint" should point you in the right direction.)

By the way, you'll notice that blue screens are available also. Blue screens can work as well as green ones, but green screens are generally better when you're shooting flesh tones (actors). You should also consider the colors of the subject you're filming. For instance, if you're shooting an Irish shamrock, you might want to film it before a blue screen, because it might not stand out against a similar green screen backdrop. On the other hand, you definitely don't want to film a character like Superman in front of a blue screen, because when you go to remove the blue screen background, you might also remove part of Superman's blue suit.

Shooting your green screen takes some practice.

You need to remember three things when you shoot an actor or other subject in front of a green screen:

- You need to illuminate the green screen evenly, so that no part of it is appreciably lighter or darker on camera. (You can illuminate the screen by shining lights at it, or you can just shoot outside in bright, even daylight.) Professionals will make sure a screen's illumination is consistent by using a light meter to measure the light falling on different parts of the screen. But if you're not ready to go to those lengths, just do your best to eyeball it. The point is that without even illumination, your computer will have a harder time isolating your subject from the screen, because the screen will appear to be a range of different light values, instead of one solid value.

We set up this green screen on the back of a flatbed truck and used natural daylight to illuminate it.

- Don't position your subject (actor, prop, whatever) so close to the screen that light reflects from the green screen onto the subject, giving it a slightly green cast. This effect will probably be subtle—for instance, a little bit of green falling on the shoulders of an actor—but it can make it harder to isolate your subject from the screen later on, because the subject shares some of the same green as the screen. Position your subject at least a few feet in front of the screen, and keep an eye out for any problematic color spill.

- Make sure your subject isn't casting prominent shadows on the green screen. (Again, positioning your subject a few feet from the screen makes this easier.) You can probably work around some subtle shadows, but harsh, high-contrast ones could give you problems down the road.

Do your compositing work in Final Cut.

Try these simple steps to remove a subject from a green screen shot and composite it into a new background. If you want to use some practice footage, I've posted a short DV video shot of the Diamone at http://www.k2films.com/greenscreen.mov. I can't promise that this clip will be available forever, but try to download it if you think that would help.

1. Import your green footage into Final Cut Express or Pro.

2. Place your footage on Final Cut's Timeline, and position the Timeline's playhead anywhere over the clip so that you can see it in Final Cut's Canvas window. (Note: See Chapter 14 for an overview of Final Cut, if you're not familiar with its windows.)

3. Select the footage clip on the Timeline by clicking it with Final Cut's selection arrow. Then choose Effects, Video Filters, Key, Blue and Green Screen. By doing this, you apply a filter that will let you remove the green background from your shot.

The goal is to isolate the Diamone twins from the green screen and composite them into a different background.

4. Double-click your green screen clip on the Timeline so that it opens in Final Cut's Viewer window. Then click the Filters tab at the top of the Viewer.

5. From the Key Mode drop-down list, select Blue or Green, depending on the color of the background. (Again, I'm assuming you went green.)

6. While keeping an eye on the image in the Canvas window, click and drag the filters, Color Level slider to a lower setting until the color of the blue or green screen disappears. You can also move the Color Tolerance slider to remove shades that are similar to the key color that you've chosen. In addition, experiment with the Edge Thin and Edge Feather sliders to see their effects.

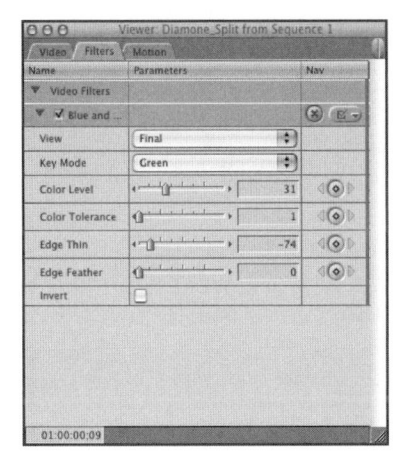

To get started, remove the green by dragging the Color Level slider.

7. You're ready to composite your green screen clip with other material. On the Timeline, click and drag the green screen clip to a track above another clip on the Timeline. Ta-da! You'll see in the Canvas window that your green screen clip is now superimposed over the clip that's beneath it on Final Cut's Timeline.

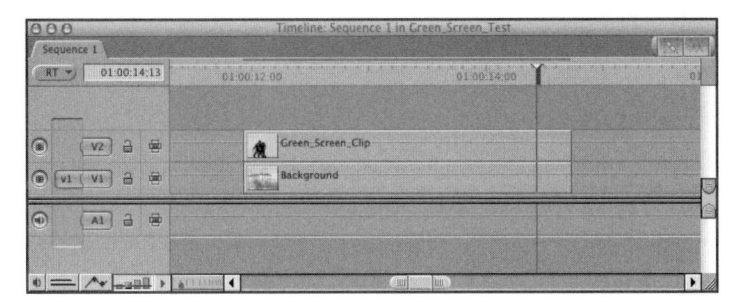

On the Timeline, stack your green screen clip over the background clip.

The twins in their new home.

This is by no means meant to be a tutorial on compositing. Numerous other tools and tactics can help you combine images. For instance, you'll want to soften the edges around your green screen subjects so that they blend better with their background. (Try the filter's Edge Feather slider after you've composited your green screen shot with its background.) Final Cut doesn't have all the flexibility for green screen compositing that an application like Adobe After Effects does. Still, my intention is to show you that the basics of compositing are pretty straightforward. Hopefully, this will give you a little courage to dive into green screen work if your film calls for it.

We worked on many of the effects remotely.

By the way, much my work with the effects guys was done remotely. All but one of the artists lived in the Los Angeles area, but L.A. is a big place, and I quickly got tired of driving around to visit everybody. We started working via phone and the Internet, meeting in person only rarely.

Basically, the artists posted their shots-in-progress on an FTP file server. (An FTP file server is like a private, password-protected Web site that lets authorized users upload and download files; if you want to set one up, you can usually do it through the same companies that host Web sites.)

Next, I downloaded the shots and watched them independently. Sometimes I cut them into an edit of *RADIUS* to see how they integrated with the rest of the film. Then I usually picked up the phone and gave the artist my feedback, or I e-mailed point-by-point written feedback so that the artist had a clear checklist to follow.

I used still images and occasionally videos to convey my feedback as clearly as possible.

To support the written feedback, I also took screenshots of individual frames, loaded them into Photoshop (http://www.adobe.com), and drew little circles or arrows directly onto the image to highlight elements I was talking about. (For instance, when the bullet impacts on the Diamone's shield began to obscure his face, I circled the impacts that had to be shifted or taken out.) The artists got these pictures attached to my e-mails so they could see exactly what I was talking about. The more visual feedback you can give an artist, the better. You've heard the saying, "A picture's worth a thousand words." Well, a single word can evoke a thousand different pictures to different people, but pointing to specific elements in a shot can help avoid misinterpretation or confusion between you and your artists.

Occasionally, some feedback was too abstract or detailed to convey efficiently in an e-mail or with still pictures, so I got out my handheld video camera, pointed it at the effects shot on my laptop's screen, and then recorded myself talking and pointing to elements in the shot as it looped repeatedly. Then I compressed the video feedback into a little QuickTime movie and e-mailed it to the artist. It was the next best thing to being there.

Speaking of being there, I should say that nothing beats being able to sit with an artist in person. It's easier to communicate, and the two of you can quickly make small changes, watch the results, and apply additional finishing touches on the spot. Working on *RADIUS* convinced me that it's entirely possible to work remotely with artists. That's especially valuable for indie filmmakers, because it significantly expands the talent pool of artists you can recruit to your film. Instead of having to find an artist who's local to your area, you can work with anyone in the world. And that makes it a lot easier to find someone who can work for whatever low budget you can scrape together.

Lesson Learned

You can piece together an effects team from all over the planet if you have to.

CHAPTER 16

Music Composition

I've always been aware of how music can help define a movie—especially an action movie—and I wanted *RADIUS* to use music to the hilt, filling almost the entire 33-minute film with a score. (In the end, a few scenes went without music to give the audience's ears a break.)

It all started with our music supervisor, Joe Fischer.

Producer Andy Trapani was friends with Joe, who donated his free time to *RADIUS* and became our music supervisor. Joe worked as an assistant music supervisor on television shows and was looking for some credits as a full-fledged supervisor, so that's why *RADIUS* had some appeal to him.

On a more elaborate film, the music supervisor's job is to recommend musical selections for a director to consider, and to work on getting the legal clearances that the music requires (which usually involves paying fees to the music's copyright holders). For instance, chances are a music supervisor recommended playing a version of Bobby McFerrin's *Don't Worry, Be Happy* in *Dawn of the Dead*'s deserted shopping mall. The same thing goes for Sonny and Cher's *I Got You Babe*, which tortured Bill Murray every morning in *Groundhog Day*.

273

Of course, *RADIUS* didn't have opportunities to use pre-existing music. Instead, we needed a composer to build a score from scratch, and that's another thing a music supervisor can help you with. Joe's job called for him to keep track of up-and-coming composers, so he provided me with a number of demo tapes, all of which showcased composers that could handle an action movie and our low budget.

I listened to a dozen or so tapes, but only a handful featured musical styles that were close to what I had in mind for *RADIUS*. And of that handful, the music of one Jeremy Zuckerman stood out especially.

Composer Jeremy Zuckerman was paid $1,000 for his 23-minute score.

Jeremy was a 24-year-old musician who was just graduating from the graduate music program of Cal Arts in Southern California. (Jeremy already had an undergrad degree from Boston's Berkeley School of Music.)

I really liked Jeremy's demo tape. Joe and I met with him, and I showed him scenes from the *RADIUS* edit we were working on. Jeremy seemed really enthusiastic about the movie and also came across as a good listener—two must-haves in a composer! But I initially had a couple of concerns. Although Jeremy's demo tape showed a lot of musical talent, only a small sample of it matched the musical style I was looking for. Plus, Jeremy had never scored a film or narrative video. Joe asked if Jeremy would be willing to score a small section of *RADIUS* as an audition, and he agreed to go that extra mile. A week later, Jeremy submitted a 3-minute piece, scored to the big shootout between the Diamone's first twin and our fleeing aircrew. It was certainly enough to give me confidence that Jeremy could get the job done, so the job was his.

Jeremy with all his gear.

Jeremy's fee was $1,000 to do about 23 minutes of solid music. Obviously, this was a small amount of money for a lot of work, but it was worth his while because he was getting his career started and needed to start building a body of work and developing contacts in the industry. This kind of forward thinking is a fact of life for most creative people in Hollywood, the equivalent of investing lots of time and money into a startup company before it breaks even.

Jeremy worked out of his "home studio," which was essentially the second bedroom of his apartment. Sitting together, we would look at the finished edit of *RADIUS*, and I would try to describe what I wanted from the music in each scene or even unique moments within a scene. Jeremy would spend a few days scoring the music on his own, and when he was ready, he would either e-mail me an MP3 file of the music that I could edit into my copy of the film, or I would drive back to his place and we would go through the work in person. I preferred meeting in person when we were doing early work on a particular section of the score, because there was often a lot to talk about and it was much easier to try new things and make adjustments when we were face to face, working in real time. But when we were just polishing a piece, we tended to use e-mail and phone conversations to get stuff done.

I liked the unique sound of Jeremy's electronic music. Besides, using a computer to "synthesize" conventional orchestral music risked sounding fake.

We worked for about 8 or 9 months, which sounds like a long time, but it was punctuated by lots of intermittent breaks when Jeremy got busy with real paying work. (He was beginning to do sound and music work for TV commercials, and he even created some music for David Lee Roth's comeback album.) This kind of stop-start process is a fact of life that low-budget indie filmmakers have to accept. You can often get people to work for low fees, but you'll also put up with downtime when those people have to go out and make a living. Fortunately, the delay in getting our music finished wasn't really a big deal, because our visual effects and sound design work was taking a while to finish, too. Taking breaks let us go back to the music, listen to it again with a fresh ear, and make more refinements with a fresh perspective.

Lesson Learned

> Finding people who are just getting started in their careers is a great way to bring talent to your film without the high price.

Run Lola Run was an initial influence on the *RADIUS* score.

Ever since I saw 1998's indie action film *Run Lola Run*, I knew I didn't want *RADIUS* to use a conventional orchestral score featuring the typical string and brass instruments. *Run Lola Run*'s music was really impressive. It had an unusual electronic, techno feel, and it felt fresh and a bit quirky. So I told Jeremy that I wanted *RADIUS*' score to draw a lot of inspiration from *Run Lola Run*, and he agreed that it was a cool direction to go in.

I edited a lot of placeholder music into *RADIUS*...

Separately, for my own purposes, I found it helpful to put placeholder music into the final edit of *RADIUS*—for instance, I used track 2 from *Run Lola Run*'s soundtrack CD for our opening crash scene, fast-paced music from *The Rock* for our running sequences, and music from *Aliens* and *Armageddon* for some of our fight scenes. From an instrumental standpoint, much of this placeholder music ran counter to the electronic style we were shooting for, because it was largely orchestral. At the same time, the placeholder tracks had the right emotional qualities our scenes called for—that is, fast, or brooding, or whatever else. The temporary tracks helped me imagine what *RADIUS* would feel like when we finally added music of our own. In addition, my placeholder music helped show Jeremy how I wanted our music to shift from slow to fast, or energetic to subdued, throughout the film.

...but I got too attached to our placeholder music.

Jeremy started his composition work by scoring a small section of the film, which was *RADIUS*' opening crash scene. We worked only on this small segment, because we wanted to perfect it first and thereby establish the musical palette that the rest of the movie's music would use. (Like a painter might choose a palette of colors to work with, composers choose a palette of instruments or sounds to work with so that their music maintains a consistent stylistic feel.)

Jeremy did an admirable job trying to create music that bore a strong resemblance to the score of *Run Lola Run* (particularly track 6), which I had cut into *RADIUS* as placeholder music. But there was still a problem: Jeremy's music wasn't actually *identical* to *Run Lola Run*. See, I had the *Lola* music edited into *RADIUS* for so long that I got too used it. In fact, I had fallen in love with it! And deep down, subconsciously, I wanted that same music. Even though Jeremy was creating something in the same vein—which was all he could be expected to do—he wasn't copying it note for note, so I was never entirely satisfied with it.

Beware the temptation to use placeholder music from favorite movie soundtracks!

We spent a couple of weeks going in circles before I realized what was really going on. When I identified the problem—that is, that I was too attached to our placeholder music, and I was holding Jeremy to an impossible standard—I realized what we needed to do. First, I cut out the *Run Lola Run* music from my edit of *RADIUS* so that I would never hear it again while watching the film. Second, I apologized to Jeremy for his trouble and asked him to take yet another pass at the music, but this time doing whatever he thought needed to be done and giving him leeway to depart from the techno style that *Lola* had established.

Within a week, Jeremy had a new version of the opening crash scene ready to go. It used electronic instruments and heavy, dramatic drums, but it didn't have a techno feel anymore. It worked great. With a little more work, we polished it and had a new style that the rest of the film's score would follow.

Suffice it to say, I'll never use placeholder music in the same way again. It sounds like a good idea, but you get addicted to music you can't have, and it's incredibly hard to see your own composer's music in an unbiased, balanced light.

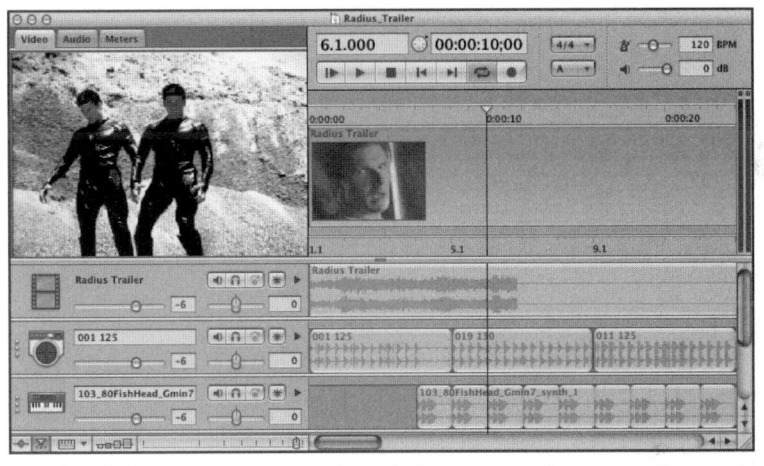

Soundtrack lets you import a movie and then arrange short, repeating music loops to build a placeholder score.

Still, placeholder music can be useful, especially while editing your film. For instance, when editing a fast-paced action scene, some editors might find it helpful to do their cutting to fast-paced music, which helps them find the right pace of cuts to use for the scene. For these purposes, I've found a helpful solution: Basically, I edit simple musical loops—for instance, repeating drum beats or other simple musical riffs—into the film, instead of full-blown, composed music. These loops are enough to get a basic feel for what your final music should feel like—fast or slow, upbeat or dark—but the loops are so simple that you can't really get attached to them. When your composer starts working, you can only be pleasantly surprised as you see (or hear) real music take shape, instead of feeling disappointed that your music isn't a 100 percent match with the placeholder tunes you've gotten accustomed to.

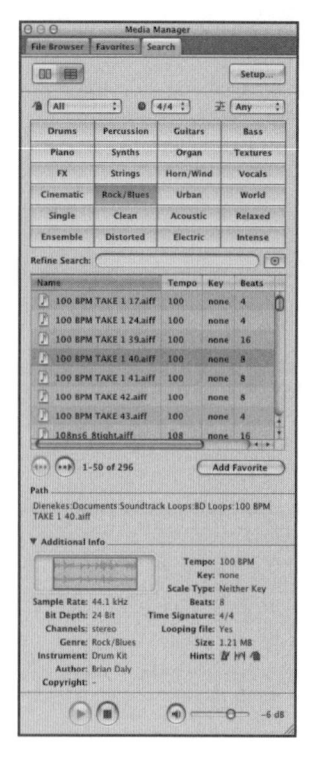

You can quickly sort through thousands of loops in different categories.

You can find loops in tons of music composition programs, but I use the broad collection that's built into Apple's Soundtrack program, which currently ships free as part of Final Cut Pro.

Lesson Learned

> Beware of getting too attached to any placeholder music you use in your film. It's best to use simple music loops that don't have an addictive quality.

Jeremy used Logic Audio software, running on a low-end Mac.

Jeremy composed *RADIUS*' music using an "ancient" Mac (a 266-MHz G3 PowerMac), a 1-gigabyte (GB) hard drive (yes, that's a measly 1-GB hard drive, no typo), and a 15-inch monitor running at only 1024×768 resolution. In other words, Jeremy's system really belonged in the Smithsonian, but he made it work.

Jeremy has since traded up to a G5 PowerMac, but this little G3 Mac will always be remembered fondly.

In terms of composition software, Jeremy used Logic Audio from Apple (now called Logic Pro, see http://www.apple.com/logic), which let him compose the whole score from start to finish and create his own digital instruments, lending *RADIUS* a sound you don't hear all the time. Logic costs $999 from Apple these days, but if you're just getting started, Apple also offers an Express version of the software for $299. Jeremy says that it's the equivalent of the version of Logic he used to compose *RADIUS*, so if you want to get into music composition without spending a lot of cash, that's a good option. And if you have a PC, a good Logic alternative would be Mark of the Unicorn's Performer and Digital Performer (http://www.motu.com).

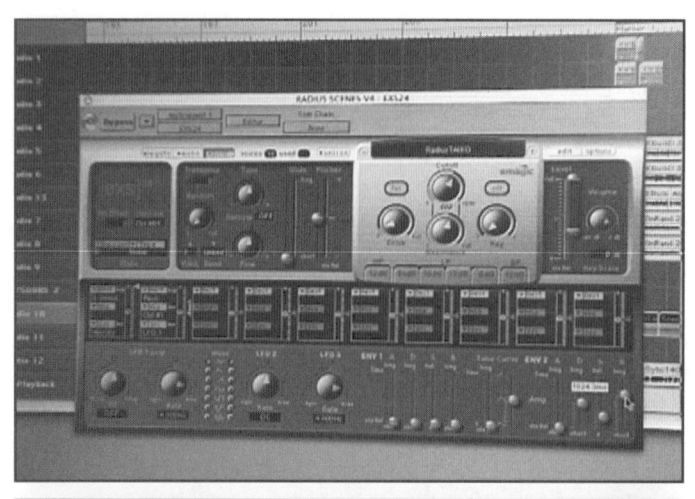

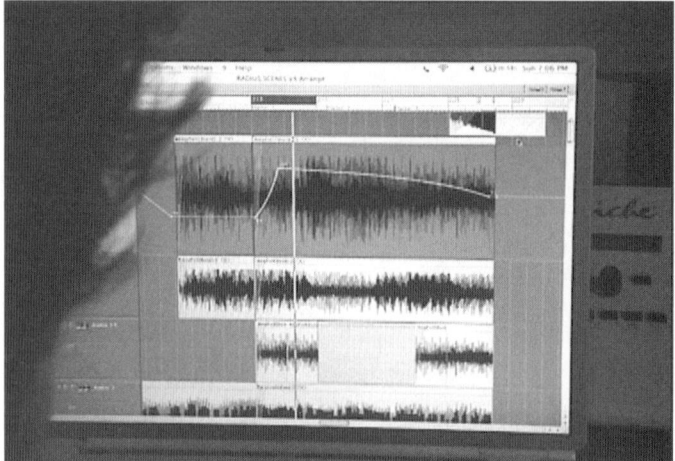

Logic Audio at work. Logic is still a mystery to me, but it's the next major application I want to teach myself. I have a book on it already, but I must admit that the interface looks rather daunting.

Lesson Learned

Jeremy's Mac-based system just goes to show that you don't need a new or high-powered computer to score music effectively.

When finished, Jeremy output *RADIUS'* score to a hard drive.

Jeremy composed *RADIUS'* music, but he didn't mix the music into the rest of our soundtrack—that is, add it to the movie's dialogue and sound effects. This mixing was done by a sound mixer, so Jeremy's last step was to prepare the music for the mixer by exporting it as a series of AIFF files to an external hard drive. He didn't mix the whole soundtrack as a single stereo mix. Instead, he created different AIFF stereo files, with each one carrying a few instrumental tracks out of the whole score. For instance, one stereo set included deep, heavy drums and other instruments that had a heavy bass quality, whereas another stereo set contained higher-pitched stringed instruments. By breaking down the final recordings into smaller sets, we could lower or raise the volume of certain instruments during our final mix. (See Chapter 17, "Post Production Sound," for more information about integrating music into the mix process.)

CHAPTER 17

POST-PRODUCTION SOUND

RADIUS' post-production sound work involved a number of different tasks, including rerecording portions of our actor's original dialogue, recording or designing hundreds of original sound effects, and mixing together all of *RADIUS'* different audio elements (dialogue, effects, and music) into a well-balanced soundtrack designed for both stereo and Surround Sound formats.

A team of young engineers at Danetracks did all our sound work.

A company called Danetracks handled all our post-production sound work. Danetracks has done sound design for a ton of Hollywood movies, including *Swordfish*, *8 Mile*, *The Forgotten*, *Kinsey*, and all the *Matrix* movies. In fact, Danetrack's founder, Dane Davis, actually won the Best Sound Academy Award for his work on the first *Matrix* film.

So why did a top-tier company like Danetracks get involved with *RADIUS*? Well, it obviously wasn't for the money. In fact, Danetracks did the work for free, and I only paid for some incidentals, such as buying a couple of cheap hard drives for sound storage and covering some fees for tape dubbing. The answer lies in the fact that Danetracks is a unique kind of company that grows its own talent. The company finds young people who want to work in the sound industry, gives them informal training onsite, and after they get to a certain level of skill, sometimes gives them a real job or helps them get other jobs in the field.

You can find the Danetracks world headquarters off of Santa Monica Boulevard in West Hollywood.

Danetracks had several young interns assisting on its various projects, but it also looked for independent films that the interns could take on and execute from start to finish, by themselves. This was a good deal for both parties. The interns would get great experience because they alone were responsible for every step of the process, and the filmmaker would get a pretty sophisticated soundtrack assembled for free.

RADIUS was one of the films that Danetracks' interns made their own. It was one of the luckiest breaks we had while making the film, and I thank my lucky stars that it fell into our lap. And luck is a pretty accurate description of how this all came to be. It turned out that the husband of our film editor had worked at Danetracks in the past and knew of its informal intern program. So he gave us a name to contact at the company, we met briefly and gave Danetracks a preview of *RADIUS*, and the next thing I knew, we had our sound team in place.

By the way, Danetracks still takes on new interns. If you're interested in getting involved, you can learn more by visiting the company's Web site at http://www.danetracks.com.

Lesson Learned

It's rare, if not impossible, to get people to work for free on your project and not give them anything in return. But that doesn't mean you have to offer monetary compensation. If you can find something else to offer—something that doesn't cost you cash—both parties can come out ahead.

Bill Dean and Stephanie Brown were employees at Danetracks. They had been interns before, but they later became employees and were assisting Danetracks' more senior engineers on various projects. Together, they became *RADIUS*' co-sound supervisors, responsible for managing the project from start to finish. It's unusual for any film to have two sound supervisors, but in this case, it was necessary. *RADIUS* called for a lot of work to be done, and Bill and Stephanie could only work on *RADIUS* during their evenings and weekends. So, for example, when Stephanie got busy with her day job or anything else, Bill could tag-team on the film to keep things moving.

Sound Supervisors Bill Dean and Stephanie Brown managed the whole process during evenings and weekends (and did plenty of sound design and editing work, too).

We kicked everything off by meeting one evening and watching *RADIUS* while I explained what I had in mind sound-wise for each scene. Next, Bill and Stephanie began assigning different sound work to a pool of about six or seven other interns, telling the interns what the scene called for and then setting a rough schedule for the work. Of course, because all the interns were also working during their free time, it was hard to set an accurate schedule. In fact, work occasionally would grind to a halt for a few weeks at a time because everybody was busy with other things. (As I've said before, though, that's what you can expect when you're not paying anybody!)

We discovered that some of our production sound was too noisy.

When we were shooting out in the desert, it was easy enough to keep our set quiet so we could record crisp, clear dialogue from our actors. (On rare occasions, though, the wind got a little gusty, and we had to wait a minute to let it die down.) Our indoor set was a lot harder to keep quiet—for instance, our spaceship cockpit made a huge amount of noise while we were filming the actors in it. Our on-set microphone had no problem picking up the actors' dialogue, but it *also* recorded the racket of the cockpit's chair's squeaking, its flight stick clanging, and plenty of reverb coming from the small enclosed cockpit space.

Usually, capturing clean sound is harder when you're shooting outside, thanks to pedestrians, traffic, construction noise, and lots of other audible factors you can't easily control. But out in the desert, we had few problems.

Our interior cockpit was so noisy that it ruined some key dialogue.

All that ambient noise was a problem because you could clearly hear it over the actors' dialogue, and it detracted from what the characters were saying. Plus, the noise obscured all the other sound effects we wanted to add to the scene later on—things like the cockpit alarms, the ship's engines, and so on.

We used ADR to record clean dialogue.

So how did we get rid of all that noise recorded over the actor's dialogue? Well, we used Automatic Dialogue Replacement (ADR), which is a fancy term for lip synching. We brought our actors into a quiet sound recording room, where they watched video of a scene they filmed earlier and lip-synched each line of dialogue that was too noisy on set. When you watch *RADIUS*' opening crash scene, keep in mind that just about all the dialogue you hear from pilots Dain and Kyle was rerecorded as ADR.

I sat with the actors in Danetracks' ADR booth as they lip-synched their lines to a video monitor. Outside, a sound engineer recorded each line to a Macintosh hard drive. Then I listened to the lines and picked the best of the bunch.

As you can imagine, doing ADR can be tricky. Our actors often needed several attempts to get a line perfectly synched, and because the actor is sitting in a small box—as opposed to a much more realistic movie set—it can be hard for them to match the emotional level of their film performance. In fact, I was never 100 percent satisfied with the rerecordings of Dain's and Kyle's dialogue. The new lines we ADRd were crystal clear, but emotionally, they felt a little flat and didn't quite match the energy of the actor's original on-set performances. Whether audience members can tell is hard to say, because no one else knows what the original, on-set dialogue sounded like. But I suspect some savvy listeners can tell that some of our ADR dialogue has a kind of removed, disconnected feel to it.

We used ADR to record clean dialogue. 291

When you're doing ADR, it also can be hard to make the microphone you use in the ADR booth match the sound quality of the original microphone used during production. This wasn't so much of a problem for Dain and Kyle's cockpit scene because all the dialogue that ended up in the film was recorded in the ADR booth, so there was no original dialogue to match. Elsewhere in *RADIUS*, we used ADR more sparingly, and we had to match it closely to the production audio around it. For instance, after killing the first Diamone twin, Dain and Vesay argue about going back to their crashed ship to protect the CraterMaker bomb. Somehow, our production microphone recorded one of Vesay's angrier lines with a lot of distortion, so we had to record it again during an ADR session. And although Mike Yavnieli had an uncanny ability to lip synch his lines, our ADR microphone had a slightly different audio quality than our production mic, and you can tell that Mike's new ADR line sounds a bit different from the lines right before and after it.

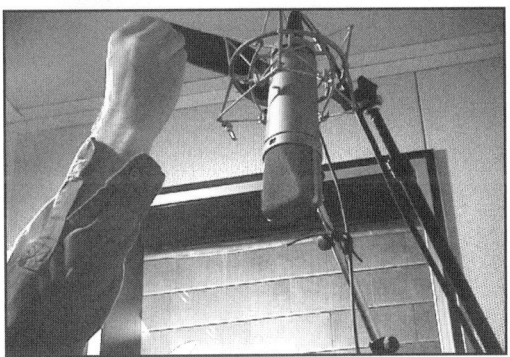

Try as we might, we had a hard time matching the audio quality of our on-set microphone to the microphone in our ADR booth. You can hear the difference when Dain and Vesay argue over the fate of the CraterMaker.

Had we been able to use the same mike in our ADR session, we probably would not have had this problem, but it wasn't available at the time. We just had to accept that fact and move on.

Lesson Learned

> ADR is a last resort, given the difficulties of matching an actor's performance and maintaining consistent audio quality. It's better to get your production audio right when you're on set. If you can't, ADR is there as a backup—but only as a backup.

We also used ADR to get dialogue that we never bothered recording.

Sometimes we used ADR to record dialogue we never got in the first place. For instance, when Dain and her crew wake up in the wreckage of their crashed ship, a lot of the crew's reactions to Dain's killing Kyle and arming the CraterMaker bomb were recorded in the ADR booth. (As I've said before, we shot those scenes in the wee hours of the morning before getting kicked off our sound stage, and we didn't have time to film proper reaction shots from crew members.)

The best example is Vesay's dialogue at the end of the movie, as he's running alone up Death Valley's canyons and eventually calls for a rescue ship. We shot these scenes a couple of months after principal photography, and by that time, I couldn't afford to bring two sound guys with us. The solution: We shot Vesay's scenes without sound and tried to keep Mike's back to the camera so that his lips were obscured for most of the scenes. Then we just recorded his dialogue in the ADR booth later on.

We tried to obscure Vesay's moving lips as much as possible to make our lip synching easier later on.

We practiced the little-known craft of dialogue editing.

Stephanie Brown also handled all the dialogue editing for *RADIUS*. She was responsible for doing anything necessary to whip our dialogue recordings into the best shape possible. That meant a number of things over the course of *RADIUS*' sound work:

- She listened to all our production audio, determining which recordings we could use and which had to be replaced with ADR dialogue.
- When possible, she cut and pasted different dialogue takes together to create a string of lines that used the best of the best recordings. This trick is possible because a lot of dialogue you hear in a film is either spoken off camera or with the actor's lips away from camera, so you can get away with using any dialogue take you want.
- When necessary, she used an audio editing tool like Pro Tools to clean up dialogue lines, cutting any possible distracting noise from the audio waveforms of the dialogue, such as heavy breathing, noise from props, or anything else.
- She applied audio filters to dialogue recordings to better match the audio quality of lines recorded with different microphones.

We recorded our own Foley sound effects.

Foley is a film industry term that describes the sounds of an actor's or a prop's physical movement onscreen. Instead of just using the sound picked up by a production microphone during the actor's performance, sound engineers usually record Foley effects later on.

294   Chapter 17 ◆ Post-Production Sound

Our on-set recording of the CraterMaker being dragged was way too wimpy, so our Foley artists invented a sound from scratch.

We recorded a bunch of our own Foley effects for *RADIUS*. For instance, when Dain drags the CraterMaker bomb away from her crashed ship, the sound you hear is actually a metal shovel being dragged across a parking lot's gravel surface—all recorded by one of our sound engineers, long after principal photography. Likewise, our engineers recorded a lot of the footsteps you hear in *RADIUS*. Case in point: Consider the scene when Dain and Crim think they hear someone coming up behind them and suddenly turn to see the rest of their aircrew. The sound of the crew's footsteps, along with Dain and Crim's sudden turn, was recorded by two engineers along a dirt road. One engineer used a handheld video camera to play that scene back while simultaneously matching the footsteps of our actors, and the other engineer recorded the steps. Yet another example of our Foley sound effects occurred early in the film, when an injured Crim fell behind the rest of the aircrew. He searched through his clothes for some kind of painkiller, and the sound of his hands brushing against his uniform was recorded by our engineers, after the fact.

Foley work included a multiple of footsteps.

You might wonder why we bothered recording these Foley sounds instead of using the sounds that our production microphone picked up on set when we were filming our actors. Well, there are a few reasons:

- First, a designed effect usually sounds a lot better than the real thing. For instance, when Dain drags the CraterMaker along the ground, I can assure you that the real sound we recorded on set was not nearly as rich or dramatic as the shovel dragged across the gravel parking lot.
- Second, many of those subtle effects, such as hands brushing against clothing, are picked up only faintly by a production microphone that's intended to record only dialogue. (That's the idea when you're recording dialogue: to get *only* the dialogue!) Recording the Foley effects later on lets us

create those subtle effects in an isolated form, in which we can adjust their volume independently of the dialogue they might play with. By the way, isolation of the Foley effects is important if a movie is dubbed into another language. This way, when dubbers remove the film's original dialogue, they don't automatically lose useful sounds (such as footsteps, or brushing against clothes) that might have been recorded with the dialogue, because those sounds are independent.

♦ Finally, you might wonder why we couldn't get our Foley sounds from a pre-existing library of sound effects, instead of having to record them ourselves. Well, for one thing, it can be harder to match a generic, prerecorded effect to the timing of footsteps or other character movement in a scene. Or, it can be hard to find a generic effect that precisely matches the physical materials involved in your particular scene. For instance, a woman walking across a marble floor in high heels might not be an effect that's common in sound libraries. In that case, you would probably need to capture the sound yourself.

Tip

And one more thought about Foley: Although you probably can't avoid using some Foley in your film, you might be able to make your post-production work easier by capturing some Foley while you're on set. Consider this: After you film some good takes for a scene, have an actor repeat his actions without dialogue and focus on recording any Foley-type sounds you can—footsteps, shuffling clothing, and so on. This takes time out of your production schedule but saves time later.

Outside of our Foley work, the Danetracks engineers created a ton of effects from scratch.

Bill and Stephanie broke down the effects work into categories. For instance, Eryne Prine did all our gun effects (shots, impacts, gun cocking sounds), and Thanos Kazakos did all spaceship sounds, such as the ship's engine noise, debris falling, and so on. Other engineers focused on various families of effects, like the CraterMaker bomb's arming and timer sounds, or the sounds of the Gemini Vortex.

We recorded our own Foley sound effects. 297

At any rate, each engineer would start by sitting at a Mac workstation, which was networked into a database of tens of thousands of basic sound effects, all searchable via keywords. (For instance, if you enter "engine" or "fire" or "gun," you'll get dozens or even hundreds of entries, all of which you can preview instantly.) By the way, Danetracks has spent years developing its own custom, proprietary library of sound effects, but other libraries are available that you can use in your own films. Some basic libraries are free, and you can download sounds off the Internet. Others you have to buy, such as the Sound Ideas library, which is popular with indie filmmakers (http://www.sound-ideas.com). Either way, if you're looking for sounds, start by typing "sound effects library" into Google, and you should be on your way.

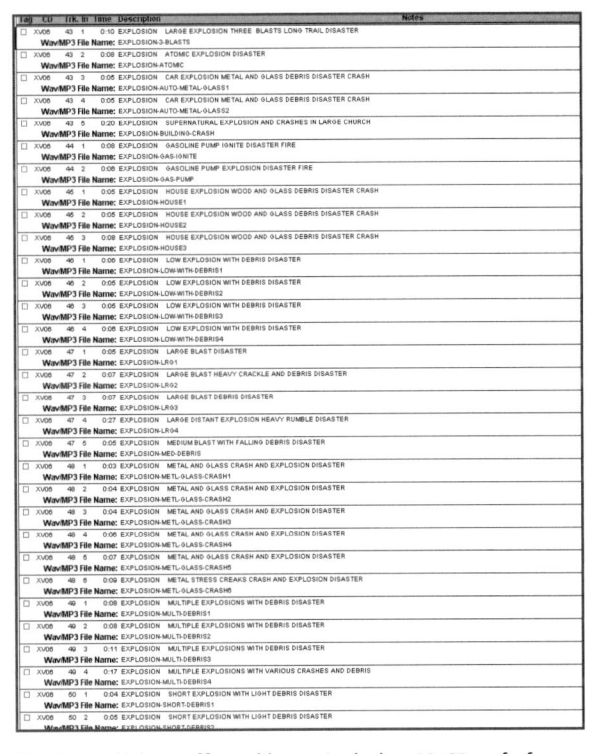

The Sound Ideas effects library includes 40 CDs of effects, which you can search and sample quickly via an included database. The library costs about $1,500, which is way too expensive for most filmmakers. However, any sound designer worth his salt will already have access to this kind of tool, so you needn't worry.

298   Chapter 17 ◆ Post-Production Sound

An engineer at a sound station. This workstation includes a small mix board (on the left) for balancing the volume of different sound channels, along with a television. If you're interested in doing sound design yourself, though, you can really do it on just about any standalone Mac or PC, without additional equipment.

It's incredibly rare that any given movie effect will use only a single sound. For instance, most sound designers would think it sloppy and unimaginative to pick a single sound of a rumbling engine and use that as Dain's ship engine effect. Instead, sound designers typically strive to create an entirely unique effect by layering multiple sounds on top of each other. It's like playing with Legos, where the final creation is not like anything that's been created before. As an example, the ambient sound effect for our Gemini Vortex was made up of about 15 different sounds. Some of those sounds have probably been used in other films but not in the same unique arrangement.

Our sound designers used a program called Pro Tools (http://www.protools.com) to design their effects. First, they imported digitized scenes of *RADIUS* into Pro Tools so that they could build their effects in synch with the film's video. (The digitized video used the same time code values as our master edit of the film, so we could easily synch each sound effect with the final film when the time came.) Next, the designers used Pro Tools to layer different sound clips together and adjust the volume of each clip so that some sounds had a prominent role in the overall effect and others added a subtle,

We recorded our own Foley sound effects. 299

almost indistinguishable touch. The designers also used Pro Tools' many different filters to affect the sounds in different ways, giving them an echo or distorting them in all sorts of strange ways. For instance, when you hear Dain arm the CraterMaker bomb at the beginning of the film, a prominent part of that arming effect is a vacuum cleaner that's been heavily tweaked with filters.

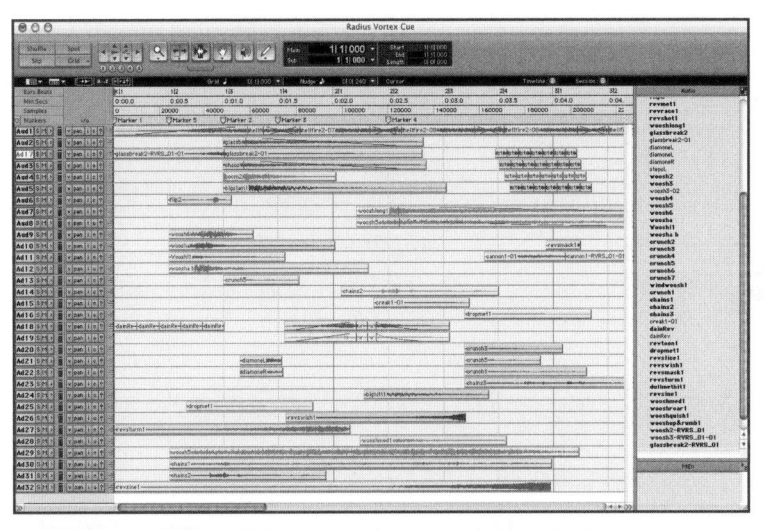

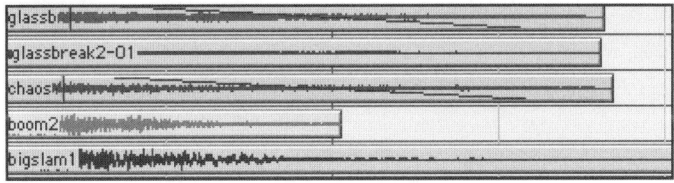

A shot of the different sound elements for the Gemini Vortex, all arranged in Pro Tools. (Each horizontal bar is a different sound that's called for.)

Our designers would usually get a rough pass of their effects ready, and then Bill and Stephanie would call me in and we would all listen together and talk about any adjustments to make. If the tweaking wasn't straightforward, Bill and Stephanie would leave me to sit with the designers and we would work out any changes on the spot. That way, there would be no guesswork on the designer's part, trying to interpret what I was looking for. It was interesting for me to learn that this isn't how mainstream Hollywood effects are done. Directors rarely meet with sound designers. Instead, all the sound design is managed by the sound supervisors, and the director usually only hears the sounds on the mix stage. If the director doesn't like an effect, the sound supervisors go back to their designers and try again—all without the director on hand. That strikes me as a workflow that respects a systematic hierarchy and division of labor but isn't necessarily one that gets the quickest results.

Finally, we were ready to start the sound mix.

After work continued on and off for about 5 months, we were finally ready to begin our sound mix, which is where we would combine all of *RADIUS*' sound effects, character dialogue, and composed music into one, well-balanced soundtrack. It's also where we would designate how our sound elements would play on Surround Sound speaker systems—that is, how much of each sound would be spread out between front speakers and rear speakers found in theaters and the living rooms of movie lovers. (For instance, when Crim's grenade explodes in the Diamone's shield, the audio effect from the grenade's whirlwind energy is constantly moved from speaker to speaker, making you feel a bit more immersed in the sound.)

Anyway, our mix was done by a guy named Jeremy Peirson, who worked as a mixing assistant on major movies. Jeremy knew the Danetracks guys because he used to work for Danetracks, and he still did freelance work for them. Bill and Stephanie, our music supervisors, thought Jeremy would be interested in mixing an action film, so he signed up.

Lesson Learned

I wondered why our sound supervisors didn't want to mix *RADIUS*. In the sound world, mixing is considered to be a particular skill that's honed over time. If you can find a specialized mixer for your film, do so.

Jeremy Peirson at his mix console.

Jeremy secured a professional sound mix stage—for free.

Besides volunteering his time, Jeremy pulled off a bit of a coup in that he secured a huge, professional mix stage for *RADIUS*' mixing work—the same one, in fact, used to mix movies like *Punch Drunk Love*, *Death to Smoochy*, and *Red Planet*. The value of a mix stage is that it's set up much like a movie theater. It's about the same size as a medium-sized theater, and it has the same kind of Surround Sound speaker systems that commercial theaters do. That's necessary, of course, because the sound mixers need to hear their work in an environment that's a close match to the theaters that moviegoers will see (and hear) the movie in.

In *RADIUS*' case, mixing on a big stage had a few benefits. First, I definitely wanted to create a Surround Sound mix, because there was always the chance that *RADIUS* would be seen in an appropriately equipped theater (probably at some film festival). I also wanted to offer it on the upcoming *RADIUS* DVD in case a customer had bothered to set up a home theater system in his living room. Second, part of Jeremy's motivation for working on *RADIUS* was to hone his skills as a mixer using professional tools that real films used. We could have mixed *RADIUS* with simpler equipment, but the process would not have given Jeremy (or our other sound guys) the same valuable experience.

Mixing on this stage was a huge perk. It let us take advantage of a first-rate Surround Sound speaker system (like you find in movie theaters), but we had to work a few hours at a time, evenings and weekends.

What's more, we didn't pay anything for the stage (which usually rents for $500 an hour, I'm told), because Jeremy worked on the same stage during the day. So, at the end of his day shift—usually around 8 or 9 p.m.—Jeremy would just stay on the stage, let us in, and we would work until about midnight. The downside to this arrangement, of course, was that the stage sometimes became unavailable as big feature films worked late into the night. The cumulative effect of all those scheduling conflicts probably delayed our mix's completion by about 4–6 weeks.

Lesson Learned

> If I do another film, I'll try to mix it on a dedicated mix stage only if we can do it without impacting our schedule quite so much. Otherwise, I'd look to do it in a more home-brew studio.

> **Don't have Pro Tools? Don't have a mix stage? No problem!**
>
> I edited and produced a couple of 2- and 3-minute promotional trailers for *RADIUS* and had to do all the sound mixing for these myself. Audio-wise, these trailers weren't nearly as sophisticated as the film itself, but they called for mixing in basic effects, dialogue, and Foley, and I did it all in my Final Cut Pro video editor. Final Cut isn't designed as an end-all, be-all audio tool, but it lets you mix up to 12 different audio tracks together in real time, and it can play up to 99 tracks of audio at once. Plus, it has tons of audio filters that can take care of bread-and-butter audio effects. So don't worry if you don't have access to dedicated audio software, because video editors like Final Cut, Avid Xpress, Adobe's Premiere, and others give you some basic functionality.
>
> And, of course, you don't need a big mix stage at your disposal either. If you intend your movie to be seen on TV or over the Internet, you really need only a stereo mix (that is, a mix that expects two speakers—a left and a right—as opposed to Surround Sound's 6–8 speakers). In that case, you can easily mix your film on your everyday computer. Just make sure you have a good pair of speakers attached to your computer or a good pair of headphones—anything that's better than the lowest common denominator speakers that are built into computers or television sets. (If you use low-end speakers to mix your film, you might not notice some audio elements that people who have better speaker systems will pick up.)
>
> But even if you want to do a surround sound mix, you don't need a big stage with all its advanced equipment. Instead, you should be able to find a freelance sound designer or mixer who has converted his bedroom or garage into a mix stage, with several speakers set up in the right locations. (There's also software that can create Surround Sound-encoded audio. That's one instance where Pro Tools will come in handy.) You might not get the same precise results as you would on a mix stage, but it would certainly be good enough.

We started our mix work by "predubbing."

Predubbing is the process of preparing all your sound effects for your final mix. Basically, it's like doing a premix of your sound effects to make the actual mix a little more manageable.

Let me explain: As mentioned earlier, sound designers create sound effects by layering multiple sounds on top of each other. For instance, consider *RADIUS*' opening scene, where Dain's ship is shot down. Multiple sound effects are going on at the same time—that is, engine noise, hull shake, cockpit instrumentation, fire from atmospheric re-entry, and so on. Each of these effects is often composed of multiple sounds, so you can have dozens of sounds playing at any given time in a scene.

Having such a multitude of sounds to work with is great for sound designers, because it lets them give their effects nuance and subtle details, making the effects more interesting and unique. But sound designers typically design one sound effect at a time, whereas mixers have to mix *all* the effects at once—that is, balancing engine noise with cockpit instrumentation with fire of re-entry, and so on—not to mention blending in music and dialogue. The prospect of balancing potentially dozens of independent sounds can be overwhelming. There are too many distinct parts to worry about all at once. That's where predubbing comes in.

Jeremy's mix console was an impressive sight. It was able to control dozens of independent sound channels, all at once. Jeremy used all the knobs and sliders to control those channels' volume and give them other audio effects.

Predubbing is a process of boiling down all the independent sounds of various effects into fewer, more manageable parts. Here's the process: Working on his mix stage, Jeremy listened to a sound effect—such as the ship's engine noise—and rerecorded its individual sound elements into a fewer number of elements. So, where an effect might have been made up of 12 independent sounds, it could emerge from predubbing as only 2 or 3. The benefit: When we did the final mix with the film's other sound effects, dialogue, and music, Jeremy (not to mention his equipment) had fewer sounds to manage. The only drawback: Jeremy lost the ability to individually adjust each unique, independent sound element that the designers used to build their overall effect. When we were in the final mix, no one could point to a subtle element of an effect and ask to change its volume. Chances are, that element was now part of a recording that included other sounds.

Losing that flexibility wasn't such a big deal. By the time we got to the final mix, we'd already used the predubbing stage to carefully balance all the effects' unique sounds. In other words, the predubbing stage is where the real fine-tuning is supposed to happen. Jeremy worked with the sound designer who created the effect in question, using the designer's balance of individual sounds within the effect as a starting point. Then Jeremy usually added his own touch to things, consulted the sound supervisors and me, and we went through the whole film that way. By the time an effect was predubbed, we were pretty confident that we wouldn't need to change anything about it later on.

At any rate, we predubbed *RADIUS* over the course of about 8 weeks, working sporadically on weekday evenings and occasional weekends. This was, of course, a long time, given that *RADIUS* was only a 30-minute film. Had we worked full time on predubbing, we probably could have finished it in roughly a week. But again, because all this work was done for free, it couldn't be the top priority in people's schedules.

Lesson Learned

The less money you spend, the more time you should expect things to take.

We mixed *RADIUS* during a weekend.

After we were finished with our predubbing, the final mix went quickly. It took a few tries, but we finally got a full weekend where the stage was available and all the major players—Jeremy, Bill, Stephanie, myself, and our composer—could come in.

We mixed the film on a Saturday and Sunday, putting in about 28 hours of work. Despite those serious hours, everything went reasonably smoothly because predubbing had taken care of the lion's share of our mix work for sound effects. We had small adjustments to make to balance different effects—for instance, ship engine noise versus cockpit instrumentation—but in general, predubbing left our sound effects in near-final states. Mixing in dialogue was also straightforward, because dialogue is a single sound element and you can be fairly objective about setting the volume of your dialogue to other sound elements. The dialogue had to be loud enough to be clearly discernible, but no more.

We had to decide whether to emphasize music or sound effects.

Music was another matter altogether. When we first included our music in the movie, it surprised me how many of our more subtle sound effects suddenly became obscure or even inaudible. I had had a couple of months to get used to these effects, so it felt like something was wrong when I couldn't appreciate them anymore.

When we lowered our music's volume, the music lost its presence in the film. You could hear the music, but it blended in with everything else and lost some of its emotional charge. (Think of great action movie soundtracks like *The Rock*, *Aliens*, or *Air Force One*, which really seem to carry the film forward.)

The problem was that I had spent months listening to our sound effects independently in the film and had gotten used to them having a certain prominence. I also had spent months listening to our music independently and had gotten used to it having the same kind of prominence. But in the final mix, our effects and music couldn't each have the same prominence that they enjoyed in their independent states. Instead, we had to choose which one to favor in the mix, and that put me in a bit of a quandary.

In the end, I knew that I wanted to err on the side of our music, because music can add that emotional charge to a film that subtle sound effects can't. But I felt a little guilty about that, given the fact that our sound designers had put a lot of work into coming up with effects that had a lot of texture and subtlety—stuff that sounded great when you're listening to the effects by themselves. The fact that the designers did all this for free, working evenings and weekends, increased my guilt factor.

In the end, though, it was my choice to make, and I had to do what felt right for the movie. I asked Jeremy to favor the music over our more subtle effects. I think it was a little painful for Bill and Stephanie, as our sound supervisors, but they accepted it and we moved on.

Lesson Learned

> Try to identify each scene's sound-versus-music priorities ahead of time, before you do all your composing and sound design work. Otherwise, you might end up building more detail than you really need into one or the other.

We were glad we recorded our music as multiple "stems."

One more thing about our music: There were a couple of cases in which the music started to feel too prominent. It wasn't an issue of the music's volume; it was that the score felt too "present," like it was playing too much of a role in a particular scene. For example, when Dain returned to her ship to defend the CraterMaker from the Diamone, our score originally featured lots of layers of eerie, discordant music. It sounded great when I approved Jeremy Zuckerman's final score. But a month later, when we finally got to the mix stage and listened with a fresh ear, I thought the score felt a little too heavy handed. After so much music throughout the film, it felt like we needed to let the audience rest its ears a little bit. That's when we thinned out the score.

Fortunately, Bill and Stephanie had told Jeremy (the composer, not the mixer) to output his music in four different sets of "stem" files, where each stem set featured some of the score's instruments, but not all. This was a safety precaution in case, during the mix, we decided we wanted to adjust the volume for only certain instruments in the music, without affecting the others. Had Jeremy output his final score as one single recording instead of multiple stems, we would not have been able to do this. But with the score divided into the stems, we had a little flexibility to isolate certain parts of the music, and that's exactly what we did. We eliminated a couple of the stems in Dain's confrontation with the Diamone and whittled the music down to only its most important elements.

Lesson Learned

> Recording final music in multiple stems gives you more options to make musical adjustments at the last minute.

I wish we could have listened to the final mix with a fresh perspective.

In true *RADIUS* fashion, we ended up finishing our mix at about 2 a.m. on Monday morning. After months of working on the project—nights and weekends—and squeezing it in between jobs and slivers of a personal life, everyone was glad to be done. We felt that we had emerged with a great mix.

For the most part, I still agree with that sentiment, but there are a few exceptions that could have been avoided had we built in a little time to come back to the mix a few days or a week or so later and listen to it with a completely fresh ear.

For instance, consider Dain's opening video letter, which kicks off the film. We tried to make it as intelligible as possible, despite all the static and interference that our sound designers had intentionally built in (according to my request). But I've since noticed that some audience members can't understand a few important lines that Dain delivers in her video. Now I wish that we had toned down the static and other sound effects even further.

Similarly, I think the ADR dialogue used in Dain and Kyle's cockpit scene is too prominent against *RADIUS*' sound effects and music. Of course, we wanted to make sure that the dialogue was clearly discernible, but it's so prominent now that you can make out its slightly flat quality. Had the dialogue's volume been turned down a bit more, that slightly odd quality would have been better masked. (And who really cares if every word is super clear, because it's a chaotic action sequence.)

At any rate, these instances and a few others sounded fine while we were in the thick of the mix. But, in fact, we were just too close to the material at the time and had gotten too used to hearing it a certain way. The only way we could have spotted problems would be to finish the mix and then return to it later and listen to it with a completely fresh ear. That way, we could have made any final small adjustments. Bringing along a couple of friends who had never heard the mix before also would have been helpful.

But that's what I know in hindsight. At the time, our confidence was high, and the crew was exhausted. Suggesting that we schedule more time on the increasingly hard-to-come-by mix stage and bringing everyone together on yet another weekend would have been tough, not to mention unpopular. The team would have felt like they had just staggered across the finish line of a grueling marathon and then been asked to jog a couple more miles. It just wasn't realistic. It was one of the many little compromises I was willing to accept.

Lesson Learned

> When it comes to your final sound mix, build some time in to go back with a fresh ear one last time.

Part 4

Marketing/ Distribution

… **CHAPTER 18**

Creating a Pro Image

Even before we started preproduction, I knew that we would have to find ways to make *RADIUS* look like it wasn't going to be yet another indie short film by a first-time filmmaker. I thought it was key for *RADIUS* to be positioned like a professional project—something that stood out from the crowd—and I believed such positioning could pay off in a number of different ways, such as these:

- Help get potential cast and crew members excited about becoming involved
- Help us convince vendors to give us great deals on equipment packages (like our camera), because vendors would be more willing to help a production that seemed legit, rather than some fly-by-night operation
- Help us get press coverage for *RADIUS*, which is rare for short films, and which would help build up an audience and fan base for the film

To create a polished, professional image for *RADIUS*, we did a number of things early on. These tactics burned precious cash, but the benefits far outweighed the costs.

I commissioned cool concept art by a student artist.

The first thing I did was commission some cool concept art to help fire up people's imaginations regarding *RADIUS*. It's one thing to talk to people and say, "We're doing this science fiction film; it's going to be cool." You'll get a much stronger response when you can show some professional artwork as you talk about your movie. Not only does good concept art bring your story to life for people, but it shows that you're putting extra effort into the project, which isn't typical on little indie films.

To get the art done, I visited the Web site for San Francisco's Academy of Art (http://www.academyart.edu) and looked through its student portfolios. I ended up finding a graduating student named Ben Craner (http://www.bencraner.com). I paid Ben $500 to do 10 concept art images in full color. Because Ben was just getting started in his career, he was willing to work for the rate I could offer.

Ben and I never met in person. Instead, we just talked over the phone and via e-mail. This kind of telecommuting gig worked, because Ben was a superb artist to begin with. I would give him a description of what I wanted for each art piece (I picked images that showed the major scenes of the movie), and then Ben would do a pencil sketch for my approval. After he got the okay, he would finish up a final color rendition about a week later. It was all pretty painless and straightforward.

I commissioned cool concept art by a student artist. 315

These are 4 of the 10 concept images that Ben Craner created for *RADIUS*.

I created a promotional card for *RADIUS*.

We also created a 4-color, 2-sided promotional card for *RADIUS*. Again, this occurred before we did preproduction work. I hired another college student to design it, and it featured our first stab at a logo and a computer-generated shot of a huge explosion and blast radius. We printed about 500 of these cards to hand out to anyone we spoke to about the project. The card had the same effect as our concept art: It helped make *RADIUS* feel like a bigger production than it really was. The total cost was $500.

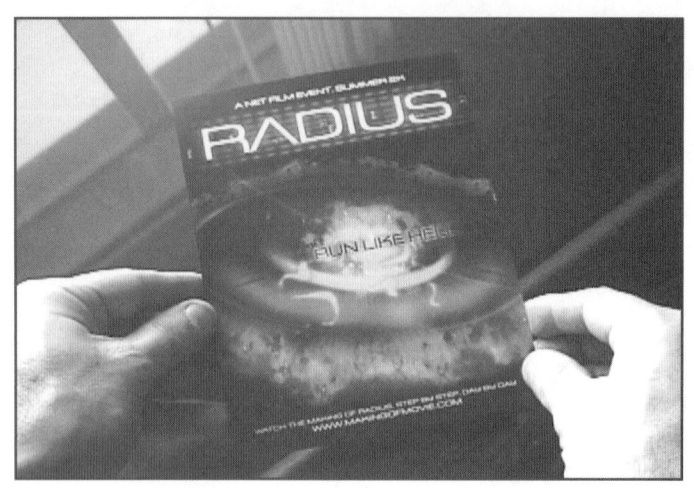

I passed out this promotional card to hundreds of people during preproduction.

I launched a Web site that tracked the making of *RADIUS*.

The most ambitious promotional tool we created for *RADIUS* was an extensive Web site that featured one big unique hook: It documented the making of the film as it was happening, step by step, day by day. The whole idea was to let the general public become silent partners in making the film, and we did this by posting daily journal entries telling readers what we were up to. We also included lots of behind-the-scenes pictures and video clips.

Nowadays, all major film productions launch Web sites ahead of time, and almost all of these sites feature some making-of elements. Plus, there have been reality TV shows like *Project Greenlight*, which take the audience behind the scenes and let them see all the gory details of the filmmaking process. But we launched the *RADIUS* Web site before everybody else started emphasizing the filmmaking process. As far as I know, we were the first to document the making of a film as it was actually happening.

That unique angle, or *hook*, helped get us some useful press attention and build up a fan base ahead of time. People really started to feel a sense of ownership in the film, because they could check in almost every day and follow all the ups and downs of the process. Before long, we were getting thousands of hits a day on the site, which was pretty unusual for a short indie film that hadn't even been shot yet.

At any rate, the Web site cost about $900 to develop. It was done by a great Web development team at http://www.feedstream.com that I found thanks to an online list of Web developers I dug up somewhere. The Feedstream guys had to create a custom database to store the site's journal entries, pictures, and video clips. They also had to create a powerful search feature so that users could look up any film-related topic—such as storyboards or cinematography or marketing—and see only the related material. Plus, we created a subscription engine that let users sign up to have future log entries e-mailed directly to them. That way, they wouldn't have to remember to visit the site.

Beyond spending the money to have all these features created, it took me a lot of time to design how everything should work, not to mention maintaining the site with new postings, pictures, and so on. It really became a quarter-time job in itself—in addition to my filmmaking job—but it was well worth it. The site was key in getting the word out about *RADIUS* and creating some buzz.

During preproduction and production, we posted log entries and pictures almost daily, which kept people coming back to the site. In post production, our progress really slowed and my posts trickled down to once every two or three weeks. It pained me to lose that sense of momentum, but you can only say so much when you're working at a crawl.

> **BUILD A WEB SITE FOR YOUR FILM.**
>
> We had to create *RADIUS'* Making Of Web site from scratch, but today, there are much easier alternatives. In fact, thanks to the popularity of Web logs and blogging, a whole industry has sprung up offering sophisticated Web sites for little money. If you're looking to create a site for your film, you should include a few essential features, such as these:
>
> ◆ A categorized journal system that lets you post time-stamped entries in specific categories and subcategories that you define (such as casting, sound design, and so on).
>
> ◆ A newsletter subscription feature that automatically e-mails news to anyone who has joined your subscriber list.

> ♦ An image database that lets you upload, annotate, and resize photos (http://www.pmachine.com), or PHP-Nuke (http://www.phpnuke.org). These are Web packages that are either free or cost around $100. They give you all or most of the functionality you'll ever need. (Note: You can also type "Web log software" into Google for more options.)
>
> Of course, if you know absolutely nothing about Web development or design, you might want to hire an expert for a couple of hours. You can let that person set up your site or design a good-looking front end so that it doesn't look so generic. (Check the community forums of these Web log sites to find people who might be able to help you.) Or, if you want something simpler and cheaper, you can look into sites such as http://www.blogger.com or http://www.typepad.com. Each of these offers Web log software that has a few less features but can still give you a ready-to-go site in minutes.

We did early public relations work.

I created a press kit for *RADIUS* months before we were ready to shoot the film. At the heart of the press kit were press releases that I wrote. For instance, our first release announced the launch of *RADIUS'* preproduction and the kickoff of our Making Of Web site. What's more, the release positioned *RADIUS* as an "Internet film," which was all the rage at the time. Sites like Atomfilms.com and Ifilm.com had recently launched, and there was an expectation that Internet film might change the movie business the way the VCR did. (It turns out, it didn't.) Given all the heat around Internet film, I thought it would be a good idea to call *RADIUS* an "Internet film event" and capitalize on all the hype.

I recruited a small public relations firm in Los Angeles called StellarQuest to place stories about us in various news and entertainment publications. StellarQuest agreed to work with us for $250 a month (plus any minor expenses, such as photocopies). The company represented *RADIUS* for about 3 months leading up to principal photography. Of course, $250 was a low rate, but StellarQuest's publicists thought they could include us with some of the other entertainment work they were already doing. They also wanted to develop a business representing filmmakers and thought we might become "up and comers" at some point.

The first thing StellarQuest did was pay about $60 to a news wire service called BusinessWire (http://www.businesswire.com), which sent our initial press release to all sorts of news outlets that covered entertainment and special interest news. This initial release didn't generate any print coverage that I was aware of, but it did lead to a number of small stories posted on online news sites. These little successes jump-started the awareness we wanted to build for *RADIUS* and increased the daily hits we were getting on *RADIUS*' Making Of Web site.

After that launch, we looked for any excuse to issue a *RADIUS* press release and add it to our press kit's collection. For instance, the hiring of Philipp Timme to be our director of photography (DP) was newsworthy, because Philipp had been the visual effects DP for big Hollywood movies such as *Armageddon* and *Independence Day*, and it was interesting that a guy who had his credentials was joining an Internet film. So I wrote another quick press release about Philipp's involvement, and StellarQuest spent another $60 to send it over BusinessWire and call some journalists who might be interested.

Sure enough, *The Hollywood Reporter* wrote a brief story about Philipp joining *RADIUS*, which was a huge thrill for us. It didn't lead to many more hits on our Web site, but it gave us more credibility in the film community—among potential cast and crew, among vendors, and other press—because it was rare for a short film to get coverage in a major Hollywood trade magazine.

We did early public relations work.   321

We loved seeing *RADIUS'* name in a major trade like *The Hollywood Reporter*.

Over time, with StellarQuest's help, we were able to get *RADIUS* in front of more and more press, which led to articles in *Variety* (another Hollywood trade), *MovieMaker* magazine, and other Internet sites. StellarQuest even got us an invitation to meet director Ron Howard and DreamWork's Jeffrey Katzenberg when they appeared at the Yahoo Internet Life Film Festival in Beverly Hills. Producer Andy Trapani and I had about 3 minutes to shake hands with the pair and tell them about our project (not that it led to any deals, of course, but it was a memorable moment nonetheless).

Lesson Learned

Getting press for your film—even before it's finished—isn't as hard as you might think. Anyone can write a press release and send it over a news wire service. And you can always call or e-mail journalists to let them know about what you're doing. See Chapter 20, "Film Marketing," for more about getting press.

Chapter 19

Film Distribution

When you're an indie filmmaker, you don't have many options for getting your film out to the general public, not to mention earning some money back for it. This chapter takes you through the thought process I followed in deciding to publish and distribute *RADIUS* myself. Chances are, the same logic can apply to your own film project.

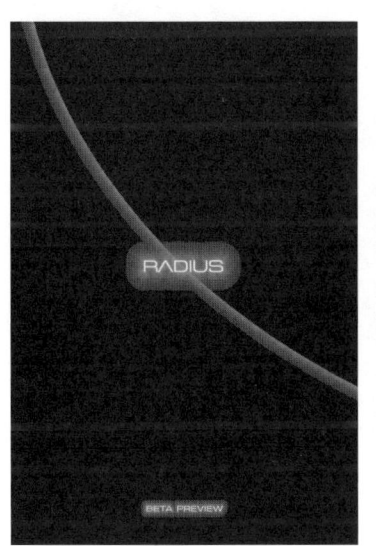

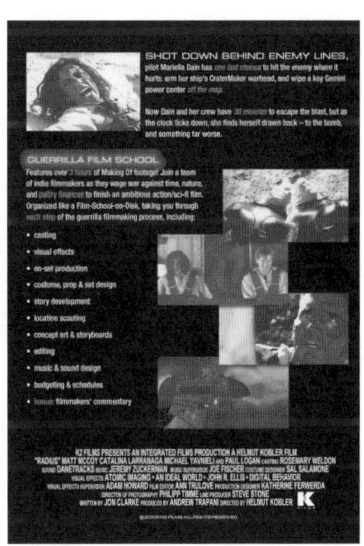

The retail *RADIUS* two-disc DVD. Many people have commented that they like the low-key design (just a small logo and graphic supporting the idea of "radius"), but we did that largely because it cost less to design.

Film festivals didn't seem like an effective distribution medium.

The only way for the general public to see the average indie film is if you enter it into film festivals, but those festivals can take you only so far. For one thing, unless your film gets into a top-tier festival like Sundance or Cannes or a couple of others, you shouldn't expect a festival appearance to raise interest from publishers and distributors that could ultimately bring your project to a wider audience. Even so, simply getting into a major festival can be tough. For instance, 2,613 films were submitted to the Sundance festival for 2005, and only 120 of them made it in.

There are film festival success stories, of course (and maybe your film could be one), but statistically speaking, you'll come away from a festival with some ego gratification and possibly a small amount of cash (provided your film wins an award). However, you probably won't be in a position to get your film distributed beyond festival audiences. Remember: Of the 120 films that got into Sundance in 2005, only about 10 of them found distribution within the United States. The rest of the films will never make it to a movie screen or video store. (Even late-night cable TV broadcasts are rare.)

I had all this in mind when I decided not to enter *RADIUS* into film festivals. (Actually, I would have entered *RADIUS* into the Slamdance festival—see http://www.slamdance.com—because it is geared toward first-time filmmakers and has a strong presence, but I missed the deadline by a couple of months.) I thought that I had a better chance of reaching an audience through other means. Because I intended to sell *RADIUS*, I didn't want to lose a portion of my audience because they had already seen the film at a festival. I should note, though, that I'm currently considering entering *RADIUS* into a couple of festivals now that some momentum has built up around the film.

Lesson Learned

> Keep your expectations down to earth and realistic when entering your film into a festival.

> **FIGURE OUT YOUR FILM FESTIVAL STRATEGY.**
>
> If you do decide to go the film festival route, there are about 2,500 film festivals around the world, so you have plenty of opportunities to find a home for your film. Of course, you can't apply to infinite festivals, because most require entrance fees (usually $20–$50), and you have to mail a copy of your film and a completed application. In other words, pick your target festivals with care so that you don't go broke or get exhausted from repeated submissions. To develop a smart festival strategy, I recommend a particularly helpful book, *The Ultimate Film Festival Survival Guide*, by Chris Gore.

> **TAKE YOUR FILM ONLINE AT ATOMFILMS AND IFILM.**
>
> Apart from conventional film festivals, you can submit short films to online film sites like AtomFilms (http://www.atomfilms.com) and iFilm (http://www.ifilm.com). These sites don't pay for your film, but they'll post it online for potentially thousands of people to see and comment on. Realistically, most films get posted and are quickly lost in a sea of other movies. But a few rise above the crowd—thanks to an audience ranking system—and get a fair amount of exposure. If nothing else, submitting your film to one of these sites is a cheap, quick way to get some feedback and see how people respond to your work.

I decided to publish and distribute a DVD myself.

Beyond festivals, I considered other venues for getting *RADIUS* to the general public. For instance, I found a company called Customflix (http://www.customflix.com). It can design your DVD and encode video from a videotape source, but it also manufactures copies on demand, and, if you like, it can handle order processing and shipping. In other words, it does almost all the work of getting your DVD published!

This initially had some appeal to me, but then I started looking at Customflix's prices and noticed that they charge a hefty premium for the various services you can pick and choose off their menu. For instance, the cost to manufacture a DVD in a case is about twice as much as what other manufacturers charge. Read later in this chapter about my ultimate DVD costs.

In my searches, I also found some companies that not only handle publishing your DVD—that is, putting it in a sellable format—but also sell it to the general public. These companies include Microcinema International (http://www.microcinema.com), Synapse Films (http://www.synapse-films.com), and Troma Studios (http://www.troma.com).

But I had a number of concerns when it came to relying on a distributor to sell *RADIUS*, starting with the fact that these distributors pass only a small percentage of a DVD's sale price to the filmmaker. You might get roughly 50 percent of online sales, and much less from retail sales, because retail stores also take a significant cut from the DVD's sale price.

If a distributor could really get my DVD into a lot of different channels or had a good track record of getting appreciable press for indie titles, I would have felt their services were worth it. But as I scanned the titles in their libraries, I noticed that I had never heard of any of the films, and I couldn't find any appreciable press about them on the Internet or any retail outlets that had the films.

To be fair, I should say that companies like Customflix and Microcinema definitely have a place in the indie film world, because a lot of filmmakers don't have the skills, time, or willpower to do the heavy lifting of getting their DVDs published and circulated. Thanks to these companies, such filmmakers still have an option for publishing and distribution, and if money isn't an issue, this path could be a good choice.

In the end, though, I had a tremendous emotional and financial investment in *RADIUS*, and I wasn't willing to cede half of the film's revenues to someone else or to leave it to an impartial third party to go out into the world and sell as many copies as possible. That's what led to my decision to do everything myself. I would publish the DVD (doing all the design, authoring, encoding, and manufacturing necessary to create a tangible product), and I would do the distribution through online sales. Read on for the details of how this process worked out.

> **Lesson Learned**
>
> You can find companies that will publish and distribute your film on DVD, but whether you give up too much money or control is up to you.

I wanted to give the DVD special features that would help make it marketable.

When I decided to create a DVD for *RADIUS*, I initially considered just putting the film on a disc and selling it for $5 or $10. But in the end, I decided that wasn't enough to get *RADIUS* the attention and sales I wanted. You can only interest so many people in an independently produced, 33-minute science fiction film unless it already has a lot of heat around it. For instance, the 1999 short film *George Lucas in Love* first became a hit on the Internet, and its now-defunct publisher, MediaTrip.com, was able to turn the film's press buzz and word of mouth into a successful DVD release. (You can still find the *Lucas* DVD on Amazon.com.) The same thing goes for 2000's Internet film *405* (http://www.405themovie.com). *405* became an overnight hit when IFILM.com put its marketing muscle behind it. The respect it built among fans and the press warranted a VHS release, even though the tape featured only 11 minutes of content!

By the time *RADIUS* was wrapping up, Internet film was as cold as a corpse, and I saw no way to get the movie the instant buzz and recognition that would have justified releasing it alone on DVD. I knew I would have to add something else to the disc, something that gave the project a bigger hook that would motivate the press to write about it and customers to buy it. That's when I decided to take all the Making Of footage we had shot while making *RADIUS* and edit it into a "Guerrilla Film School on Disc." My idea was to create an entire second DVD, filled with "chapters" dedicated to each step of the filmmaking process—casting, location scouting, costume design, film editing, set design, music composition, visual effects, marketing, you name it.

Every good product needs a hook, and the hook of the *RADIUS* two-disc DVD was to show other aspiring filmmakers all the ups and downs of making an ambitious but ultra-low-budget indie film.

For each of these DVD "chapters"—26 in all—I wrote a script, recorded it as voice narration, and then edited together my Making Of video to support the commentary. I spent almost a full year creating more than 4.5 hours of Making Of content for the two-disc DVD. (I ended up adding another 25 behind-the-scenes videos to the 26 tutorial videos I initially set out to create.) The *RADIUS* DVD is more extensive than the vast majority of Hollywood DVDs you can buy. Although some Hollywood DVDs do offer great Making Of content, *RADIUS*' material is geared, as the title states, to guerrilla filmmaking, not movies with huge budgets. It's a unique DVD that's especially useful to filmmakers who are just getting started.

Note: This book, of course, is an extension on the whole idea. The DVD included with this book contains about half of the Making Of content that *RADIUS*' two-disc DVD originally featured (although this book goes into greater detail than I could in the original DVD's how-to videos).

> **BE SURE TO DOCUMENT THE MAKING OF YOUR PRODUCTION AS IT HAPPENS.**
>
> Looking back, I'm really glad that we went to the lengths we did to document the making of *RADIUS*; otherwise, we wouldn't have had all the footage to create the original two-disc *RADIUS* DVD or the DVD included with this book. Likewise, you should try to document the making of your own film. You can put pictures or video on the film's Web site and other marketing materials, plus you'll have a fun memento from the experience—to go along with the scars!
>
> If nothing else, buy a small, easy, point-and-shoot digital camera and snap pictures as you go along. Just make sure the camera has quick autofocus in low light conditions (because you might find yourself working in dim light), a flash that reaches more than a couple of feet, and a resolution of at least 1.3 megapixels. (This resolution lets you capture images that will easily fill up a TV screen's 720×480 pixel resolution, with room to spare.) These days, you should have no problem finding such a camera for a couple hundred dollars, and even cutting-edge cell phones now include cameras that can do the job.
>
> Better yet, try to take a small handheld video camera with you to document the important moments of your production. For *RADIUS*' preproduction and post production, I used Sony's smallest handheld MiniDV camcorder, along with an extended battery that lasted for more than 3 hours per charge. This camera made it easy for me to document meetings and other events. I had to be there anyway, so why not just kill two birds with one stone and pull out the little video camera for a few minutes? For production, I had no time to videotape things myself, but my oldest friend, Dan Field, volunteered to come out with the cast and crew and shoot all our Making Of footage during *RADIUS*' six days of principal photography. Dan took along a friend of his, Erin Milnes, who recorded sound with a rented boom microphone, while Dan shot video on a borrowed Canon XL-1 camera. The two of them documented the entire production. Without this huge contribution, I would have had a fraction of the Making Of footage that we ended up getting.

I hired a menu designer to create the DVD's menus.

Always a big believer in making strong first impressions, I wanted *RADIUS*' DVD menus to immediately set a high quality bar, because those menus would be the first thing the movie's audience would see when they loaded the DVD. I didn't want just a simple, static menu system; instead, I wanted menus that incorporated lots of video and background music and used short but cool transitions to move between each menu that you could select.

I had neither the design skills to create the animated menus myself nor the money to pay a designer to create an elaborate set of menus from scratch. So I used video clips from the film as the background images for our menus and then hired a designer to create some cool but limited text that sat over the video images. It was a cost-effective way to create motion menus with content that I already had and with a minimum of new work to be done.

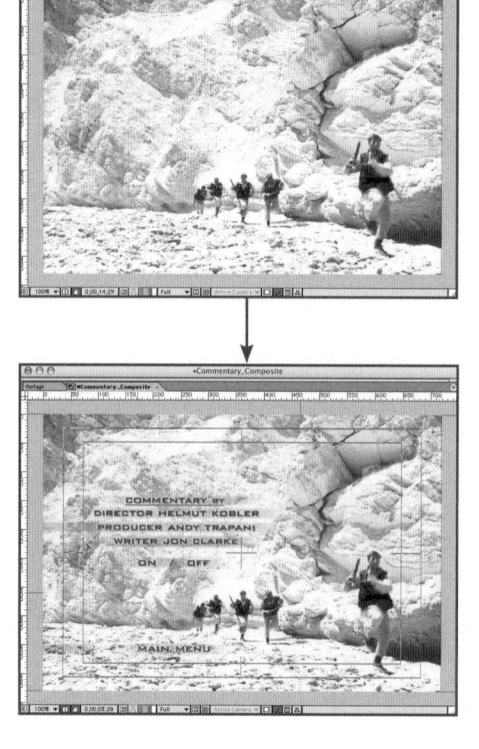

I figured out what menus we needed, what they should say, and what video clips to use as background. I uploaded everything to Designer Nachiket Katti, and he used Adobe After Effects to add cool animated text over the video.

Here's how we created the menus: For the DVD's main menu, I used Final Cut Pro to edit a 60-second montage of action footage from *RADIUS*. For each additional menu, I picked a single shot from *RADIUS* (each shot lasted only a couple of seconds) and decided which menu text needed to appear on the screen. Finally, I met Designer Nachiket Katti (http://www.netkarma.net) via an ad I placed on Craigslist.com looking for a motion graphic artist who had experience with Adobe After Effects. Working remotely from Minnesota, Nachiket animated a subtle-but-cool text effect onto the 20 or so menus that made up the two-disc DVD (fee: $500). By the way, DVD authoring programs such as Apple's DVD Studio Pro also include plenty of great menu templates that you can adapt to your own projects for free. Personally, I wanted *RADIUS*' menus to feel completely original, but using pre-existing templates is an even more cost-effective alternative.

I authored the DVD myself.

As Nachiket and I prepared the DVD's menus, I fully expected to hire another person to author the DVD (in other words, to do the "scripting" of menu buttons so that they led to the right menus, submenus, and video content). DVD authoring seemed like a huge, unexplored world to me, and I didn't think I would be able to teach myself how to do it with professional results.

I turned to online sites like Craigslist.com, 2pop.com, and Creativecow.net, looking for a DVD expert who could do the job. To my great shock, everyone wanted what I considered absurd amounts of money to author my two-disc DVD. (The lowest bid I got was $1,500, and in some cases, the fee was much higher.) This seemed crazy to me because I had already done all the menu work. All my menus were rendered and ready to go, and I had designed the DVD's *information architecture*, or which menus connect to which submenus, and so on.

Chapter 19 ♦ Film Distribution

Apple's iDVD is about the easiest and cheapest way to create a good-looking DVD for your film. (It features many slick-looking "themes" to help get your design started.) It can't handle advanced features such as subtitles or commentary tracks, though.

One day, I borrowed a friend's copy of Apple's DVD Studio Pro and bought a $25 book on the subject. You know what? It turned out that DVD authoring wasn't as complicated as I thought, and that revelation made me think about doing my own authoring. Shortly after that, Apple released a new version of DVD Studio Pro, which was even easier to use and offered a few other features I needed for some of the *RADIUS* DVD's special features.

So I ended up doing the authoring myself, which was a really great experience for a couple of reasons. First, I was able to constantly make tweaks and minor adjustments to the DVD's content myself, which saved a lot of time and potentially money. (Having to pass small tweaks to another person would have become inefficient pretty quickly.)

Just as importantly, I learned a new skill that was really useful for digital filmmaking. Remember: The more things you can do yourself, the better off you'll be in the long run.

If you have a spare weekend, I highly recommend that you teach yourself how to author your own DVDs. These days, there are plenty of inexpensive and easy authoring programs for the Mac and PC. For instance, you can buy Apple's iDVD as part of its iLife package for $49, or you can buy Sonic's MyDVD Studio on the PC, to name just a couple. Although the higher-end, professional applications such as Apple's DVD Studio Pro or Adobe's Encore DVD are considerably more expensive (DVD Studio Pro currently goes for $499), they're well worth it in the long run.

Lesson Learned

> Authoring a DVD—even one with lots of advanced features—isn't as complicated as it seems. Get a good book on the subject, and you can teach yourself what you need to know in a weekend.

How does DVD authoring work?

DVD Studio Pro has a lot to look at.

Here's a quick overview of how a DVD authoring program such as Apple's DVD Studio Pro actually works. (The same overall concepts apply to other DVD programs.) Sure, when you look at the software's overall interface—stuffed with various windows and tabs—it looks really complicated, but appearances can be deceiving. In fact, DVD Studio Pro follows a pretty simple, logical workflow. First you import your video and audio clips. Then you create menus containing one or more buttons, which you can easily program to play your various video/audio clips. Anyway, here's a closer look at some of major elements of DVD Studio Pro.

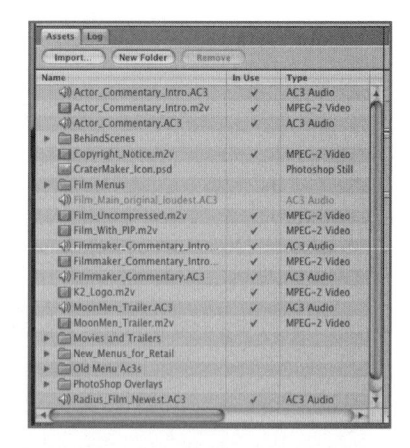

The Assets tab showcases what you've imported.

The Assets tab shows you all the video and audio files you've imported into your project so that you can find them easily.

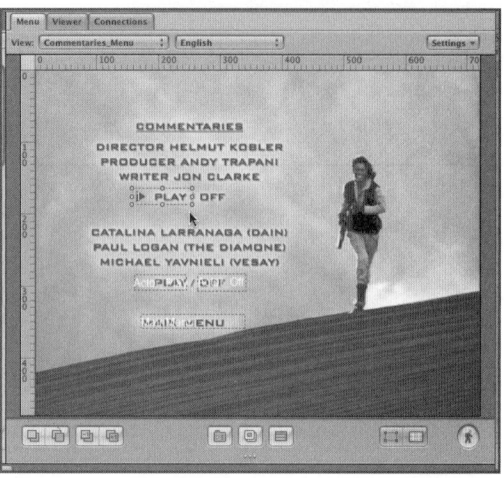

The Menu tab allows you to create button hotspots.

Create a new menu by clicking the Add Menu button from DVD Studio's palette. You can see your menu in the making by clicking the program's Menu tab. From here, you can drag a still picture or video clip from the Assets tab directly onto your menu. That file—either static or moving—will become the menu's background. Next, you can click and drag your mouse over menu areas to create button hotspots. (A menu isn't a menu without a few buttons for users to choose from, right?) At that point, you can easily link the buttons to other menus or video/audio tracks, such as your film. When the user chooses a menu button, the DVD plays whatever is linked to that button.

The inspector lets you program menu bottons.

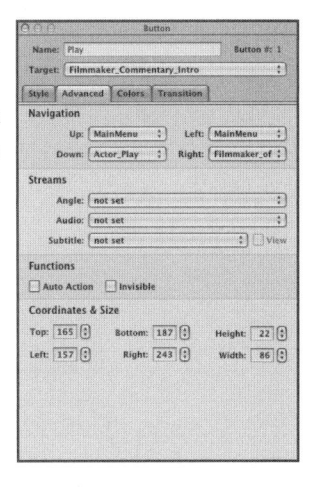

The menu inspector lets you program exactly what a menu button should do when it is clicked.

The Track tab lets you play the video and audio stream.

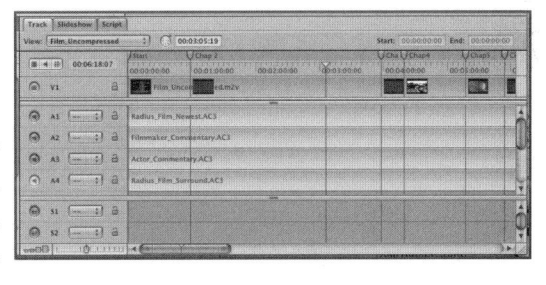

A track is typically a video and its corresponding audio that you want your DVD to play at some point. Your film would be a track, and another track could be a Making Of video that you've created or a trailer for a friend's film. Tracks can feature multiple *streams*. For instance, the track for a commercial Hollywood DVD typically has one video stream (the movie's imagery) but three audio streams (a stereo sound mix, a 5.1 Surround Sound mix, and a d3), besides several subtitle streams that feature subtitles in different languages. Only one video, audio, and subtitle stream can play at once, but you can easily determine which streams play. For instance, let's say that a viewer clicks the Play Movie button you've created on your main menu. In that case, you can easily set DVD Studio Pro to play the video stream, the first audio stream, and no subtitle stream of your movie's track. But let's say that a viewer goes to your DVD's Special menu and chooses to watch your film with director's commentary turned on. For that menu, you'll set DVD Studio Pro to play your film's video stream, its *second* audio stream, and no subtitle stream of your movie's track. If the viewer goes to your Languages menu and chooses the French option, that menu option will be programmed to play the movie track's video stream, its first audio stream, and one of the subtitle streams you've created (whichever stream features your French subtitles).

To create a track, click the Add Track button from DVD Studio Pro's palette. Next, click and drag a movie file from the Assets tab to whatever row (stream) you want in the Track tab. In the Track tab, you can also easily set chapter markers with a track. For instance, you can set up multiple chapter markers throughout your film, and then you can create a separate Scenes menu that jumps directly to each of those markers.

The graphical view is a good way to see the flow of your DVD content.

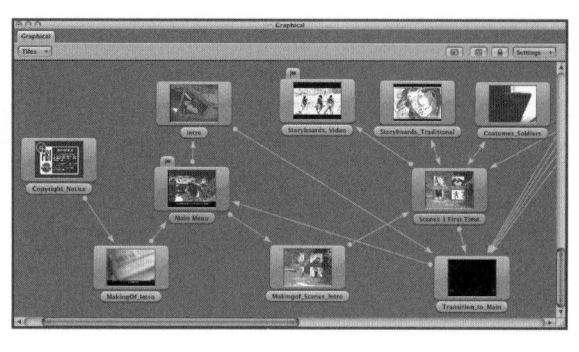

Optionally, DVD Studio Pro lets you work in a bird's-eye view of your DVD's content, where each menu and track is represented by a tile (like a thumbnail graphic), with arrowed lines connecting related menus and tracks. This graphical view is the best way to see how all of your DVD's content flows together.

Video and audio encoding should be done before the authoring process.

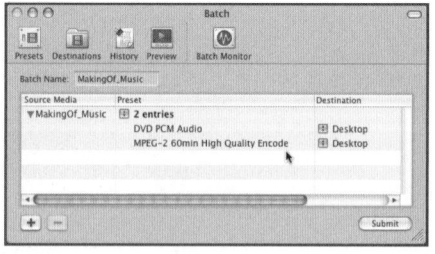

Before your video clips can play on a DVD, you need to encode them in the MPEG-2 file format, which is a high-quality, compressed video format that all DVDs use.

DVD Studio Pro can do this automatically when you're ready to burn your DVD, but I prefer doing it before the authoring process begins. I use Apple's free Compressor software to perform the MPEG-2 encoding. The same goes for DVD audio: For best results, you should encode your audio files in the highly compressed AC3 format (as conventional Hollywood DVDs do). For this, you can use Apple's included A.Pack utility.

I replicated the DVDs as DVD-9s, which is a unique process.

I had toyed with the idea of burning copies of the *RADIUS* DVD directly off my Mac on an as-needed basis, as orders came in one by one. This would have been the cheapest route to DVD distribution (blank DVD-R discs cost only about 50 cents each in bulk), but in the end, I decided against this grassroots approach for three reasons:

- I knew that if I started getting more than a couple orders per day, I would quickly tire of manually burning the twin DVDs on my computer and then stuffing them into a DVD case. It would be much more convenient to have hundreds manufactured at one time, ready to distribute when needed.

You now can burn dual-layer DVDs—equivalent to *RADIUS'* DVD-9s—on your computer, but you might still encounter older DVD players that can't play them.

- Some people don't realize that DVDs burned on a computer aren't 100 percent compatible with consumer DVD players. In fact, computer-burned discs are estimated to be only 90–95 percent compatible with set-top DVD players, and those discs are more easily damaged and rendered unplayable by dust and scratches. This was a big concern for me, because I didn't want to send the DVDs to customers, film agents, or journalists and then hear that the discs wouldn't play. It wasn't a professional scenario, and I wanted *RADIUS* to appear as professional as possible.

- At the time, discs that were burned on a computer could store only 1 hour of high-quality video, but I was counting on each disc to carry more than 2 hours' worth. (Today, some computer DVD drives can burn dual layers of data on a disc surface, meeting my 2 hours requirement, but those burners weren't available when I was launching the DVD.)

The answer to all these concerns was to *replicate* the DVDs, meaning that I would take the data for each disc to a factory, which would use a special process to manufacture them as DVD-9 discs. DVD-9 is a format that can store about 2 hours of high-quality video—or about 8 gigabytes (GB) of data—per disc. When you buy or rent a commercial Hollywood DVD, chances are it's a DVD-9. Besides storing a lot of video, DVD-9s are fully compatible with set-top DVD players. You can ship the discs to customers and journalists and know that they'll play without a hitch.

There's one drawback to DVD replication: Most replication factories manufacture a minimum of 1,000 discs, so you'll have to make a moderate financial commitment before getting a single disc in your hands. And besides the per-disc charge for replication, most manufacturers charge a separate fee to create the *glass master* for a DVD-9, which is the master disc that's used to make all other copies.

All these little gotchas were okay with me, so I typed "DVD replication" into Google and came up with a bunch of companies that could do the job. Ultimately, after a lot of comparison shopping, I chose a company called Dub-It (http://www.dub-it.com). Dub-It didn't have the cheapest prices, but it was located in Los Angeles, and I could drive over there and meet the people who would be replicating my DVDs and printing the cover artwork. Because I hadn't made a DVD before, I felt more comfortable knowing that I could meet face to face with these people. That peace of mind was worth a couple hundred dollars extra. Also, Dub-It had a good reputation among indie filmmakers in Los Angeles, so I didn't have to worry much about screw-ups on their part.

In the end, the costs to make my first round of 1,000 *RADIUS* DVDs broke down like so:

- $300 for a glass master of disc 1
- $300 for a glass master of disc 2
- $820 for 1,000 copies of disc 1
- $820 for 1,000 copies of disc 2
- $300 for 1,000 DVD cases and 4-color printed sleeves

With tax and a few other minor costs, I spent a little less than $3,000—or $3 per unit. I consequently decided to sell each package for $19.95, which seemed like a fair price given all the content that the DVDs included. It's also worth noting that reprints of the DVDs were significantly cheaper. After I sold my first 1,000 copies, reprinting 1,000 more units was $600 cheaper because I had already paid for the glass masters.

I created a Web site to promote and sell the DVD.

As I said, I had decided to sell *RADIUS*' DVD online, which meant that I needed a Web site that could quickly and clearly convey to customers what was special and unique about the film and all its Making Of material. I retired the first Web site I had built for *RADIUS* (the site that documented the making of the film step by step as it was happening—see Chapter 18, "Creating a Pro Image") and launched a new Web site that was much more promotional in nature and that projected a polished image for the project. (Anything less would fail to persuade customers to part with their $19.95!)

To get started, I studied the Web sites for major Hollywood films, checking out all the different ideas that various designers used and noting what I liked best. My intention was to adopt (or, um, copy) an existing site design, because I didn't have the time or money to design a new site from scratch. Obviously, it was much more efficient to identify an existing site that some big Hollywood studio had paid thousands of dollars to create and use that as a model. If this strikes you as not very creative, you're right. But my attitude was, "Who cares?" I wasn't trying to build a career as a Web publisher. I was a filmmaker, and I needed a good-looking but affordable site to promote my film. Modeling my site on an existing one was the easiest path to that goal.

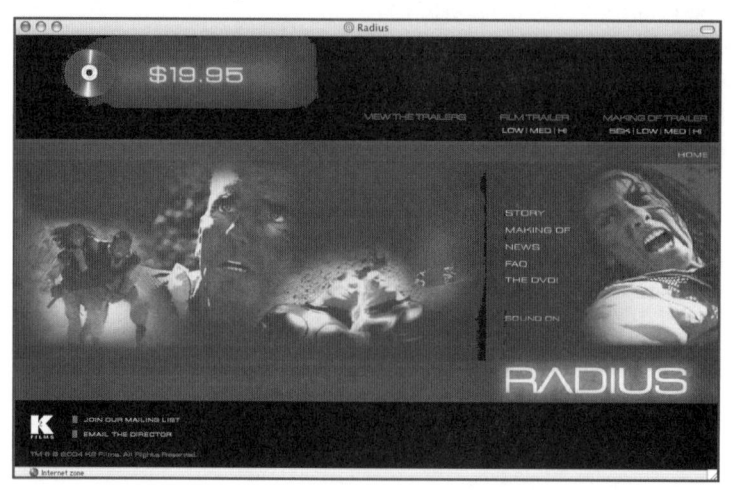

The *RADIUS* promotional site replaced our Making Of site when the film was finished.

After looking at plenty of promotional film sites, I settled on one that New Line Cinema had launched for the Denzel Washington movie *John Q*. (See http://www.iamjohnq.com; the site is still up as of this writing.) I liked New Line's site for a number of reasons. It had an unconventional aspect ratio, which reminded me of a widescreen film, and it used lots of animated graphics and sound clips from the movie.

Thanks to a mutual friend, I had met a talented young Web designer named Calvin Sun (http://www.superesc.com). I asked Calvin if he could build *RADIUS*' site along the lines of *John Q*. but with a look that was unique to *RADIUS*. It took Calvin about a week's worth of evenings to come up with a sleek, professional design, which you can see at http://www.radiusmovie.com. Total cost for the Web site was about $750. (By the way, Calvin lives in Canada, and he did all the work remotely.)

I also edited a number of promotional video clips for *RADIUS*' site, including a 2-minute film trailer, a 5-minute Making Of trailer, and a 3-minute overview of the DVD, narrated by me and explaining what was unique about the discs. You can still see these video clips at http://www.radiusmovie.com. Let me tell you, I worked long and hard putting these things together! Not only did I edit them, but I also wrote and recorded the dialogue scripts where applicable, got custom music scored for the trailers, and had to teach myself the art of video compression (compressing the video clips into small but good-looking formats that customers could download). It took weeks of solid work to produce this stuff and refine it, but I really think it was essential, because video clips can sell your film better than anything else.

Lesson Learned

> If you're going to be selling your own film, go the extra mile with an effective promotional Web site. It will be a big factor in persuading strangers to order your film.

I got set up to accept credit cards.

With a promotional Web site ready to go, I had to figure out how to charge customers for their orders. The easiest way to do this would have been to accept PayPal payments. Many people already have PayPal accounts (thanks to the popularity of eBay), and it's easy and nearly free to set yourself up as a PayPal "merchant." In the end, though, I decided not to go the PayPal route, because I was worried that some customers would still not have PayPal accounts and wouldn't bother setting them up just to order my DVD.

Instead, I decided to accept major credit cards such as Visa and MasterCard, which made ordering the *RADIUS* DVD from our Web site as convenient for customers as ordering from, say, Amazon.com. Fortunately, in this day and age of online commerce, it's pretty easy to set yourself up for credit card payments over the Internet. The first thing you need to do is sign up with a credit card merchant, which is basically a bank that processes credit card payments on your behalf.

To find a merchant, I typed "credit card merchant" into Google and came up with a long list of companies that offer the service. If you do the same, you'll see that these companies charge a small percentage fee for each transaction they process. Not all fee structures are alike, though. Some are good only if you sell a small amount of merchandise per month but become more costly if you have greater sales, or vice versa. I tried to guess what my monthly sales would be and picked the vendor that offered the best rates within those sales. Getting signed up is easy. In most cases, you fill out a short online application and provide the bank account number you want your sales deposited into. Companies usually make deposits every two weeks.

The second thing you need to set up, beyond a credit card merchant, is an online shopping cart. This is basically like a Web page that displays a thumbnail image of your product, allows customers to indicate how many units they want to order, and then lets them enter their address and credit card info. (All that is passed to your credit card merchant for processing. Shipping addresses are e-mailed to you for shipping.) Shopping cart software comes in many flavors (some are simple, whereas others are built with huge mail order businesses in mind), and renting it can add yet another expense to your business.

I looked at a bunch of different credit cart merchants, including Yahoo's offerings (http://www.smallbusiness.yahoo.com), but I settled on a company called 2Checkout (http://www.2checkout.com). I liked 2Checkout for two reasons: Its fees were pretty reasonable for low-volume business (I had no idea how many units *RADIUS* would sell per month, but I wanted to err on the conservative side), and it offered a simple but adequate shopping cart that I could use with the service, free of charge. (Many merchants require you to find a separate shopping cart, and that was too much work for me.)

I got set up to accept credit cards. 343

It took about 15 minutes to set up the *RADIUS* Web site for credit card orders via 2Checkout.com.

Getting my existing Web site integrated with 2Checkout's shopping cart was easy. I just created an Order Now button on the *RADIUS* site and linked it to the shopping cart that 2Checkout created for my business on its own secured Web site. It's that simple. My customers click the Order Now button, and then 2Checkout's Web site handles all the data entry and processing and returns customers to my *RADIUS* site after they've placed an order. For each order, I get an e-mail from 2Checkout stating how many units the customer wants and where to send then. I just pack up the order in bubbled shipping envelopes (bought in bulk from http://www.staples.com) and print a shipping label using a handy label printer called the LabelWriter 330 ($119, http://www.dymo.com).

That's pretty much how the process works. I've sold a little more than 1,900 DVDs—or almost $40,000 worth of merchandise—this way.

Lesson Learned

> In this day of online commerce, pretty much anyone can get set up to accept credit card payments—in minutes.

By the way, when I send a customer the *RADIUS* DVD, I enclose a small sheet of paper thanking them for the order and saying that we would love to hear feedback. That little gesture has led to dozens of fans writing in with praise, which we post on our site as customer testimonials.

I've since added Amazon.com distribution.

Shortly after I started taking orders for *RADIUS* at http://www.radiusmovie.com, I signed up to have it distributed via Amazon.com. Amazon has a program for small publishers called Amazon Advantage; you can learn more about it by going to http://www.amazon.com/advantage.

Selling through Amazon has some pros and cons. In the con category, I only get about 55 percent of each unit's sale price, whereas I get almost 98 percent of the sale price when customers order through the *RADIUS* site. But in terms of pros, Amazon makes distributing your film about as easy as it can get. It handles all credit card processing and shipping for you, so if you don't want to bother with finding a credit card merchant, setting up an online shopping cart, and physically mailing out movies, you'll appreciate Amazon's convenience factor.

I've since added Amazon.com distribution.　345

Your DVD appears on Amazon like any other product. You send Amazon a few copies of your film at a time, and it orders more copies on an as-needed basis.

What's more, telling customers that your movie is available on Amazon gives you extra credibility in their eyes, and that's why I signed up. I thought that as I tried to get journalists to write about *RADIUS* (for instance, trying to get it covered in the *New York Times* or *Entertainment Weekly*), it would help legitimize the movie if it was sold by the world's largest bookstore rather than just my private site.

In the end, the vast majority of *RADIUS*' orders come through the official *RADIUS* site (largely because all the press we've gotten to date has pointed people there). Amazon, so far, has only been good for show.

CHAPTER 20

FILM MARKETING

After I had finished making the *RADIUS* DVD and got everything set up to sell online (see Chapter 19, "Film Distribution"), the only thing left to do was market the film—in other words, look for ways to get the public to notice it and buy it online.

I had no budget for advertising.

Running paid product advertisements is a major marketing tactic, but I never really considered advertising *RADIUS*, because it's such an expensive proposition (by low-budget, indie film standards, at least). For starters, buying print ads in film magazines was certainly *way* out of my reach (thousands of dollars, not to mention the cost of designing a good-looking, compelling advertisement). But I discovered that even online ads on film and entertainment Web sites were expensive. For instance, iFilm.com currently charges a minimum of $10,000 for an ad campaign, and even smaller sites with less traffic and more specialized focuses are expensive by barebones, indie-film standards.

My marketing strategy focused on getting free press.

Because I had no budget for advertising, my only option was to pursue public relations (or PR for short). In other words, I had to look for ways to get journalists to write about *RADIUS* in magazines and online Web sites, which could lead to readers checking out the *RADIUS* Web site (http://www.radiusmovie.com) and possibly buying my DVD.

The best part about this approach is that getting PR is absolutely free. If you get a Web site or a magazine to write up some quick news blurb about your movie—or better yet, do a review—you don't pay a dime. Journalists will cover your product because they think it will be interesting to their readers. Coverage is really a reader service, which costs you nothing. And that, of course, is why free press is the indie filmmaker's best friend!

Here's the bad news: Because free press is free, everyone tries to get it. You'll face an uphill battle trying to convince a journalist that your movie is somehow unique and will offer the journalist's audience something useful or interesting that other movies in the crowd don't. (That's why, throughout this book, I've often seemed obsessed with making *RADIUS* stand out in one way or another.)

Lesson Learned

> If you have no money to work with, seeking free press is your best bet for getting broad exposure for your film.

I came up with multiple marketing "hooks."

Before I took steps to execute my marketing plan (that is, writing a press release and then contacting journalists), I had to figure out what *RADIUS*' hook would be. In other words, what was really unique about *RADIUS* that would have the best chance of getting the press interested in covering it? I thought *RADIUS* had a few unique qualities, but my sense was that I needed to pick one thing—the best quality—that I could really focus on and that would have the best chance of being relevant to whatever journalists I'd be talking to.

But I also knew that I might be talking to journalists who had different priorities—for instance, a journalist who covers movies wouldn't have the same interests or perspective as a journalist who covers technology. But *RADIUS* had something interesting to offer movie journalists *and* tech journalists. Although I never used more than one hook with a journalist, I came up with multiple hooks that would let me tailor my message to the particular journalist I happened to be talking to.

So for film-related press, I chose a hook that went something like this:

> A first-time filmmaker made an impressive sci-fi action film on a budget of only $60,000 and now takes other aspiring filmmakers through every step of the filmmaking process, showing them how they can make their own films, using *RADIUS* as the example.

But I also thought that there were things about *RADIUS* that might appeal to journalists who cover the Macintosh computer, because so much of *RADIUS* was done on the Mac. So for Mac journalists, my hook would be something like this:

> Ambitious guerrilla film achieved impressive quality on a low budget, thanks to the Macintosh.

And because *RADIUS* was a science fiction film, and there's a big press contingent that covers science fiction specifically, my hook for this audience became the following:

> Science fiction fan creates his own sci-fi epic on guerrilla budget of $60,000 and then shows other sci-fi fans how to make their own films.

The differences between these hooks are not extreme; they're a question of emphasis. But that's what marketing is—figuring out what quality of your product will be interesting to your immediate audience and then emphasizing that.

Lesson Learned

> There might several unique qualities of your product, but if you try to tick all of them off to someone, their eyes will glaze over. Figure out the *one* thing that's really compelling and unique about your film, and then hammer on that.

> **READ UP ON MARKETING.**
>
> If you're going to try to market your film, there are plenty of marketing books that can help you formulate a strategy and tactics. I'd recommend browsing your local bookstore's shelves to see what jumps out at you. One that seems interesting to me but that I haven't read yet is *The Anatomy of Buzz: How to Create Word of Mouth Marketing*.
>
> I can recommend one book in particular that's been out for years, and it's called *Positioning: The Battle for Your Mind* ($14.95, by Al Ries and Jack Trout). This book is short, focused, and all about how to position products so they have a clear and unique identity in the public's mind (with plenty of real-world case studies to demonstrate its points). If you read only one book on marketing philosophy, make this the one.

I wrote press releases for each of my hooks.

I wrote a two-page press release for each of my hooks (film, sci-fi, and Macintosh). I had experience writing press releases from my video game days, so I knew some of the basic do's and don'ts of writing them. For instance, *do* be to-the-point, getting the core of your message (or hook) across in the press release's headline and first couple of sentences, because journalists might not continue reading past that point. But *don't* treat a press release like a promotional advertisement, filled with lots of marketing copy, subjective claims, or hype. Instead, focus on conveying objective information, because the press will want to draw its own conclusions about your product. I allow myself to use a few subjective words like "groundbreaking" or "epic," but that's about it.

Anyway, if you want to get a feel for how real-world, genuine press releases read, just visit a Web site like PR Web (http://www.prweb.com) and look for a link called News Releases by Category on the site's home page. Or you can download *RADIUS*' film and Macintosh-oriented releases at http://www.k2films.com/press/film_release.pdf or http://www.k2films.com/press/mac_release.pdf.

Anyway, as I did for the early press releases I had sent out during *RADIUS*' production (see Chapter 19), I paid $60 to a wire service called BusinessWire (http://www.businesswire.com) to send *RADIUS*' film-oriented press release to general interest and entertainment news organizations. Doing so got a couple of little blurbs written about the *RADIUS* DVD in a few offbeat Web sites, but the real work lay ahead, which required me to approach hand-picked publications one by one and pitch them my story.

I prioritized the list of print and Internet publications I would approach.

I wrote down every publication I could think of that might be interested in running a review of *RADIUS* or at least a short one- or two-paragraph blurb announcing its availability. These target publications included everything from the *New York Times* and *Entertainment Weekly* to *Film Threat* and *Ain't It Cool News* to the Sci-Fi Channel's *SciFi Wire*, along with lots of others. (By the way, even major, national publications will cover small, off-the-beaten-path products. Columnists often like citing unknown little gems, even if they're not appropriate for major editorial coverage, so don't think that these publications are out of your reach simply because they're well-known.)

Then I looked over my master list of publications and started prioritizing each publication by order of importance and order of feasibility. For instance, getting *RADIUS* mentioned in the *New York Times* would be a major coup, generating good sales exposure and great prestige. But the chances of getting coverage in *The Times* were naturally lower than my chances of getting coverage in smaller publications, so I had to factor that into my ultimate plans. In other words, given the fact that I'd be doing all the promotional work myself, what would be a better use of my time when I kicked off *RADIUS*' so-called PR campaign? If my goal was to get people to visit the *RADIUS* Web site and order the DVD, would it be good to spend time pursuing the *New York Times* or, say, Macintosh news sites, which would be easier to get stories into?

I strongly considered going for A-list publications first—names like the *New York Times*, *Entertainment Weekly*, and whatever else. It was tempting. I looked forward to the ego boost that would come from being covered by this press. I also thought that getting coverage from an A-list publication—although harder to pull off—would make it easier to get coverage everywhere else, since I'd already had a "seal of approval" from big-name press.

But in the end, I opted to go after my easier targets first. For starters, I realized that getting early press coverage for *RADIUS*—any coverage—would bring in much-appreciated DVD sales sooner than later. Second, I thought that getting any coverage would give me a morale boost and build my confidence in the DVD, which would help me go after the bigger fish later on. Finally, I tend to think that news travels up toward the bigger publications. First a story is picked up by smaller, special-interest publications, and then it sort of snowballs, getting more and more coverage until it reaches the national publications, who are more apt to pick it up because it's already been "proven" on a more specialized or localized scale. That's just my theory, and I'm sure there are exceptions, but that's how things seem to work generally. I made my plans accordingly.

Then I started contacting publications and journalists.

I went down my prioritized list, contacting one publication at a time. If I had a phone number for the publication, I'd start by calling and asking for the editor of whatever section of the publication I thought *RADIUS* might fit into (entertainment, technology, and so on). Or sometimes I'd already know that a particular journalist at the publication covered products like *RADIUS*, so I'd ask for that person. (While I was making *RADIUS*, I would clip out articles I saw written on any subject roughly related to *RADIUS*—guerrilla films, Internet film, sci-fi fan films, Mac-made films, and so on—and then note the journalists' names for future reference.)

If I didn't have a phone number to reach these publications or journalists (which was often the case, because I initially wanted to focus on online publications that would drive traffic to my Web site), I'd use e-mail.

Obviously, getting someone on the phone was preferable. The journalist could hear the energy and enthusiasm in my voice, which could go a long way, and I could spend a minute giving the journalist a brief pitch for *RADIUS* in a couple of sentences, all based on whatever hook I thought was appropriate. (I'd also throw in some nuggets I hoped would help my case, like the fact that the film was made by some film industry veterans, or that we shot during a 120-degree heat wave in Death Valley.) And then I'd ask if I could send them a press kit and a copy of the DVD.

If the journalist seemed open to considering *RADIUS* (and most were, if only to avoid rejecting me right over the phone), I'd send out my DVD immediately and then call a few days later to make sure he got it. Finally, I'd call *again* a week or two after that to see if he'd had a chance to check out the DVD. Basically, without being too much of a pest, I'd call as many times as I had a good excuse to do so, to keep *RADIUS* on the journalist's radar; otherwise, he might simply forget about it.

Working through e-mail was a little tougher, because I couldn't make a personal connection with the journalist—my message was yet another anonymous piece of mail crowding someone's In box. But if e-mail was my only option, I'd start by sending a concise but energetic message with a short, single-paragraph introduction, followed by three or four bullet points citing what was unique about *RADIUS*. The goal was to get across the essential, interesting points about *RADIUS* in as few words as possible, because nobody wants to read much verbiage in an initial e-mail. Then I'd attach a bunch of promotional pictures from the movie (resized to be downloaded easily), a link to *RADIUS*' online, 2-minute film trailer, and a link to my DVD's trailer, which explains, in a semi-amusing way, what's special about the DVD. (You can see both of these trailers at http://www.radiusmovie.com.) Being able to attach pictures and easy links is the one benefit of using e-mail to contact journalists, because they can quickly see your stuff and hopefully be intrigued. And if all these tricks compelled the journalist to respond to my e-mail, I'd again send a press kit and DVD in the mail.

At any rate, the result of all these machinations was a mixed bag. Sometimes I got coverage immediately. For instance, a number of Macintosh news sites ran stories about *RADIUS* right away and led to thousands of hits to the *RADIUS* site and dozens of sales a day, for several days at a time. Apple Computer picked up the story and ran a three-page story about *RADIUS* on its pro page (http://www.apple.com/pro/video/helmut). Likewise, Chris Gore, who runs the popular indie film site, FilmThreat (http://www.filmthreat.com), responded to my initial e-mail immediately and ran a great 4-star review a couple of weeks later. There were lots of other write-ups on small film fan sites and Web logs.

But plenty of leads didn't pan out. I really hoped *RADIUS* would get a mention on the indie news site IndieWire, but it didn't. I also hoped for a small mention on the site Ain't It Cool News, because that site has a soft spot for truly indie, off-the-radar films, but no dice there either.

But *RADIUS*'s marketing campaign is still a work-in-progress. I continue to approach press and get some stories written… or don't. What's clear about this whole process is that marketing your own indie film takes a thick skin. I'm enthusiastic and excited about my film, but no journalist is going to have that same mindset. Journalists have their own lives to lead, they're busy, they have a million other people pitching them products, and to a degree, they develop a "been there, done that" outlook on things because they've seen so much. Plus, they simply might not see the same qualities in *RADIUS* that I do. So it can be really hard, if not impossible, to cut through all the noise and get coverage. Sometimes it's hard even to get hold of them—even when they have a phone, they might never answer it, and the same goes for e-mails. In other words, it can feel like you're pitching your product to a black hole.

Lesson Learned
> As an indie filmmaker doing your own PR, you'll experience a low success rate, where you make more pitches that go nowhere than pitches that actually lead to coverage. Dealing with this kind of rejection can be unpleasant to say the least, but it's something you've got to do if you want to get the word out about your film and can't afford to pay a public relations agency to take the arrows in the back for you.

To build credibility, I also sought out promotional quotes for *RADIUS*.

Besides going after free publicity, I sought out any and all promotional quotes from working filmmakers and other professionals in the film industry. Promotional quotes are a tried-and-true marketing tool—you get someone whose name or work is already respected to say something about your product, and that helps build your product's credibility, the same way a good review in a magazine or other publication might.

So I went after as many promotional quotes as I could get and posted them at the top of *RADIUS*' Web site:

> *RADIUS* is a text book example of how a little ingenuity, determination and talent can produce a film that defies its humble budget. On top of that, Helmut goes so far as to chronicle the entire process in such a way as to make this venture a classic example of how to get the most out of what you have to work with.
> **Daniel Myrick**, director of *The Blair Witch Project*

> Full of fun anecdotes and interesting stories of filmmakers in the heat of production!
> **David Bertman**, editor of *Gilmore Girls*

> An impressive film done with little resources, and for any aspiring filmmakers, it's a great guide for what to expect and what you can accomplish. It really is like a whole film school on disc!
> **Jeffrey Reddick**, writer of *Final Destination* and *Final Destination 2*

> I found disc 2 to be one of the most thorough, honest, and fascinating looks behind the scenes that I've ever seen. I wish I could have seen something like this when I was in film school.
> **Joe Nussbaum**, director of *George Lucas in Love* and *Sleepover*

How did I get these quotes? In some cases, I knew someone who knew the person who gave me the quote. For instance, *RADIUS*' producer, Andy Trapani, is the friend and manager of writer Jeffrey Reddick (the *Final Destination* movies), so Andy made that connection. Likewise, editor David Bertman (*Gilmore Girls*) is a friend of mine, so it wasn't too hard to get a quote from him.

But I got most of my quotes by cold-calling or e-mailing each filmmaker and asking if he would help me out. To reach Joe Nussbaum, I called the Director's Guild of America (310-289-2000) and asked for the name of Joe's agent. (The DGA will give this information to the public—all you have to do is ask.) Joe's agent agreed to e-mail my request for a quote to Joe, and he responded pretty quickly with an e-mail back to me. Likewise, I used the Internet Movie Database (http://www.imdb.com) to find the phone number for the production company of Daniel Myrick.

When I got someone via e-mail or on the phone, I'd convey a lot of key information in a couple of sentences:

- I was an indie filmmaker who had just finished my first film.
- I was a big fan of theirs and had been inspired by their work (which was always true—I approached guys like Joe Nussbaum and Daniel Myrick because they had been low-budget indie filmmakers and their movies had given me inspiration to do *RADIUS*).
- My film was unique because a) it was done on a very low budget, but with some impressive production values, and b) it included a Guerrilla Filmmaking School for other aspiring filmmakers going through the same thing I did.
- I was marketing the film myself and was wondering if they'd consider checking out the film and giving me a promotional quote if they liked it.

So that's what I did. Everyone I ever got a chance to make that pitch to agreed to take a look at the film. So I'd write a one-page cover letter reiterating everything I had said in my original pitch, package it with a shrink-wrapped DVD and a press kit (always in a sleek, white bubbled envelope—much better than the ugly manila variety), and send the whole thing via Priority Mail ($3.95 from the Post Office).

I wish I could say that all my pitches led to getting quotes, but they didn't. There were a couple of instances in which someone agreed to watch *RADIUS* but then didn't respond to my follow-ups, so I had no idea if they got around to it.

Even worse, my first three attempts to get promotional quotes never even got that far. Way before I finished *RADIUS*, I intended to ask three of my favorite filmmakers for a quote: Steven Soderberg (*Sex, Lies, and Videotape* and *Traffic*), Sam Raimi (*Evil Dead* and *Spider-Man*), and Robert Rodriguez (*El Mariachi* and *Sin City*). Because all of these guys have strong indie roots, I thought at least one of them might, if they liked *RADIUS* or its Film School, be willing to give me a quote. But to increase my chances of getting a "Yes," I decided to create a unique video-based Web site where I could introduce myself on camera and show them clips of *RADIUS* and its Making Of footage, along with a request to send them a DVD. If you want to see one of these sites, check out http://www.k2films.com/rrodriguez, which I made for Robert Rodriguez.

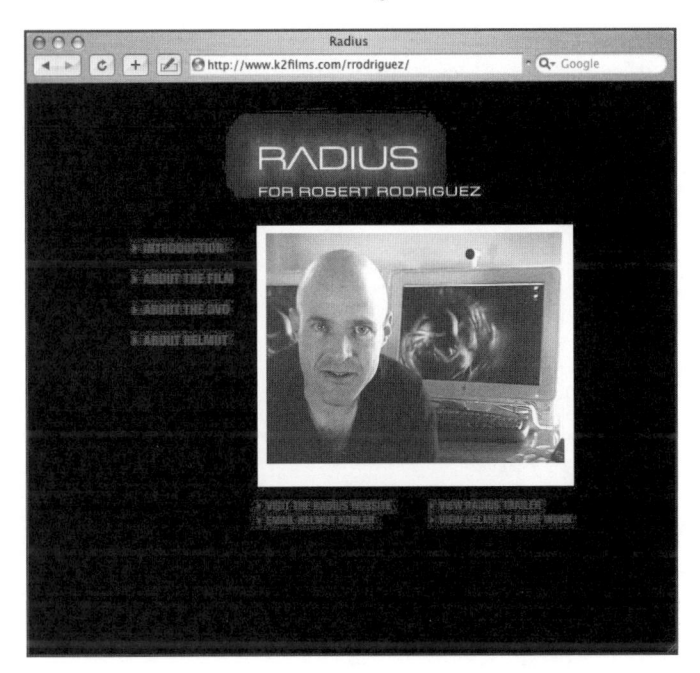

A scene from my video letter, asking some favorite directors for a promotional quote.

Did any of this help? Nope! On multiple occasions, I contacted the agents or production companies for all three directors, gave them the Web site link, and asked if they could pass it on. Later on, I also used some other contacts (friends of friends of friends) who had leads at these places. But the result was always the same: I never heard a single thing back and still have no idea if my request was even passed on.

Obviously, that's painful, especially because I went the extra mile in contacting these guys in a unique way by creating the whole video site. But that's just the price of doing business as an indie filmmaker. As I said, the odds are against you, and failures are a guaranteed part of the equation. You do what you can and then move on. You just have to keep in mind that if you keep trying, you're going to have some successes to go along with all the failures, and those are doubly satisfying given what it took to get them.

Lesson Learned

> Approach people who can identify with your film or your own experience. I wouldn't ask Michael Bay for a promotional quote, because I don't think he'd identify with an indie filmmaker making a film by hook or by crook. (Bay's career took off right after film school.) But Robert Rodriguez, Joe Nussbaum, or Daniel Myrick certainly would.

Chapter 21

Lessons Learned

In this last chapter, I want to review some of the biggest lessons I took away from my experience of making *RADIUS* and its two-disc DVD. I've cited these lessons throughout the book, along with many others, but these are worth reiterating, because they'll certainly be the ones that apply first to any projects I get the chance to do in the future. Of course, these are my lessons, learned from my particular experience. They might not apply to you or your project, but for what they're worth, here they are.

Come up with a unique hook.

You can skip this advice if you're making a film purely for yourself, an audience of one. But if you want other people to see your work, you'll have an easier time getting attention if you come up with some unique angle that separates your film from the crowd.

Your hook can be one of many different things. For instance, the hook for the film *Memento* was that it featured a hero who couldn't remember anything from one moment to the next. The director used clever time shifting to convey the movie's story in the same jumbled, confused way that the story's hero struggled with in his own memories. That's an original story hook! And the hook of *The Blair Witch Project* was that it gave a fictitious story an authentic documentary feel, making people feel as if it all really happened.

When we started making *RADIUS*, our hook was that we positioned ourselves as a high-quality Internet film, way back when Internet film seemed like a hot commodity but was filled with lots of examples of amateurish content. As an Internet film, we stood out from the crowd because we had recruited some talented film industry veterans to work on the project, and we had launched a Web site that let fans track the making of the film day by day, which hadn't been done before. So that was our first hook. But after Internet film went cold, I created the *Guerrilla Film School* DVD for *RADIUS*, and our unique hook became the fact that a first-time filmmaker was taking other aspiring filmmakers through every step of the production process, looking at everything that worked and didn't.

I think you get the point: Come up with something story-related or market-related that is special about your film. It doesn't have to be special to everyone, but it should be special to at least a select audience, so *someone* is compelled to embrace your film a little more than the next one.

Do a small project better, instead of a big project worse.

If you have limited resources, it's better to focus them on a smaller project than a bigger one. Honestly, would you rather have a 90-minute feature with tons of rough, unpolished edges, or a 20-minute or even 10-minute film that looks, sounds, and feels really sharp and doesn't compel you to make excuses about how you just didn't have the time or the money to do what you wanted to do? I guarantee that between these two choices, doing a more polished film with a narrower scope will serve you better in the long run. Remember: You can always do bigger stuff later on, but if you can't show that you can make a small, quality film now, you might never develop the momentum you need to do bigger things down the road.

I was already aware of this issue when I started *RADIUS*, which is why I did a 33-minute film instead of a feature. But looking back, I should have scaled back my ambitions even further. There are still plenty of spots in *RADIUS* where we spread our limited resources too thin to accomplish the quality I ultimately wanted, and if I had done a shorter film, or one with not quite so many effects or tough locations, *RADIUS* either would have been stronger for it or would not have taken so long to finish.

My advice to you is to pick a project with a scope you think you can handle with a high degree of quality and then reduce your film's scope *even further* to protect you from too many optimistic expectations. (And what is an indie filmmaker if not optimistic?)

You want something that's just ambitious enough to make your film stand out from the crowd of films that have similar resources to work with, where hard work and good planning can really carry the day. But hard work and good planning can be overwhelmed by an overly ambitious agenda, and that's what you should be careful to avoid.

Find as many experienced crew members as you can.

RADIUS would have cost a little less to make but its quality would have suffered significantly had we done it with an inexperienced crew, where each person was learning his job *on* the job.

It's important to remember that you don't have to pay significantly more for experience. Potential crew members aren't always looking for a payday. Catch someone at the right time, and you'll find that he has other reasons for getting involved with your production—for instance, a chance to do some different creative work, gain a little more experience, fill up some free time, or just have a mini-adventure. These people are out there—you just need to find them and figure out how your film can give them what they're looking for, in return for their services.

Find good people—don't settle!

By "good," I mean a few things: people who keep their cool under pressure, are reliable in that they follow through on their commitments, and are fun to work with.

I know this sounds obvious, but in practice, when you're trying to piece together a team on a low budget, you might find yourself tempted to work with people who don't feel quite right. Maybe they become unresponsive for stretches of time. Maybe they continually seem to have an attitude that they're doing you a huge favor. Maybe they regularly come up with things they need from you before they can continue with their tasks. Maybe they're not conscientious with their work and don't check it for problems that they could easily catch, but instead leave you to worry about it. Maybe they never want to take time to experiment. Maybe they're natural cynics or complainers. The point is, these potential crew members might come in all shapes and forms, and to get your project done, you might find yourself willing to work with them, just grinning and bearing it along the way.

But I would really caution against doing so, unless you have to deal with it in isolated and limited cases. It's better to find the right kind of person for your film, even if it takes you longer to do so, or even if you have to stop progress for a little while and find someone new.

Making an indie film on limited resources is already a stressful, iffy proposition—a little bit like building a house of cards—and having people who drive you crazy in one way or another can truly derail the whole production. I've seen that happen on other projects, but by some incredibly lucky stroke, we managed to avoid such a fate on *RADIUS*. It started with Andy Trapani, our producer, who was great with people, a resourceful, entrepreneurial thinker, and completely able to function independently. Andy hired people he respected and who worked like him, and those hires did the same thing. Our cast proved similarly strong and reliable, as were the vast majority of people we recruited to work on *RADIUS*' post-production. These people went the extra mile for the film, even after going the extra mile a few times already.

That's not to say that there weren't stressful moments or frank discussions with crew members on the production, or moments when a crew member had to push back and say, "I think this is all I can do." There were. But these exchanges happened in a spirit of cooperation and a sincere desire to help finish the film and to see it succeed. And so our house of cards managed to stand.

Work with equipment you have easy access to.

RADIUS used a lot of the same high-end equipment that "real" movies use. We shot on 35-mm film cameras. We edited the film on an Avid that was especially designed for cutting film (as opposed to video). We did our color correction at a professional post-production company, with the same equipment that TV shows and slick commercials use. Some of our visual effects were done on high-end workstations (like an Inferno or Jaleo), and we mixed our soundtrack on a huge mix stage used for big Hollywood movies.

It was exciting to use all this "grown-up" equipment for *RADIUS*, and it was a near miracle that we did so for so little money. But the drawback to this approach was that we often had sporadic access to the gear—usually a few hours at a time on nights and weekends, when paying clients went home—and this limited access really hurt our ability to finish the film in a timely manner.

So I recommend that you take a different approach and build your whole production and post-production strategy around equipment that your team members have easy, constant access to. For instance, make sure your film editor has his own editing system, with all the tools needed for editing and color correction. For audio work, find a sound designer and mixer who can do the work on his own computer and speaker setup. (Plenty of audio guys have created mini-production studios in second bedrooms and garages.)

These days, digital production tools have gotten really sophisticated, yet they still run on everyday desktop computers (like a mid-level Macintosh). So there's nothing stopping a talented person from getting professional results from affordable, readily available equipment.

Go ahead—get discouraged!

If you've set ambitious goals for your film, you might experience moments of utter frustration, depression, and despair when nothing seems to be going right, and you wonder if you'll ever finish the film or if it will be a disaster when it's done. There were certainly moments like these on *RADIUS*, such as when we fell further and further behind schedule in the Death Valley heat or when we experienced a snail's pace of progress while finishing our visual effects and sound design.

During these dark moments, friends and family would try to be helpful, saying, "Don't get discouraged." But in the end, that well-meaning advice wasn't all that helpful, because I *was* discouraged. So I'd start thinking that I must be wimp, because I wasn't able to spring heroically into all these challenges without letting them get me down. Such feelings of inadequacy often nagged at me while making *RADIUS*, but I gradually came to realize that I was trying to hold myself to an unrealistic standard, and I suggest you come to the same conclusion, sooner than later.

The fact is, you *will* get discouraged, and there's no getting around it. So don't feel guilty or beat yourself up about it. The trick is to accept that you're going to get discouraged but to remain *moderately functional* during your discouragement. That's the key. If you can keep moving, keep plugging away—even at a slower pace—you're doing fine, and the good news is, you'll eventually dig yourself out of your hole. *Just keep going.*

Create a polished image.

Although you might already be spreading your resources thin, I highly recommend putting a little money—and more than a little time—into creating some polished promotional materials for your film. At a minimum, create a good-looking postcard (even if it's just a slick logo and a creative tagline for your film) that you can print at Kinko's and later hand out to potential cast, crew, or audience members. Another helpful step is to set up a Web site—even if it's a single page—that has a professional feel. Finally, while you're still in post production, edit a short trailer (even if it's just a montage of scenes cut to some good music) that shows off some of your movie's best shots. Create a link for this video on your Web site, and make sure that the trailer's video is encoded well. (I can't tell you how many indie film trailers I've seen that play at stuttery frame rates, with heavy pixilation, because the filmmakers didn't know how to encode their video properly. Hint: Use a video codec like Sorenson Pro that features two-pass variable bit rate encoding.)

These basic steps don't have to be expensive, but they can help give your film a polished, professional feel that plenty of low-budget indie films don't have. And my experience on *RADIUS* tells me that creating a semi-pro image can aid your film in plenty of ways, from helping to get potential cast and crew members excited about what you're doing to building an audience for your film in advance.

Invest in yourself.

As an indie filmmaker, the more you can do yourself, the better off you'll be. Learn as many new skills as you can, especially digital ones. I started *RADIUS* with virtually no specific film experience or skills, but by the end of the project, I had taught myself video editing, DVD authoring, video encoding, some Web publishing, and bare-bones skills in Adobe PhotoShop and After Effects.

This wasn't exactly easy, and it took a few years, but there are many long-term benefits to taking this tack. For starters, it saves money, because you won't have to hire someone every time you want to do basic filmmaking chores. Besides, even if you manage to hire someone else at bargain-basement rates, you'll probably spend a lot of time waiting for him to finish the work, because it's simply not a top priority for him given the meager pay he's working for. So being able to do things yourself steers clear of the quagmire of waiting for near-volunteers to get things done.

Of course, I'm not advocating trying to do everything yourself. You can't be an expert at everything (unless you're Robert Rodriguez, apparently!), but even if you could, there are only 24 hours in a day, and you wouldn't have the bandwidth to accomplish everything a film production requires in a timely manner. So leave really critical things to an expert. For instance, I can't imagine serving as the director of photography on my own film, or the music composer. I doubt I'd ever be quite as good at those jobs as a specialist, and each of those jobs is pretty critical to a film's success. But it can never hurt to have *some* experience even with the things you ultimately leave to others. That way, you're a lot more informed when you talk to people about their work.

Anyway, you don't have to learn everything at once. It took me a few years to learn what I do know, and it's going to take me a similar amount of time to work on the new skills on my To Do list: color correction, effects compositing, sound mixing, and more. Also, it doesn't have to cost you money to learn new skills. I've noticed there's now a big industry offering classes on various software programs, but most of these options seem way overpriced to me. For instance, why pay $500 for a weekend course when you can buy a good book for $30 and teach yourself the same thing? Really, the trouble with formal classes is that a lot of people take them without having an immediate, pressing need for the skills they'll learn. By the time they actually have a real project to apply the skills to, they've forgotten much of what they learned in that focused classroom environment and have to go back to a book anyway. It's better to wait until you have a *real need* for some skill, and then learn what you immediately need. You can do it with a good technical book, sitting at home or at Starbucks for a few hours at a time. Chances are, you'll retain a lot more in the long run.

Do a "postmortem" review afterward.

Shortly after you finish your film, I highly recommend taking some time to sit and think about what went right on your production and what went wrong. In fact, don't just think about these things—organize your thoughts into a written report for yourself. Adding a little written formality to the process will help you uncover details that you might not think of otherwise and will provide you with a written record that you can go back and review whenever you start your next project.

You should have two objectives during this postmortem process. First, be as detailed as possible in considering every factor that had a positive or negative influence on your film. For instance, was your scheduling accurate? Where was it accurate, and where was it not? And if not, why not? Ask those kinds of pointed questions about every aspect of the project, especially the budget. In general, what were the obstacles you didn't quite anticipate when you were planning your film but that hurt your progress in one way or another? Leave no stone unturned.

Second, be truly honest during this process. Be sure to recognize and give credit to yourself or your crew for all the things that went right, but honestly admit where you really blew it. (You don't have to show your document to anyone, if that helps open things up a little!) In fact, imagine you're in the boardroom of *The Apprentice*, and you're opposite Donald Trump. Ask the same questions you could imagine him asking, and draw the same conclusions.

I went through the postmortem process about three weeks after finishing *RADIUS*. Three weeks was a good time for me; it gave me some time to relax, recover a bit, and clear my head, but it wasn't long enough for me to forget any details. I spent more than a full day writing up a formal document with an overall summary of how the project went and then included a further breakdown by preproduction, production, post-production, and marketing. All the victories and setbacks I've talked about in this book made their way into the document—along with some stuff I'll probably never share with anyone!

Finally, I wrapped up the postmortem with a section dedicated to what I'd do differently in the future, described with one bullet point after another. This whole process had a therapeutic effect and left me feeling excited that even the various mistakes I made on *RADIUS* would lead to some good down the road in terms of lessons learned.

> **IS FILM SCHOOL NECESSARY?**
>
> Indie filmmakers like to ask each other this question, and I asked it myself before making Radius.
>
> I didn't attend a film school but have met plenty of alumni from schools like USC, NYU, and UCLA to have developed an opinion on the utility of a film school education. Here are my two cents: When it comes to learning the technical and creative aspects of making a film, I don't think film school is necessary. (It can be helpful, especially if you're not a real self-starter, but it's not really necessary.) In the dark ages (before digital video cameras and desktop computers could handle video editing, sound mixing, and so on), film schools gave you access to lots of specialized, costly equipment that you couldn't easily get your hands on otherwise. Now, however, you can make films with tools that you can afford yourself.
>
> *(continued on next page)*

> **IS FILM SCHOOL NECESSARY?**
>
> *(continued from previous page)*
>
> Of course, those films might not be *good* films, but they'll be excellent learning experiences in that they'll give you tons of hands-on practice, which is all you can hope for. In fact, many film students spend surprisingly little time actually making films as part of their curriculum, and even fewer students get the chance to direct significant projects.
>
> Similarly, you don't need film school to refine your creative film "instincts" (that is, what makes a good, compelling film). A perfect substitute is to watch a lot of movies, talk with friends about them, read a couple of books you can find at major bookstores, and listen to the commentary tracks that genuine directors, writers, and producers now record on commercial Hollywood DVDs. Observing real films on your own is just as good as talking about films with a professor in a classroom environment.
>
> There's one big advantage I see to film school, though, and that's that it automatically puts you in a filmmaking track where you can develop a network of professional contacts, which is as important as your filmmaking skills. At a respectable film school, you'll meet lots of people who will go on to jobs in the film industry[md]few as directors, but more as producers, writers, editors, sound engineers, and so on. These people can help you get paying work down the road and can help you make your first couple of projects outside of school. Film schools are also where established companies and producers go to look for hot new talent. For instance, a commercial production company might sign up some lucky filmmakers right out of school, or a producer might see some promising work some students have done and help them move forward.
>
> Of course, just one of these networking breaks can have a hugely positive effect on your career, which is a strong case for film school. On the other hand, I truly believe that you can build a network without film school, even if it takes a couple of years longer and requires you to be an extrovert[md]getting out there and mixing with different people in the industry, making friends, and keeping up contact.

So that's about it. These are the big lessons I've taken away from *RADIUS*—some learned more painfully than others. I hope you can apply at least some of them to your own films. And again, I'd be curious to hear about any interesting projects you have going, so feel free to let me know by e-mailing me at director@k2films.com. Good luck!

INDEX

Numbers

3ds max, 262
35-mm cameras, 160-162
  Arriflex, 162-164
  checking gates, 173-174
  cleaning, 173-174
  costs, 249
  cranes, 185-189
    costs, 185
    setup, 189
    time, 189
  crew, 174
  dollies, 180-185
    costs, 183-185
    setup, 182-183
    substitutes, 183-185
    time, 182-183
    zooming, 181
  film, changing, 173-174
  handheld, 175-177
  ladder pods, 185-189
    costs, 185
    setup, 189
    time, 189
  lenses, 164-168
    depth of field, 168
    focus, 168-172
    long, 168
    prime, 167-168
    wide-angle, 167, 183-185
    zoom, 164-166, 181
  maintenance, 173-174
  measuring distance, 169-172
  quality, 249
  shooting, 248-249
  time, 169-175
  tripods, 177-180
48 Hour Film Web site, 19

A

Academy of Art Web site, 314
accessibility (locations), 58, 67-69
accommodations
  actors, 42-43
  crew, 154
  locations, 59, 63
action scenes
  choreography, 148-151
  conventional storyboards, 110-111
  pickup shots, 219
  shooting
    actors, 169-172
    handheld cameras, 175-177
    tripods, 177-180
  video storyboards, 113-115
actors. *See also* **crew**
  action scenes. *See* action scenes
  ADR, 289-292, 308-309
  choreography
    changing, 148-151
    pickup shots, 211

Index

costs
  advertising, 27-29
  insurance, 121-122
costumes. *See* costumes
dialogue
  ADR, 289-292, 308-309
  pickup shots, 213
  shooting, 177-178
doubles, 216
established actors
  credentials, 36-37
  hiring, 36-38
  McCoy, Matt, 36-38, 41-42
  Schroeder, Rick, 38
  screenwriters, scripts, 24-25
green screens, 267
hiring
  accommodations, 42-43
  advertising, 27-29
  atmosphere, 31-32
  auditions, 29-35
  casting directors, 29, 36
  casting rooms, 30
  colleges, 29
  costs, 41-44
  credentials, 36-37
  demo reels, 42
  established actors, 36-38
  etiquette, 31-32
  exposure, 42, 44
  film groups, 29
  food, 42
  head shots, 27-29
  IFP, 29
  McCoy, Matt, 36-38, 41-42
  notes, 32-33
  points, 41-42
  production offices, 30
  quitting, 38-40
  reading scenes, 30-35
  referrals, 38-41
  SAG, 44-45
  schedules, 44
  Schroeder, Rick, 38
  sides, 30-31
  theaters, 29
  videotapes, 32-33
  morale/motivation, 151-155
  pickup shots, 205-208, 216
shooting
  blocking scenes, 137-138
  makeup artists, 138-139, 142
  moving, 169-172
  wardrobe supervisors, 138-139, 142
video storyboards, 115
Adobe
  After Effects, 260-263, 270
  Photoshop, 271
ADR (Automatic Dialogue Replacement), 289-292, 308-309
advertising
costs
  actors, 27-29
  marketing, 347
hiring
  actors, 27-29
  crew, 49-50
  screenwriters, 18-19
  visual effects artists, 256-257
After Effects, 260-263, 270
agents, 18
Alias Maya. *See* **Maya**
Amazon.com, 344-345
ambient noise, 288-289
Apple
  Final Cut Express, 268-270
  Final Cut Pro, 218-219, 234-241, 258, 268-270, 280, 303
  Logic Pro, 281-282
  Shake, 263
  Soundtrack, 280
Arriflex cameras, 162-164
art directors, 133
artifacts (digital video cameras), 198-199
artists. *See* **visual effects artists**
aspect ratio (digital video cameras), 197, 199
assistant art directors, 133

A

assistant directors
  hiring, 48
  managing sets, 123-124
  responsibilities, 131, 144
  schedules
    call sheets, 124, 133-134
    communication, 125-126
    creating, 123-126
    meetings, 125-126
    software, 124-125
  shooting, 137-144
AtomFilms Web site, 325
attorneys, 18
audiences. *See* test audiences
audio. *See* sound
auditions (actors), 29-35
authoring DVDs, 331-337
Automatic Dialogue Replacement (ADR), 289-292, 308-309
Avid, 234-237

B

Backstage West, 27-28
backstory, 21-23
backup costumes, 80-81
blocking scenes, 137-138
Blogger.com Web site, 319
blogs, 353
blue screen/green screen comparison, 266
bombs, 99-101
books, marketing, 350
boom operators, 133
breaking even, 9
brightness, 190-194
broadsides (actors), 30-31
budgets. *See* costs
burning DVDs, 337-339
Business Wire Web site, 320, 350

C

cable television distribution, 201
call sheets, 124, 133-134

cameras. *See also* shooting
  35-mm cameras, 160-162
  Arriflex, 162-164
  checking gates, 173-174
  cleaning, 173-174
  costs, 249
  cranes, 185-189
  crew, 174
  depth of field, 168
  dollies, 180-185
  film, changing, 173-174
  focus, 168-172
  handheld, 175-177
  ladder pods, 185-189
  lenses, 164-172, 181, 183-185
  maintenance, 173-174
  measuring distance, 169-172
  quality, 249
  shooting, 248-249
  time, 169-175
  tripods, 177-180
  zooming, 164-166, 181
  choosing, 160-162
  conventional storyboards, 110-112
  costs
    film, 161-162
    insurance, 121-122
    line producers, 160
  digital video cameras, 160-162
    artifacts, 198-199
    aspect ratio, 197, 199
    cable television, 201
    colors, 198
    compression, 197-200
    converting film, 226
    costs, 200, 249
    distribution, 200-201
    DV, 197-198, 219, 226, 236-237, 248-249
    editing, 236-237
    festivals, 200
    frame rates, 197, 199
    HD, 198-201, 226, 236-237, 248-249

Index

HD TVs, 200-201
lenses, 199
overview, 196
pickup shots, 219
quality, 249
resolution, 197-201
shooting, 248-249
exterior shots, 189-194
film. *See* film
frame rates
  digital video cameras, 197, 199
  TV monitors, 95-96
green screens
  actors, 267
  blue screens comparison, 266
  compositing, 268-270
  costs, 266
  creating, 266
  finding, 266
  lighting, 266-267
  overview, 265-266
  props, 267
  set design, 88-90
  shadows, 267
  shooting, 266-267
heat, 146
interior shots
  lighting, 194-196
  set design, 85-90
operating, 163
pickup shots, 162, 213, 215, 218-219
sets
  set design, 85-90
  setup, 163-164
shot lists, 115-116
TV monitors, synchronizing, 95-96
video storyboards, 113-115
campgrounds, 59
career, portfolios, 8
cast. *See* **actors**
casting. *See* **hiring**
casting directors, 29, 36
casting rooms, 30

character development, 24-25
choreography
  changing, 148-151
  pickup shots, 211
Cinematographer.com Web site, 158
cleaning cameras, 173-174
clouds, shooting, 190-192
cockpits, 93-96
colleges (actors), 29
color correction
  costs, 245
  editing film, 245-246
  shooting, 190-192
color timing. *See* **color correction**
colors
  color correction
    costs, 245
    editing film, 245-246
    shooting, 190-192
  digital video cameras, 198
  lighting, 190-192, 196
communication
  contacting journalists, 351-354
  e-mail (marketing), 353
  etiquette (hiring), 31-32
  interpersonal conflicts, 153
  meetings
    composers, 274-276
    schedules, 125-126, 134
    sound supervisors, 288, 300
    visual effects, 270-272
  telephone (marketing), 352-353
compatibility (DVD distribution), 338
composers
  costs, 275
  experience, 274
  hiring, 274-276
  meetings, 274-276
  music
    costs, 281
    final mixes, 306-309
    loops, 279-280
    placeholders, 277-280

Index 373

software, 280-282
stems, 307-308
style, 277-280
portfolios, 275
schedules, 276
time, 276
compositing
green screens, 268-270
visual effects, 261-263
compression (digital video cameras), 197-200
computer graphics (storyboards), 111-112
computer monitors, 95-96
concept art
promotion, 313-315
storyboards. *See* storyboards
conflicts, 153
contracts. *See also* **hiring**
SAG, 44-45
screenwriters, scripts, 18
contrast, visual, 66-67
conventional storyboards. *See* **storyboards**
converting film to videotapes, 225-226
costs. *See also* finding; hiring
advertising, actors, 27-29
Alias Maya, 262
cameras
35-mm cameras, 183-185, 249
cranes, 185
digital video cameras, 197, 199-200, 249
dollies, 183-185
insurance, 121-122
ladder pods, 185
film, 161-162
line producers, 160
casting directors, 29
color correction, 245
composers, 275, 281
costumes, 71, 74-75, 77-79
credit cards, 10-12

DVD distribution, 325-326, 331-333, 337-344
film
cameras, 161-162
cutting negatives, 245
developing, 225
editing, 233-236
film editors, 224
financing, 10-12
going over budget, 5-7
green screens, 266
hiring
actors, 41-44
crew, 52
directors of photography, 52
grips, 52
producers, 52
production designers, 52
initial, 3-5
insurance
actors, 121-122
cameras, 121-122
equipment, 121-122
line producers, 121-123
locations, 122
production companies, 122-123
props, 98, 121-122
investors, 10-12
lighting, 189
line producers
cameras, 160
creating budgets, 117-121
experience, 119, 160
insurance, 121-123
software, 120-121
locations
deposits, 64
finding, 58-60, 64-67, 69-70
insurance, 122
permits, 60, 64-65, 69-70
marketing, 347
music, 275, 281
pickup shots, 211-213
prioritizing, 4
promotion, 314, 316-317, 320

props/prop masters, 98, 104, 121-122
public relations, 320
quality, 4
schedules relationship, 117
screenwriters, scripts, 5, 13, 17, 21
sets, 211
  design, 83, 93
  pyrotechnics, 88, 92
shooting, crew, 130
sound
  sound mixers, 301-303
  sound stages, 89
  sound supervisors, 285, 297
visual effects, 262
  visual effects artists, 257
  visual effects supervisors, 252-255

costume designers. *See also* **wardrobe supervisors**
costumes
  backup costumes, 80-81
  creating, 74-81
  design, 72-74
  materials, 74-81
  replacements, 80-81
hiring, 71-72
pickup shots, 217

costumes
costs, 71, 74-75, 77-79
costume designers
  backup costumes, 80-81
  creating, 74-81
  design, 72-74
  hiring, 71-72
  materials, 74-81
  pickup shots, 217
  replacements, 80-81
pickup shots, 208-210, 217
wardrobe supervisors, 79-80
  actors, shooting, 138-139, 142
  costume maintenance, 79-80
  responsibilities, 132
coverage (scenes), 229-233
Craiglist Web site, 256

Craner, Ben, Web site, 314
cranes, 185-189
  costs, 185
  setup, 189
  time, 189
creating
  budgets, 117-121
  costumes, 74-81
  dolly substitutes, 183-185
  green screens, 266
  props, 99-101, 104-107
  schedules, 123-126
credentials (actors), 36-37
credit card merchants, 341-344
credit cards, 10-12
crew. *See also* **actors**
  accommodations, 154
  cameras, 174
  food, 154-155
  heat exhaustion, 145
  hiring
    advertising, 49-50
    assistant directors, 48
    costs, 52
    costume designers, 48
    directors of photography, 49-50, 52
    experience, 50-52, 54-55, 361
    groundbreaking work, 53
    line producers, 48
    morale/motivation, 52-55, 361-362
    portfolios, 54-55
    producers, 48
    production designers, 48
    production managers, 48
    referrals, 47-50, 159-160
    schedules, 51-52, 54
    script supervisors, 48
    sound recordists, 48
  interpersonal conflicts, 153
  medical emergencies, 147
  morale/motivation, 151-155
  pickup shots, 205-208
  responsibilities, 131-133, 144

shooting
  costs, 130
  overview, 129-133
  scripts, 142-143
  time, 130
Customflix Web site, 325-326
cutting
  negatives, 244-245
  scenes
    scripts, 25
    shooting, 148-151

D

dailies (editing), 225
Danetracks
  sound supervisors. *See* sound supervisors
  Web site, 286
deadlines. *See* **schedules; time**
Death Valley
  finding locations, 60-65
  shooting, 144-147
demo reels (actors), 42
deposits (locations), 64
depth of field, 168
design
  costumes, 72-74
  sets
    cockpits, 93-96
    costs, 83, 93
    details, 90-93
    green screens, 88-90
    interior shots, 85-90
    lighting, 90-93
    pickup shots, 90
    production designers, 83-85
    props, 90-96
    schedules, 89, 91
    sound stages, 88-90
    TV monitors, 95-96
details (set design), 90-93
developing
  characters, 24-25
  film, costs, 225
  self, 365-366

dialogue
  ADR, 289-292, 308-309
  conventional storyboards, 110
  editing, 293
  pickup shots, 213
  sets, ambient noise, 288-289
  shooting, 177-178
Digital Behavior, 111
Digital Performer, 281
digital video cameras, 160-162
  artifacts, 198-199
  aspect ratio, 197, 199
  cable television, 201
  colors, 198
  compression, 197-200
  converting film, 226
  costs, 197, 199-200, 249
  distribution, 200-201
  DV, 197-198, 219, 226, 236-237, 248-249
  editing, 236-237
  festivals, 200
  frame rates, 197, 199
  HD, 198-201, 226, 236-237, 248-249
  HD TVs, 200-201
  lenses, 199
  overview, 196
  pickup shots, 219
  quality, 249
  resolution, 197-201
  shooting, 248-249
  software, 198
digitizing film, 227
directors, 131
Directors' Guild of America, 355
directors of photography
  hiring, 158-160
    costs, 52
    crew, 49-50, 52
  responsibilities, 132
  shooting
    overview, 157-160
    pickup shots, 205

Discreet 3ds max, 262
distance, cameras, 169-172
distribution
  cable television, 201
  digital video cameras, 200-201
  DVDs
    Amazon.com, 344-345
    authoring, 331-337
    burning, 337-339
    compatibility, 338
    costs, 325-326, 331-333, 337-344
    credit card merchants, 341-344
    features, 327-329
    marketing, 327-329
    menus, 330-331
    players, 338
    profit, 344-345
    promotion, 339-345
    publishing, 325-327
    replicating, 337-339
    selling, 339-345
    shipping, 343
    shopping carts, 342-343
    Web sites, 339-345
  festivals, 200, 324-325
  HD TVs, 200-201
  overview, 323
  Web sites, 325
documenting shooting, 329
dollies, 180-185
  costs, 183-185
  setup, 182-183
  substitutes, 183-185
  time, 182-183
  zooming, 181
doubles (actors), 216
Dr. Raw Stock Web site, 160
Dub-It Web site, 338
DV digital video cameras, 197-198, 219, 226, 236-237, 248-249
DVDs (distribution)
  Amazon.com, 344-345
  authoring, 331-337
  burning, 337-339
  compatibility, 338
  costs, 325-326, 331-333, 337-344
  credit card merchants, 341-344
  features, 327-329
  marketing, 327-329
  menus, 330-331
  players, 338
  profit, 344-345
  promotion, 339-345
  publishing, 325-327
  replicating, 337-339
  selling, 339-345
  shipping, 343
  shopping carts, 342-343
  Web sites, 339-345

E

Easy Budget, 120-121
editing
  dialogue, 293
  digital video cameras, 236-237
  film
    color correction, 245-246
    converting to videotapes, 225-226
    costs, 233-236, 245
    coverage, 229-233
    cutting negatives, 244-245
    dailies, 225
    digitizing, 227
    hardware, 241-243
    locking, 243
    Macintoshes, 241-243
    PCs, 241-243
    scenes, 228-233
    schedules, 233-236, 245
    self, 224-225, 237
    software, 234-243
    telecine, 225
    time, 233-236, 245
    visual effects, 246-247
  video storyboards, 114
  visual effects, 270-272
education, 9

Index

effects. *See* Foley sound effects; visual effects
e-mail (marketing), 353
emergencies (medical), 147
Entertainment Partners Web site, 120
EP Budgeting, 120
EP Scheduling, 124-125
equipment
  costs, insurance, 121-122
  finding locations, 68-69
  heat, 146-147
  schedules, 363
  time, 363
established actors
  hiring, 36-38
    credentials, 36-37
    McCoy, Matt, 36-38, 41-42
    Schroeder, Rick, 38
  screenwriters, scripts, 24-25
etiquette (actors), 31-32
Excel, 120-121, 259-260
experience
  composers, 274
  costs (line producers), 119, 160
  film editors, 223-224
  hiring crew, 50-52, 54-55, 361
  skills, 365-366
exposure (actors), 42, 44
exterior shots, 189-194

F

feature creep, 20-21
features (DVDs), 327-329
Feedstream Web site, 317
festivals
  digital video cameras, 200
  distribution, 200, 324-325
  screenwriters, 19
fill light, 189-190
film
  changing, 173-174
  costs, 161-162
    cameras, 161-162
    cutting negatives, 245

developing, 225
editing, 233-236
film editors, 224
editing
  color correction, 245-246
  converting to videotapes, 225-226
  costs, 233-236, 245
  coverage, 229-233
  cutting negatives, 244-245
  dailies, 225
  digitizing, 227
  hardware, 241-243
  locking, 243
  Macintoshes, 241-243
  PCs, 241-243
  scenes, 228-233
  schedules, 233-236, 245
  self, 224-225, 237
  software, 234-243
  telecine, 225
  time, 233-236, 245
  visual effects, 246-247
film editors
  collaborating, 224-225, 237
  costs, 224
  experience, 223-224
  hiring, 223-224
  pickup shots, 212, 214
  rough cuts, 212, 214
frame rates
  digital video cameras, 197, 199
  TV monitors, 95-96
recans, 161
short ends, 161
used, 161
film editors. *See also* film
  collaborating, 224-225, 237
  costs, 224
  experience, 223-224
  hiring, 223-224
  pickup shots, 212, 214
  rough cuts, 212, 214
Film Emporium Web site, 122
film festivals. *See* festivals

film groups (actors), 29
Final Cut Express, 268-270
Final Cut Pro, 218-219, 234-241, 258, 268-270, 280, 303
Final Draft, 26
final mixes, 306-309
financing, 10-12
finding. *See also* costs; hiring
  green screens, 266
  locations
    accessibility, 58, 67-69
    accommodations, 59, 63
    campgrounds, 59
    costs, 58-60, 64-67, 69-70
    criteria, 57-58
    Death Valley, 60-65
    deposits, 64
    equipment, 68-69
    location scouts, 59
    permits, 60, 64-65, 69-70
    referrals, 59
    road trips, 59-60
    salt flats, 68-70
    size, 60
    terrain, 57-58
    transportation, 63
    visual contrast, 66-67
  props, 98-99, 101-104
  sound
    Foley sound effects, 297
    libraries, 296-297
    sound stages, 90
first assistant cameramen, 132
fliers, 316
focus (cameras), 168-172
Foley sound effects
  finding, 297
  sound supervisors, 293-300, 308
food
  crew, 154-155
  heat, 146
  hiring actors, 42
  schedules, shooting, 133
  transportation, 155

frame rates
  digital video cameras, 197, 199
  TV monitors, 95-96

G

gaffers
  lighting, 194-196
  responsibilities, 132
gates (cameras), 173-174
gels (lighting), 196
goals (scripts), 23-25
going over budgets, 5-7
graphics
  storyboards, 111-112
  TV monitors, 95-96
  Web sites, 319
green screens
  actors, 267
  blue screens comparison, 266
  compositing, 268-270
  costs, 266
  creating, 266
  finding, 266
  lighting, 266-267
  overview, 265-266
  props, 267
  set design, 88-90
  shadows, 267
  shooting, 266-267
grenades, 98, 104-107
grips
  hiring, 52
  responsibilities, 132
guns, 101-104

H

handheld cameras, 175-177
hardware
  film editing, 241-243
  visual effects, 260-263
  visual effects supervisors, 252
HD digital video cameras, 198-201, 226, 236-237, 248-249
HD TVs, distribution, 200-201

head shots (actors), 27-29
heat
  cameras, 146
  crew, 145
  equipment, 146-147
  food, 146
  props, 146
  setup, 146-147
  shooting, 144-147
  time, 146-147
heat exhaustion, 145
hiring. *See also* **costs; finding**
  actors
    accommodations, 42-43
    advertising, 27-29
    atmosphere, 31-32
    auditions, 29-35
    casting directors, 29, 36
    casting rooms, 30
    colleges, 29
    costs, 41-44
    credentials, 36-37
    demo reels, 42
    established actors, 36-38
    etiquette, 31-32
    exposure, 42, 44
    film groups, 29
    food, 42
    head shots, 27-29
    IFP, 29
    McCoy, Matt, 36-38, 41-42
    notes, 32-33
    points, 41-42
    production offices, 30
    quitting, 38-40
    reading scenes, 30-35
    referrals, 38-41
    SAG, 44-45
    schedules, 44
    Schroeder, Rick, 38
    sides, 30-31
    theaters, 29
    videotapes, 32-33
  contracts
    SAG, 44-45
    screenwriters, scripts, 18

  crew
    advertising, 49-50
    assistant directors, 48
    costs, 52
    costume designers, 48, 71-72
    directors of photography, 49-50, 52, 158-160
    experience, 50-52, 54-55, 361
    grips, 52
    groundbreaking work, 53
    line producers, 48
    morale/motivation, 52-55, 361-362
    portfolios, 54-55
    producers, 48, 52
    production designers, 48, 52, 85
    production managers, 48
    prop masters, 97
    referrals, 47-50, 159-160
    schedules, 51-52, 54
    script supervisors, 48
    sound recordists, 48
  film editors, 223-224
  screenwriters, 15-19
  sound
    composers, 274-276
    music supervisors, 273-274
    sound mixers, 300-301
    sound recordists, 48
    sound supervisors, 285-288
  visual effects
    visual effects artists, 255-258
    visual effects supervisors, 251-252
hooks (marketing), 348-354, 359-360

I

iFilm Web site, 325, 347
IFP, 29
Instant Films Web site, 19
insurance
  actors, 121-122
  cameras, 121-122
  equipment, 121-122

380 Index

line producers, 121-123
locations, 122
production companies, 122-123
props, 98, 121-122
interior shots
  lighting, 194-196
  set design, 85-90
Internet Movie Database Web site, 356
interns (sound), 285-288, 296-300
investors, 10-12

J-K

job descriptions. *See* **responsibilities**
journalists, contacting, 351-354

Katti, Nachiket, Web site, 331
key grips, 132

L

labeling visual effects, 258
ladder pods, 185-189
  costs, 185
  setup, 189
  time, 189
lawyers, screenwriters, 18
lenses
  35-mm cameras, 164-168
    depth of field, 168
    focus, 168-172
    long, 168
    prime, 167-168
    wide-angle, 167, 183-185
    zoom, 164-166, 181
  digital video cameras, 199
libraries (sound), 296-297
lighting
  costs, 189
  screenwriters, scripts, 24
  set design, 90-93
  shooting
    brightness, 190-194
      clouds, 190-192

color correction, 190-192
colors, 196
exterior shots, 189-194
fill light, 189-190
gaffers, 194-196
gels, 196
green screens, 266-267
interior shots, 194-196
pickup shots, 214-217
reflectors, 189-190
setup, 194-196
shadows, 192-193, 267
sunset, 194
time, 190-196
LightWave, 262
limitations, conventional storyboards, 110-111
line producers
  costs
    cameras, 160
    creating budgets, 117-121
    experience, 119, 160
    film, 161-162
    insurance, 121-123
    software, 120-121
  hiring, 48
  responsibilities, 131
lip-synching (ADR), 289-292, 308-309
location scouts, 59
locations. *See also* **sets**
  changing, 147-148
  conventional storyboards, 110-112
  costs
    deposits, 64
    finding, 58-60, 64-67, 69-70
    insurance, 122
    permits, 60, 64-65, 69-70
  finding
    accessibility, 58, 67-69
    accommodations, 59, 63
    campgrounds, 59
    costs, 58-60, 64-67, 69-70
    criteria, 57-58

Death Valley, 60-65
deposits, 64
equipment, 68-69
location scouts, 59
permits, 60, 64-65, 69-70
referrals, 59
road trips, 59-60
salt flats, 68-70
size, 60
terrain, 57-58
transportation, 63
visual contrast, 66-67
pickup shots, 211-217
representatives, 134
shooting. *See* cameras; shooting time, 147-148
video storyboards, 113-115
viewfinders (storyboards), 114
locking film, 243
lodging. *See* accommodations
Logic Pro (Apple), 281-282
long lenses, 168
loops (music), 279-280

M

Macintoshes, film editing, 241-243
magazine, *Backstage West*, 27-28
maintenance
 cameras, 173-174
 costumes, 79-80
makeup artists
 actors, 138-139, 142
 pickup shots, 217
 responsibilities, 132
managing sets, 123-124
Mark of the Unicorn Digital Performer, 281
marketing. *See also* promotion
 advertising costs, 347
 books, 350
 DVD distribution, 327-329
 public relations
  blogs, 353
  contacting journalists, 351-354

costs, 320
Directors' Guild of America, 355
e-mail, 353
hooks, 348-354, 359-360
press, 320-322, 347-354
press releases, 350-354
promotion, 319-322
promotional quotes, 344, 354-358
telephone, 352-353
Web sites, 353-354
wire services, 320, 350-351
matching pickup shots, 218-219
materials (costumes), 74-81
Maya, 260-263
 costs, 262
 Web site, 260
McCoy, Matt, hiring, 36-38, 41-42
meals. *See* food
measuring distance, 169-172
medical emergencies, 147
meetings
 composers, 274-276
 schedules
  assistant directors, 125-126
  shooting, 134
 sound supervisors, 288, 300
 visual effects, 270-272
menus (DVDs), 330-331
Microcinema International Web site, 326
Microsoft
 Excel, 120-121, 259-260
 PowerPoint, 218
 Word, 26
MiniDV digital video cameras, 197-198, 219, 226, 236-237, 248-249
mix stages, 301-303
mixing (sound)
 costs, 301-303
 final mixes, 306-309
 hiring, 300-301

mix stages, 301-303
music, 283
predubbing, 303-305
schedules, 302, 305
software, 303
stems, 307-308
time, 302, 305
money. *See* **costs; profit**
morale/motivation
    actors, 151-155
    crew, 52-55, 151-155, 361-362
    self, 363-364
music
    composers
        costs, 275, 281
        experience, 274
        final mixes, 306-309
        hiring, 274-276
        loops, 279-280
        meetings, 274-276
        placeholders, 277-280
        portfolios, 275
        schedules, 276
        software, 280-282
        stems, 307-308
        style, 277-280
        time, 276
    sound mixers, 283
    music supervisors, 273-274
music supervisors, 273-274

N

negatives, cutting, 244-245
networking. *See* **referrals**
newsletters, 318
Newtek LightWave, 262
notes, hiring actors, 32-33

O

operating cameras, 163
outdoor shots, 189-194
overruning budgets, 5-7

P

P Machine Web site, 319
padding schedules, 212-213
pay. *See* **costs**
PCs, editing film, 241-243
permits, 60, 64-65, 69-70
PHP-Nuke Web site, 319
Photoshop, 271
pickup shots
    action scenes, 219
    actors, 205-208, 211, 216
    cameras, 162, 213, 215, 218-219
    causes, 203-204
    choreography, 211
    costs, 211-213
    costume designers, 217
    costumes, 208-210, 217
    crew, 205-208
    dialogue, 213
    digital video cameras, 219
    directors of photography, 205
    Final Cut Pro, 218-219
    lighting, 214-217
    locations, 211-217
    makeup artists, 217
    matching, 218-219
    overview, 204-205
    post-production sound, 213
    props, 208-210, 215-216
    reference shots, 217-219
    rough cuts, 212, 214
    schedules, 205-206, 212-213
    sets, 90, 211-217
    software, 218-219
    videotapes, 219
    visual effects supervisors, 205
placeholder music, 277-280
planning schedules, 363
players, DVDs, 338
Point Zero, 120-121
points, hiring actors, 41-42
portfolios, 8
    composers, 275

crew, 54-55
visual effects artists, 257
post-production
  conventional storyboards, 111-112
  screenwriters, scripts, 21-23
  sound, pickup shots, 213
postmortems, 366-367
Power Production Web site, 112
PowerPoint, 218
PR Web Web site, 350
predubbing, 303-305
preproduction scripts, 19-21
press
  Backstage West, 27-28
  marketing, 320-322, 347-354
  press releases, 350-354
press releases, 350-354
prime lenses, 167-168
print media. *See* press
Pro Tools, 293, 298
problems (schedules), 203-204
process (shooting), 137-144
producers
  costs, 52
  hiring, 48, 52
  responsibilities, 131
production assistants
  responsibilities, 131
  schedules (call sheets), 133-134
production companies, 122-123
production designers
  costs, 52
  hiring, 48, 85
  responsibilities, 133
  set design, 83-85
production managers
  hiring, 48
  responsibilities, 131
production offices, 30
profit, 7-9, 344-345
programs. *See* software
project scope, 360-361
projecting budgets, 3-5

promotion. *See also* marketing
  concept art, 313-315
  costs, 314, 316-317, 320
  DVD distribution, 339-345
  overview, 313, 364-365
  promotional cards, 316
  promotional quotes, 344, 354-358
  public relations, 319-322
  Web sites, 316-319
    graphics, 319
    newsletters, 318
    timestamps, 318
promotional cards, 316
promotional quotes, 344, 354-358
props/prop masters
  bombs, 99-101
  costs, 98-104, 121-122
  creating, 99-101, 104-107
  green screens, 267
  grenades, 98, 104-107
  guns, 101-104
  heat, 146
  hiring prop masters, 97
  insurance, 98, 121-122
  pickup shots, 208-210, 215-216
  radios, 98, 104-107
  renting, 98-99, 101-104
  replacements, 104-107
  responsibilities, 132
  screenwriters, scripts, 25
  set design, 90-96
  stolen, 104-107
  test audiences, 107
  timers, 98
public relations (marketing)
  blogs, 353
  contacting journalists, 351-354
  costs, 320
  Directors' Guild of America, 355
  e-mail, 353
  hooks, 348-354, 359-360
  press, 320-322, 347-354
  press releases, 350-354
  promotion, 319-322

promotional quotes, 344, 354-358
telephone, 352-353
Web sites, 353-354
wire services, 320, 350-351
publications. *See* **press**
publishing DVDs, 325-327
pyrotechnic costs, 88, 92

Q

quality
cameras, 249
costs, 4
quitting (actors), 38-40

R

radios (props), 98, 104-107
readers (scripts), 23
reading scenes, 30-35
recans (film), 161
recording ADR, 289-292, 308-309
reference shots, 217-219
referrals
finding locations, 59
hiring
actors, 38-41
crew, 47-50, 159-160
reflectors (shooting), 189-190
renting props, 98-99, 101-104
replacements
costumes, 80-81
props, 104-107
replicating DVDs, 337-339
resolution
digital video cameras, 197-201
visual effects, 257
responsibilities (crew), 131-133, 144
resume pieces. *See* **portfolios**
revisions (scripts), 17, 19-23, 26
road trips, finding locations, 59-60
rough cuts, 212, 214

S

SAG (Screen Actors Guild), 44-45
salt flats, 68-70
scenes
action scenes. *See* action scenes
blocking, 137-138
coverage, 229-233
cutting, scripts, 25
dialogue
ADR, 289-292, 308-309
conventional storyboards, 110
editing, 293
pickup shots, 213
sets, ambient noise, 288-289
shooting, 177-178
editing, 228-233
reading (actors), 30-35
shooting. *See* cameras; shooting
schedules. *See also* **setup; time**
assistant directors
call sheets, 124, 133-134
communication, 125-126
creating, 123-126
meetings, 125-126
software, 124-125
costs relationship, 117
composers, 276
editing
cutting negatives, 245
film, 233-236
equipment, 363
hiring
actors, 44
crew, 51-52, 54
padding, 212-213
pickup shots, 205-206, 212-213
planning, 363
problems, 203-204
production assistants, 133-134
set design, 89, 91
shooting, 129, 133-137
call sheets, 133-134
food, 133

Index   385

location representatives, 134
meetings, 134
setup, 134-137
transportation, 134
wake-up calls, 133
sound mixers, 302, 305
sound stages, 89
visual effects, 258-260, 263-265
visual effects supervisors, 253-256
Schroeder, Rick, hiring, 38
scope (projects), 360-361
scores. *See* music
scouting. *See* finding
scouts, 59
Screen Actors Guild (SAG), 44-45
screenwriters (scripts)
advertising, 18-19
agents, 18
backstory, 21-23
character development, 24-25
collaborating, 15
contracts, 18
costs, 17, 21
cutting scenes, 25
established actors, 24-25
feature creep, 20-21
festivals, 19
Final Draft, 26
hiring, 15-19
lawyers, 18
lighting, 24
Microsoft Word, 26
post-production, 21-23
preproduction, 19-21
props, 25
revisions, 17, 19-23, 26
sets, 24-25
software, 26
spec scripts, 16, 19
strategic goals, 23-25
synopses, 19
test audiences, 21-23
test readers, 23
Web sites, 19

script supervisors
hiring, 48
responsibilities, 132
shooting, 143
scripts
costs, 5, 13, 17, 21
crew, shooting, 142-143
passion, 13-15
screenwriters
advertising, 18-19
agents, 18
backstory, 21-23
character development, 24-25
collaborating, 15
contracts, 18
costs, 17, 21
cutting scenes, 25
established actors, 24-25
feature creep, 20-21
festivals, 19
Final Draft, 26
hiring, 15-19
lawyers, 18
lighting, 24
Microsoft Word, 26
post-production, 21-23
preproduction, 19-21
props, 25
revisions, 17, 19-23, 26
sets, 24-25
software, 26
spec scripts, 16, 19
strategic goals, 23-25
synopses, 19
test audiences, 21-23
test readers, 23
Web sites, 19
script supervisors
hiring, 48
responsibilities, 132
shooting, 143
subject matter, 13-15
second assistant cameramen, 132
second assistant directors, 131

self
  development, 365-366
  editing film, 224-225, 237
  morale/motivation, 363-364
selling DVDs, 339-345
sequences. *See* scenes
sets. *See also* locations
  cameras, 163-164
  conventional storyboards, 110-112
  costs, 211
    design, 83, 93
    pyrotechnics, 88, 92
  design
    cockpits, 93-96
    costs, 83, 93
    details, 90-93
    green screens, 88-90
    interior shots, 85-90
    lighting, 90-93
    pickup shots, 90
    production designers, 83-85
    props, 90-96
    schedules, 89, 91
    sound stages, 88-90
    TV monitors, 95-96
  dialogue (ambient noise), 288-289
  managing (assistant directors), 123-124
  pickup shots, 211-217
  screenwriters, scripts, 24-25
  setup, 147, 163-164
  shooting. *See* cameras; shooting
  video storyboards, 113-115
setup. *See also* **schedules; time**
  cameras, 163-164
    cranes, 189
    dollies, 182-183
    ladder pods, 189
    tripods, 179-180
  heat, 146-147
  sets, 147, 163-164
  shooting
    lighting, 194-196
    schedules, 134-137

  visual effects, 256
shadows
  green screens, 267
  lighting, 192-193
Shake (Apple), 263
shipping, 343
shooting. *See also* cameras
  action scenes
    actors, 169-172
    handheld cameras, 175-177
    tripods, 177-180
  actors
    action scenes, 169-172
    blocking scenes, 137-138
    dialogue, 177-178
    makeup artists, 138-139, 142
    moving, 169-172
    wardrobe supervisors, 138-139, 142
  assistant directors, 137-144
  crew
    costs, 130
    overview, 129-133
    scripts, 142-143
    time, 130
  cutting scenes, 148-151
  Death Valley, 144-147
  digital video cameras, 248-249
  directors of photography. *See* directors of photography
  documenting, 329
  exterior shots, 189-194
  film. *See* film
  frame rates
    digital video cameras, 197, 199
    TV monitors, 95-96
  green screens, 266-267
    actors, 267
    blue screens comparison, 266
    compositing, 268-270
    costs, 266
    creating, 266
    finding, 266
    lighting, 266-267
    overview, 265-266
    props, 267

set design, 88-90
shadows, 267
heat, 144-147
interior shots
  lighting, 194-196
  set design, 85-90
lighting
  brightness, 190-194
  clouds, 190-192
  color correction, 190-192
  colors, 196
  exterior shots, 189-194
  fill light, 189-190
  gaffers, 194-196
  gels, 196
  green screens, 266-267
  interior shots, 194-196
  pickup shots, 214-217
  reflectors, 189-190
  setup, 194-196
  shadows, 192-193
  sunset, 194
  time, 190-196
locations. *See* locations
pickup shots
  action scenes, 219
  actors, 205-208, 211, 216
  cameras, 162, 213, 215, 218-219
  causes, 203-204
  choreography, 211
  costs, 211-213
  costume designers, 217
  costumes, 208-210, 217
  crew, 205-208
  dialogue, 213
  digital video cameras, 219
  directors of photography, 205
  Final Cut Pro, 218-219
  lighting, 214-217
  locations, 211-217
  makeup artists, 217
  matching, 218-219
  overview, 204-205
  post-production sound, 213
  props, 208-210, 215-216

reference shots, 217-219
rough cuts, 212, 214
schedules, 205-206, 212-213
sets, 90, 211-217
software, 218-219
videotapes, 219
visual effects supervisors, 205
process, 137-144
sets. *See* sets
scenes. *See* scenes
schedules, 129, 133-137
  call sheets, 133-134
  food, 133
  location representatives, 134
  meetings, 134
  pickup shots, 205-206, 212-213
  setup, 134-137
  transportation, 134
  wake-up calls, 133
script supervisors, 143
shot lists, 115-116
takes, 140-142
time, 148-151
  crew, 130
  lighting, 190-196
  locations, 147-148
shopping carts, 342-343
short ends (film), 161
shot lists, 115-116
ShowFax Web site, 31
sides (actors), 30-31
Six String Samurai Web site, 60
size
  aspect ratio, 197, 199
  locations, 60
skills, building, 365-366
Slamdance Web site, 324
software
  Adobe
    After Effects, 260-263, 270
    Photoshop, 271
  Alias' Maya, 260-263
    costs, 262
    Web site, 260

388　Index

Apple
　Final Cut Express, 268-270
　Final Cut Pro, 218-219, 234-241, 258, 268-270, 280, 303
　Logic Pro, 281-282
　Shake, 263
　Soundtrack, 280
Avid, 234-237
budgets, 120-121
conventional storyboards, 112
digital video cameras, 198
Discreet 3ds max, 262
Easy Budget, 120-121
EP Budgeting, 120
EP Scheduling, 124-125
film editing, 234-243
Final Draft, 26
Mark of the Unicorn Digital Performer, 281
Microsoft
　Excel, 120-121, 259-260
　PowerPoint, 218
　Word, 26
Newtek LightWave, 262
pickup shots, 218-219
Point Zero, 120-121
Pro Tools, 293, 298
schedules, 124-125
screenwriters, scripts, 26
sound
　composers, 280-282
　sound mixers, 303
　sound supervisors, 293, 298, 303
visual effects
　visual effects, 260-263, 271
　visual effects supervisors, 252
sound
　dialogue
　　ADR, 289-292, 308-309
　　conventional storyboards, 110
　　editing, 293
　　pickup shots, 213
　　sets, ambient noise, 288-289
　　shooting, 177-178
　finding
　　Foley sound effects, 297
　　libraries, 296-297
　Foley sound effects
　　finding, 297
　　sound supervisors, 293-300, 308
　music
　　costs, 275, 281
　　experience, 274
　　final mixes, 306-309
　　hiring composers, 274-276
　　loops, 279-280
　　meetings, 274-276
　　music supervisors, 273-274
　　placeholders, 277-280
　　portfolios, 275
　　schedules, 276
　　software, 280-282
　　sound mixers, 283
　　stems, 307-308
　　style, 277-280
　　time, 276
　pickup shots, 213
　sound mixers
　　costs, 301-303
　　final mixes, 306-309
　　hiring, 300-301
　　mix stages, 301-303
　　music, 283
　　predubbing, 303-305
　　schedules, 302, 305
　　software, 303
　　stems, 307-308
　　time, 302, 305
　sound recordists
　　hiring, 48
　　responsibilities, 133
　sound stages
　　costs, 89
　　finding, 90
　　schedules, 89
　　set design, 88-90
　sound supervisors
　　ADR, 289-292, 308-309

ambient noise, 288-289
costs, 285, 297
editing dialogue, 293
final mixes, 306-309
Foley sound effects, 293-300, 308
hiring, 285-288
interns, 285-288, 296-300
meetings, 288, 300
software, 293, 298, 303
stems, 307-308
sound effects. *See* Foley sound effects
Sound Ideas, 297
sound mixers
costs, 301-303
final mixes, 306-309
hiring, 300-301
mix stages, 301-303
music, 283
predubbing, 303-305
schedules, 302, 305
software, 303
stems, 307-308
time, 302, 305
sound recordists
hiring, 48
responsibilities, 133
sound stages
costs, 89
finding, 90
schedules, 89
set design, 88-90
sound supervisors
costs, 285
final mixes, 306-309
hiring, 285-288
interns, 285-288, 296-300
meetings, 288, 300
sound
ADR, 289-292, 308-309
ambient noise, 288-289
costs, 297
editing dialogue, 293
Foley sound effects, 293-300, 308

software, 293, 298, 303
stems, 307-308
Soundtrack, 280
Southwest Films, 121-123
spec scripts, 16, 19
special effects. *See* **Foley sound effects; visual effects**
stems (music), 307-308
stolen props, 104-107
StoryBoard Lite Web site, 112
StoryBoard Quick Web site, 112
storyboards
conventional
action scenes, 110-111
cameras, 110-112
computer graphics, 111-112
dialogue, 110
limitations, 110-111
locations, 110-112
overview, 109
post-production, 111-112
sets, 110-112
software, 112
visual effects, 111-112
shot lists, 115-116
video
action scenes, 113
actors, 115
cameras, 113-115
editing, 114
locations, 113-115
overview, 113
sets, 113-115
viewfinders, locations, 114
subject matter, 13-15
substitute dollies, 183-185
sunset, shooting, 194
Synapse Films Web site, 326
synchronizing cameras, TV monitors, 95-96
synopses, 19

T

takes, 140-142
telecine, 225

Index

telephone (marketing), 352-353
television
  cable television distribution, 201
  HD TV distribution, 200-201
  monitors, 95-96
terrain, 57-58
test audiences
  props, 107
  scripts, 21-23
test readers (scripts), 23
theaters (actors), 29
third assistant directors, 131
time. *See also* **schedules; setup**
  cameras, 169-175
    cranes, 189
    dollies, 182-183
    ladder pods, 189
    tripods, 179-180
  composers, 276
  editing
    cutting negatives, 245
    film, 233-236
  equipment, 363
  frame rates
    digital video cameras, 197, 199
    TV monitors, 95-96
  heat, 146-147
  planning, 363
  shooting
    crew, 130
    lighting, 190-196
    locations, 147-148
    scenes, 148-151
  sound mixers, 302, 305
  visual effects, 258-260, 263-265
  visual effects supervisors, 253-256
timers (props), 98
timestamps, 318
timing color. *See* **color correction**
tracking. *See* **schedules; time**
transportation
  finding locations, 63
  food, 155
  shooting schedules, 134
  visual effects, 256, 270-272

tripods, 177-180
Troma Studios Web site, 326
truck dollies, 183-185
TypePad Web site, 319

U-V

used film, 161

VFX Pro Web site, 256
video cameras. *See* **digital video cameras**
video storyboards. *See* **storyboards**
videotapes
  converting film, 225-226
  hiring actors, 32-33
  pickup shots, 219
viewfinders (storyboards), 114
visual contrast, locations, 66-67
visual effects
  compositing, 261-263
  conventional storyboards, 111-112
  costs, 262
  editing, 270-272
  editing film, 246-247
  green screens
    actors, 267
    blue screens comparison, 266
    compositing, 268-270
    costs, 266
    creating, 266
    finding, 266
    lighting, 266-267
    overview, 265-266
    props, 267
    set design, 88-90
    shadows, 267
    shooting, 266-267
  hardware, 260-263
  labelling, 258
  meetings, 270-272
  overview, 251
  resolution, 257
  schedules, 258-260, 263-265

setup, 256
software, 260-263, 271
time, 258-260, 263-265
transportation, 256, 270-272
visual effects artists. *See* visual effects artists
visual effects supervisors. *See* visual effects supervisors
visual effects artists
advertising, 256-257
costs, 255, 257
hiring, 255-258
portfolios, 257
visual effects supervisors
costs, 252-255
hardware, 252
hiring, 251-252
pickup shots, 205
responsibilities, 133
schedules, 253-256
software, 252
time, 253-256
vortex. *See* sets; visual effects

W-Z

wake-up calls, 133
wardrobe. *See* **costumes**
wardrobe supervisors. *See also* **costume designers**
actors, shooting, 138-139, 142
costume maintenance, 79-80
responsibilities, 132
Web sites
48 Hour Film, 19
Academy of Art, 314
Adobe After Effects, 260
Alias Maya, 260
Amazon.com, 344
AtomFilms, 325
Backstage West, 27-28
Blogger.com, 319
Business Wire, 320, 350
Cinematographer.com, 158
Craiglist, 256
Craner, Ben, 314

Customflix, 325-326
Danetracks, 286
Discreet 3ds max, 262
distribution, 325
Dr. Raw Stock, 160
Dub-It, 338
DVD distribution, 339-345
Easy Budget, 120
Entertainment Partners, 120
Feedstream, 317
Film Emporium, 122
Final Draft, 26
iFilm, 325, 347
IFP, 29
Instant Films, 19
Internet Movie Database, 356
Katti, Nachiket, 331
marketing, 353-354
Microcinema International, 326
Newtek LightWave, 262
P Machine, 319
PHP-Nuke, 319
Point Zero, 120
Power Production, 112
PR Web, 350
Pro Tools, 298
promotion, 316-319
screenwriters, scripts, 19
ShowFax, 31
Six String Samurai, 60
Slamdance, 324
Sound Ideas, 297
Storyboard Lite, 112
Storyboard Quick, 112
Synapse Films, 326
Troma Studios, 326
TypePad, 319
VFX Pro, 256
Zebra Development, 112
wheelchair dollies, 184-185
wide-angle lenses, 167, 183-185
wire services, 320, 350-351
Word, 26

Zebra Development Web site, 112
zooming, 164-166, 181

… THOMSON
COURSE TECHNOLOGY

Professional ■ Technical ■ Reference

STEP INTO THE 3D WORLD OF ANIMATION WITH THE *INSPIRED* SERIES!

Inspired 3D Modeling and Texture Mapping
1-931841-50-0

Inspired 3D Character Setup
1-931841-51-9

Inspired 3D Lighting and Compositing
1-931841-49-7

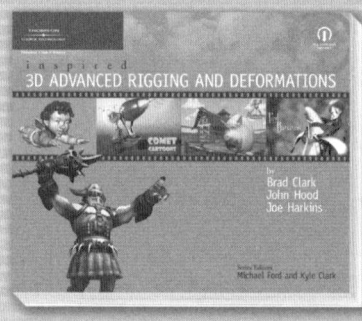

Inspired 3D Advanced Rigging and Deformations
1-59200-116-5

Filled with tips, tricks, and techniques compiled by the animators of blockbuster films at Hollywood's biggest studios, these four-color books are a must-have for anyone interested in character creation.

Series Editor Kyle Clark is a lead animator at Microsoft's Digital Anvil Studios. His film credits include *Star Wars Episode I— The Phantom Menace*, *Sleepy Hollow*, *Deep Blue Sea*, *The Adventures of Rocky and Bullwinkle*, *Harry Potter and the Sorcerer's Stone*, and *Brute Force* video game for the Xbox.

Series Editor Michael Ford is a senior technical animator at Sony Pictures Imageworks. He is a certified Level 2 Softimage instructor whose film credits include *Stuart Little*, *Stuart Little 2*, *The Perfect Storm*, *The Mummy*, *Godzilla*, *Species II*, *Mortal Kombat II*, and *The Faculty*.

Inspired 3D Short Film Production
1-59200-117-3

THOMSON
COURSE TECHNOLOGY
Professional ■ Technical ■ Reference

Call 1.800.354.9706 to order
Order online at www.courseptr.com

COURSE TECHNO

Professional ■ Technical ■

aspiring filmmaker's library

Take a behind the scenes look at Do-it-Yourself filmmaking with industry secrets from film veterans.

24P: Make Your Digital Movies Look Like Hollywood
ISBN: 1-59200-599-3 ■ $34.99

Packed with tips and advice, this book discloses the secrets of Hollywood-style production. It includes an 8-page color insert and offers an insider's view of the complete chronological sequence of professional film-style production, helping you give your film a polished, commercial look.

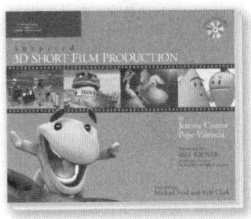

Inspired 3D Short Film Production
ISBN: 1-59200-117-3 ■ $59.99

Cover every aspect of the short-film production pipeline as you master each concept and technique through a combination of general theories, examples, exercises, case studies, and interviews with short-film directors and industry specialists. This book includes a robust DVD full of dozens of award-winning short films.

$30 Film School
1-59200-067-3 ■ $30.00

$30 Film School is an alternative to spending four years and a hundred thousand dollars to learn the trade. It includes numerous interviews from insightful independent filmmakers and artists, as well as a host of practical advice, knowledge, and resources.

Digital Filmmaking for Teens
1-59200-603-5 ■ $24.99

Learn how to tell your story on a budget, using tips from industry veterans as you cover each step—from developing your idea and writing a script to planning for production, shooting, and editing. The accompanying DVD is packed with advice, instructional videos and examples.

To order, call 1.800.354.9706
Order online at www.courseptr.com

License Agreement/Notice of Limited Warranty

By opening the sealed disc container in this book, you agree to the following terms and conditions. If, upon reading the following license agreement and notice of limited warranty, you cannot agree to the terms and conditions set forth, return the unused book with unopened disc to the place where you purchased it for a refund.

License:

The enclosed software is copyrighted by the copyright holder(s) indicated on the software disc. You are licensed to copy the software onto a single computer for use by a single user and to a backup disc. You may not reproduce, make copies, or distribute copies or rent or lease the software in whole or in part, except with written permission of the copyright holder(s). You may transfer the enclosed disc only together with this license, and only if you destroy all other copies of the software and the transferee agrees to the terms of the license. You may not decompile, reverse assemble, or reverse engineer the software.

Notice of Limited Warranty:

The enclosed disc is warranted by Thomson Course Technology PTR to be free of physical defects in materials and workmanship for a period of sixty (60) days from end user's purchase of the book/disc combination. During the sixty-day term of the limited warranty, Thomson Course Technology PTR will provide a replacement disc upon the return of a defective disc.

Limited Liability:

THE SOLE REMEDY FOR BREACH OF THIS LIMITED WARRANTY SHALL CONSIST ENTIRELY OF REPLACEMENT OF THE DEFECTIVE DISC. IN NO EVENT SHALL THOMSON COURSE TECHNOLOGY PTR OR THE AUTHOR BE LIABLE FOR ANY OTHER DAMAGES, INCLUDING LOSS OR CORRUPTION OF DATA, CHANGES IN THE FUNCTIONAL CHARACTERISTICS OF THE HARDWARE OR OPERATING SYSTEM, DELETERIOUS INTERACTION WITH OTHER SOFTWARE, OR ANY OTHER SPECIAL, INCIDENTAL, OR CONSEQUENTIAL DAMAGES THAT MAY ARISE, EVEN IF THOMSON COURSE TECHNOLOGY PTR AND/OR THE AUTHOR HAS PREVIOUSLY BEEN NOTIFIED THAT THE POSSIBILITY OF SUCH DAMAGES EXISTS.

Disclaimer of Warranties:

THOMSON COURSE TECHNOLOGY PTR AND THE AUTHOR SPECIFICALLY DISCLAIM ANY AND ALL OTHER WARRANTIES, EITHER EXPRESS OR IMPLIED, INCLUDING WARRANTIES OF MERCHANTABILITY, SUITABILITY TO A PARTICULAR TASK OR PURPOSE, OR FREEDOM FROM ERRORS. SOME STATES DO NOT ALLOW FOR EXCLUSION OF IMPLIED WARRANTIES OR LIMITATION OF INCIDENTAL OR CONSEQUENTIAL DAMAGES, SO THESE LIMITATIONS MIGHT NOT APPLY TO YOU.

Other:

This Agreement is governed by the laws of the State of Massachusetts without regard to choice of law principles. The United Convention of Contracts for the International Sale of Goods is specifically disclaimed. This Agreement constitutes the entire agreement between you and Thomson Course Technology PTR regarding use of the software.